I0214643

By Antonio Escohotado

Reality and Substance (1986)

Philosophy and Methodology in the Sciences (1987)

The Spirit of Comedy (1991)

Whores and Wives (1993)

From Physis to Polis (1995)

The Question of Cannabis (1997)

Portrait of a Libertine (1998)

Chaos and Order (2000)

Learning About Drugs (2002)

Sixty Weeks in the Tropics (2003)

Elementary History of Drugs (2003)

Four Myths on Sex and Duty (2003)

The Enemies of Commerce (2008)

THE GENERAL HISTORY OF DRUGS

Volume Two, Part One

Antonio Escohotado

translated and edited by
G. W. Robinette

GRAFFITI MILITANTE PRESS
Valparaiso, Chile
2018

Graffiti Militante Press
Valparaiso, Chile

First English Edition

ISBN 978-0-98207-877-8

Acknowledgments to Volume One

For Albert Hofmann and Tom Szasz, who with their friendship and advice helped to distill the essence of this chronicle.

"This endeavor to achieve that everyone should approve that which one loves and hates is, in reality, ambition; and thus we see that each naturally desires that the rest should live according to his own nature. But as all desire this at the same time, at once each one gets in the way of the other, and as everyone wishes to be praised and loved by everyone else, they end by hating one another." – B. Spinoza, Ethics (Book III, Proposition XXXI)

I owe gratitude also to Pablo Fernandez-Florez, who was always distrustful of the project even though he ended up writing various portions and who contributed valuable documentation for the rest; to Luis Gil, who guided me decisively through Greco-Latin antiquity, moreover remediating some inappropriate remarks in the proofs; to Ramon Sala, for making accessible to me many sources about the contemporary period; and to Monica Bacazar, my wife, who stoically supported the birth of the whole book, collaborating also in the typewritten transcription. With their economic assistence, the Center for Sociological Investigations first, and later the Ministry of Culture, permitted an undivided attention to the work in its initial and final stages.

Author's Preface to Volume One

It has not been very common to unite theory and practice in the matter of drugs, and this explains perhaps some adventures that accompanied the composition of *La historia general de las drogas*. In 1988 – being then a professor of Sociology – the criminal court of Palma condemned me to two years and a day of prison, having found me guilty of drug trafficking. The punishment requested by the prosecutor – six years – was reduced by two-thirds, because for one judge of the court the offence was found to be *en grado de tentativa imposible* [literally, a crime impossible to commit]. Effectively, those who were offering to sell and those who were offering to buy – by means of three interposed users (one of whom was myself) – were agents of the police or their pawns. Just one week after this judgment, the criminal court of Cordoba declared a verdict of pure entrapment upon similar facts, whereupon they proceeded to annul all the charges, an interpretation that in time would become the accepted jurisprudence in Spain.

Apprehensive over what might end up happening on an appeal to the Supreme Court – in a litigation where a certain citizen was alleging to have been blackmailed by the authorities, while they were accusing him of being an opulent drug dealer who hid his criminal empire behind the lectern of the scholar – I preferred to serve the sentence without delay. As a then magistrate of the Supreme Court made clear, the matter was poisoned by the fact of my being a spokesperson for reform on the issue, already well-known since 1983. Given the facts of the case, to absolve without conditions would incriminate in some manner the incriminator, and would open a path toward a demand for a scandalous reparation.

After some inquiries, I discovered that the jail at Cuenca – thanks to its understanding Director – would concede me the three things necessary to take advantage of such a stay: a light switch inside the cell, an ancient PC, and isolation. During that fully-paid (albeit humble) vacation, four-fifths of this work was written. Naturally, I had entered into that establishment with no small number of kilos of index cards and notes, gathered during many long years. I had only to structure them, polishing the final exposition.

It could be added that I did not lose much time, and for this same reason neither was I downhearted. However, the conditions for bibliographic consultation are not ideal in a penitentiary and before I could abandon it this book began to be published,[1] so that it was dogged from the beginning by innumerable imprecisions, more than those which trouble any really extensive work. Some of them were remediated in the third edition, thanks above all to the effort of the chemist and ethnobotanist Jonathan Ott who tirelessly inserted the many changes and additions necessary, thoroughly revising the system of references and transforming entire sections of the text.

With this new English edition, the degree of precision demanded in a scientific work has been perfected once more, completed by a researcher who has been able to confirm and amplify my work making use of various libraries and the internet. As a result, the edition that the reader now holds in his hands not only suffers from far fewer errors and oversights, but also hopes to fulfill even closer the goal of an academic standard with regards to the precision of its information. No doubt, in twenty years this history will need to be revised again as new data becomes available. I look forward to reading that book.

La Navata
February 2010

---

[1] Volumes I and II in the *Alianza* edition.

Translator's Preface

It's been eight years since the publication of an English language translation of the first book of Antonio Escohotado's multi-volume, encyclopaedic *La historia general de las drogas*. At this rate, the last one should appear in 2050. *Mea culpa.* Life, in the form of several other books and a number of jobs, got in the way.

Partly for that reason, here is only the first half of volume two. The second reason is to keep the size of each volume down to less than a door-stopper. The third reason is that these translations have obviously been annotated, even considerably so. I'm keeping to the basic themes. But Antonio finished the work at the height of the drug war, had little access to primary resources and zero access to the internet. In spite of all these deprivations, or because of them, he's clearly written the best book ever on the history of drugs.

During the interregnum, the War on Cannabis continued to be lost as state after state in the US legalized first medical use and second recreational use. Two countries, Uruguay and Canada, legalized recreational. This has not been any less or any more related to the Great Worldwide Recession of 2009 than the legalization of alcohol was to the Great Worldwide Depression of 1933. In both cases, the eternal moral arguments against a social evil were suddenly found to be unaffordable as cities, counties, states and even countries searched for new sources of tax revenue. In each era a new drug war (in 1937 cannabis, in 2013 the government sponsored opiod epidemic) was slouching toward Bethelem, waiting to be born.

In the midst of this recurring prohibitionist spiral of fear, hatred and greed, it is still useful to discover the antecedents that led to the current confusion, and to search diligently for solid information based on verifiable facts. May such be found within these pages. Best,

G. W. R.

Contents of Volume Two, Part One

Introduction to Volume Two, Part One

This part of the story begins with the end of the Roman Empire and carries us through to the beginning of the Renaissance. In chapter eight, a thousand shops selling opium disappear as if by magic along with scientific medicine and rational thought. The nascent cult of orthodox Christianity abhors the non-alcoholic psychotropic drugs, represses the remnants of competitive mystery cults, and censors the history of its own Dionysiac/orgiastic beginnings, betraying the original entheogenic promise of the Eucharist. Euphoria is eschewed and unorthodox consciousness persecuted while the body is declared the personal property of a deity. All magic, white or black, is now satanic. Superstition, idol worship and sacrifice are abolished. The Visigoths condemn equally fortune tellers, apostates, dissidents and root cutters. Charlemagne punishes the possession of any diabolic plant not grown on the imperial estates. In a few centuries Europe falls back economically and spiritually a millennium. Yet, both urban and rural witches continue to flourish.

In chapter nine, a different monotheism, Islam, arises in a different desert and conquers by conviction (and a few scimitars) what the Papacy could not. In its early years it is tolerant, not only toward other religions but also the use of drugs, especially alcohol. Drunks are prescribed mercy in Cordoba and Omar Khayyam sings the praises of hashhish and wine. The great Persian, Arab and Jewish physicians of this era with confidence prescribe opium and strong solanaceas. The crusaders learn courtesy and medicine as Saladin heals their wounded. The Old Man of the Mountain founds his sect of Assassins with either opium, wine or hashish. Coffee arives via the Yemen, probably as a result of a shortage of khat. This gift of *Waqa* is prohibited for the first time at Mecca, then rapidly expands via the caravan routes to all parts of the Ottoman Empire, where it is officially prohibited and unofficially enjoyed. As Turkish fortunes decline, the heads of rebellious coffee drinkers litter the streets of Istanbul while their live bodies are sewn into leather sacks and dumped into the Bosphorus. Tobacco users are mutilated. After their loss at the Battle of Vienna (1683), the Turks license, tax and regulate both.

In chapter ten, individual witches and sorcerers in Europe are converted into mere members of a universal epidemic. The only medical cures permitted are prayers to icons and holy relics. The science of Satanism or demonology becomes a well-developed disclipine, creating its own inverted pyramidal monotheism. The Great Hunger and the Black Death shake the foundations of society and the Christian kingdoms of Europe prohibit the reading of their own Old and New Testaments. Editors, translators and witches meet the same fate at a public pyre. Inquisitors torture the poor found in possession of unguents, pomades and diabolic herbs. Yet, as the Renaissance gathers force, some begin to question whether it is less the Devil and more the natural plants themselves which are responsible for the witches' trances. Eroticism and lust are still crimes regardless of how aroused. Cardan and Porta publish the recipes for the witches' flying ointments and meet the iron cuffs of the Inquisition. A number of modern psychonauts recreate the medieval potions and lotions to verify their pharmacological action. Schools of physicians dispute over who should enjoy a monopoly on the elaboration and dispensing of drugs capable of altering the soul. The European alquimists connect the serpentine coil to the Arab still and begin to produce large quantities of flammable *aquae*. Yet these enjoy a special dispensation from the authorities, at least for a while.

Monotheisms with Dreams of Universal Empire

Figure 77 (previous page).
The Temptation of St. Anthony, copperplate engraving by Martin Schongauer (c. 1435 – 1491), British Museum. Known as the father of Christian Monotheism, St. Anthony (c. 251 – 356), hermit and cenobite, founded a number of monasteries in the Thebaid region of Upper Egypt. Düring his first fifteen years of solitary life in the desert, he was beseiged by visions and temptations which will later exercise a decisive influence on Christian demonology.

8
Christianity and Ebriety (I)

Impostors! who vaunt that to others they'll show
A path which themselves neither travel nor know.
Since they promise wealth, if we pay for their pains,
Let them take from that wealth, and bestow what remains.
-- Q. Ennius[1]

---

[1] Sometimes called the "Father of Roman Poetry," (c. 239 – 169 BC). Dunlop, John Colin. History of Roman Literature from Its Earliest Period to the Augustan Age, vol. I. London: Longman, Hurst, Rees, Orme, Brown, and Green, 1823 (GB), p. 103, ftnt. 1. See also the 1827 edition at archive.org and gutenberg.org.

A more or less implicit consensus among historians supposes that during the death rattles of GrecoRoman paganism the knowledge of psychoactive drugs was lost through a mixture of capricious events, unforeseen circumstances and a lack of any special appreciation. In the same way that philology was forgotten so was the smoking of the flowers of cannabis; just as the study of astronomy fell into disuse, so did the cultivation of the opium poppy. These substances emigrated voluntarily and accidentally to oriental locales, without anything to cause their exile; their return at the end of seven or eight centuries – within an awakening rationalism that favored a return to scientific medicine – was simply another accident.

Without making any noise, a thousand Roman shops dedicated to selling opium, the tons guarded in the imperial storehouses, the commercial emporiums based upon the exportation of the juice of the poppies of Asia Minor from Alexandria, the enormous plantations of cannabis cultivated by the Celts, the "vain imaginings, though very agreeable to the senses"[2] mentioned by Dioscorides,[3] the "leaves of laughter" of Democritus "taken in myrrh and wine,"[4] the social use of

---

2 Said to have been caused by a decoction of the roots of deadly nightshade (*Atropa belladonna*), found in Andrés Fernandez de Laguna, tr. *Pedacio Dioscorides Anazarbeo, Acerca de la Materia Medicinal, y de los Venenos Mortiferos*. Antwerp, NL: Casa de Juan Latio, 1555 (GB), p. 420, book IV, ch. LXXV: *Beuida con vino una drama de su rayz, representa ciertas imagines vanas, aunque muy agradables à los sentidos: y beuiendose en quantidad doblada, tiene fuera de-si a hombre tres dias: y de hecho le mata si-se beue quadruplicada* (Drunk with wine, a dram of its roots produces certain vain imaginings, though very agreeable to the senses; if the quantity should be doubled, it drives a man out of his mind for three days, and kills him if it be quadrupled), tr. gwr. See also Ch. 6, Vol. I, GHD, p. 294.

3 Pedanius Dioscorides (c. 40 – c. 90), Greek military surgeon born at Anazarbos (present day Nazarba), near Tarsus, Turkey. His *Materia Medica* was "one of the most influential and prized pharmacological treatises in the ancient world" (GHD, vol. I, ch. 6, p. 313).

4 "The gelotophyllis grows in Bactria and along the Borysthenes. If this be taken in

insufficiently separated hemp seed noticed by Galen[5] occurring in the salons of good society in Athens and Rome, the *kyphy*, the saunas of hashish, the intoxicating darnel of the Greeks, the resinous wine and other liquors that required the addition of eight or ten parts water, the

---

myrrh and wine all kinds of phantoms beset the mind, causing laughter which persists until the kernels of pine-nuts are taken with pepper and honey in palm wine" (Jones, W. H. S., tr. Pliny Natural History, vol. VII, book 24, ch. 102, sect. 164. Cambridge, MA: Harvard University Press, 1966 (Loeb), p. 117). Jones literally translates gelotophyllis as "leaves of laughter" (p. 116, ftnt. e). After listing three other options, the translation by Bostock and Riley notes that "Desfontaines suggests that hemp (prepared in the form of *hasheesh*) is meant" (J. Bostock and H. T. Riley, trs. The Natural History of Pliny, vol. V. London: Henry G. Bohn, 1856 (GB), p. 66, ftnt. 1). They suggest the same for the *potamaugis* (p. 65, ftnt. 98). The two plants are sometimes confused (see Rätsch, Christian. The Encyclopedia of Psychoactive Plants, tr. J. R. Baker, et al. Rochester, VT: Park Street Press, 2005, p. 146). Gaius Plinius Secundus (23 – 79 AD) attributes these "marvelous phenomena" to Democritus, living some four centuries earlier: "In this chapter Pliny uses indirect speech, as if to disclaim responsibility for the truth of the account he is giving" (Jones, 1966, p. 119, ftnt. f). The problem of precise plant identification is compounded by the fact that only some 300 fragments exist of the many works of the "physicist ... cosmologist, geologist, medical writer, and ethical and political philosopher" Democritus (c. 460 – 385 BC). Today he is "ineluctably identified with Atomism" but at the beginning of the Christian era he was better known as the "laughing philosopher" (Cartledge, Paul. Democritus. New York: Routledge, 1999, pp. 7-8, 46).

[5] Claudius Galen (c. 129 – 200), born at Pergamon (present day Bergama), Turkey, educated at Alexandria, practiced at Rome, physician to Marcus Aurelius, the "greatest of the Greco-Roman physicians, and first experimental physiologist [whose] influence on medicine [extended] over more than fourteen centuries" (Veith, I. "Galen," New Catholic Encyclopedia, vol. VI, Fra to Hir. New York: McGraw-Hill, 1967, p. 247). Of "the Indian hemp plant" he noticed "some people roast and eat it with other sweetmeats. ... The seeds are quite warming, and consequently when they are taken in quantity over a short period they affect the head, sending up to it a vapour that is both warm and like a drug" (Powell, Owen, tr. On the properties of Foodstuffs (*De alimentorum facultatibus*). Cambridge, MA: Cambridge University Press, 2003 (GB), p. 68, book I, section 34); see also Ch. 6, Vol. I, GHD, p. 292.

fumigations of henbane and mandrake, the preparations of *cantharides*, and many other ancient forms of therapy, commerce, and recreational pastime evaporated silently like so much smoke. Also evaporating were the aches and pains, insomnia, asthma, dysentery and many other local or general afflictions which thanks to certain drugs could be treated effectively, the fear of being poisoned and the desire to become immune to various toxins which had led to the development of the theriacal tradition, as well as the need for anesthetics in major or minor surgery. All this disappeared from memory like Euclidean geometry or the Corinthian capital.

A. The Censor and the Censored

In order to be able to believe such things, some scholars have proposed that drug use has always sought the shameful shadows.[6] The abrupt cessation of news about drugs in Europe was simply obedient to this principle of inherent shamefulness abetted by more fortuitous events; it was equally fortuitous that the use of drugs should seek the light of day (due to the lack of shame) in zones not dominated by Christianity like China, India, Persia or Arabia.

Those who do not feel themselves inclined to assimilate so many accidental occurrences at the same historical moment might rely upon well known facts, though facts not often mentioned by historians of this subject. It is known (1) that non-alcoholic psychoactive drugs – and even alcohol – were radically abhorred by the nascent cult of

[6] See for example Lewin, Louis. Phantastica Narcotic and Stimulating Drugs, tr. P. H. A. Wirth. New York: E. P. Dutton & Co., Inc., 1964, p. 37: "Time has preserved some testimonies of this abuse [eating opium], which in all periods has shunned the light"; "Now this evil [morphia] continues to develop clandestinely [p. 44]"; Lewin, Louis. Phantastica Narcotic and Stimulating Drugs. London: Routledge & Kegan Paul, 1964 (1931), "Morphia, a scourge of recent date, has established itself all over the world. It is always ready for use ... a dark corner [is] all that is needed [p. 46]."

orthodox Christianity not only as entheogens but in all their uses; (2) that from its earliest beginnings Christianity directly and indirectly persecuted with great tenacity the focal points of pharmaceutical culture; and, (3) that if this is not better understood by us today, it is due to massive bonfires of books encouraged by Christian bishops and emperors and the secrecy of the Christian censors.

1. The Orthodox Alteration of Consciousness. The rejection of cults linked to entheogenic plants can be explained from two perspectives, the one connected to the sacerdotal estate in the widest sense and the other to certain specific priests.

The ritualistic castes (Roman pontiffs, Greek basileis, Confucian priests, Hebrew rabbis, etc.) exhibit a professional sobriety that not only excludes the trances and ecstatic voyages of characters divinely summoned to and endowed with entheogenic power (like the wizards and shamans) but also the idiosyncrasies in clothing and conduct characteristic of ascetics like the hermit, fakir or yogi. The ritualists collaborate loyally with the established social order but also oppose it when the political power fails to fulfill the agreements on which such collaboration is based, as these figures are not marginalized but socially well integrated. The religions they administer – though they also claim to deal with revealed truth – can be easily contrasted with the customs of sorcery in general; this is the distinction already analyzed in Volume One between cults based on the learning of creeds and ceremonies whose essence is the following of a scripture that reassures the believer with a preconceived model of how one should act within the world and cults based upon isolated experiences, sometimes occurring only once in a lifetime, where the essential is an intense and unforgettable mental and emotional experience.

For a long time the ritualistic priest and the sorcerer lived together without serious conflict, since in reality they minister to very different but compatible needs. The Greek basileis coexisted with hierophants of the mystery cults, the Roman pontiffs with the mystagogues, the Confucian priests with the Taoist and Buddhist shamans, the rabbis with the prophets. War without quarter only explodes when a certain caste linked to primitive modalities of communion (with antecedents in the ecstatic or in sorcery) attempts to establish itself as the *only* estate, seeking to administer both tumultuous, natural religion as well as its civil, prosaic avatar. This can be observed in Brahmanism, where the original *drinkers of soma* ultimately became the vanguard of an essentially anti-ecstatic cult; it can be observed with still greater clarity in Christianity, a mystery cult that adopts ceremonies from analogous cults and in which, from the beginning of the fourth century, the Eucharist has preserved features of the more authentic meaning of the *sacer mysterion.*[7]

Figure 78. Catacombs in the Maius cemetery, Rome. A sub-terranean chamber with a chair for the bishop and stone benches for the deacons, who would have been seated around a table for the caena caelestis or Eucharist repast.

[7] The 'sacred mystery' or sacrament.

CHAPTER EIGHT -- CHRISTIANITY AND EBRIETY (I)

As it was in the rites of Bacchus, Attis and Mithra, in the Christian communion wine is also considered divine blood. The noteworthy quantity and variety of drinking cups found in the catacombs – many with filigree and the inscription *bibe in pace*[8] – explain the warnings of the Apostle Paul when he demands that early Christians keep themselves separate from "drunkenness" and "revellings."[9] Already at the end of the third century, one of the Fathers of the Church, Novatian,[10] was expounding with severity on the disorderly love of drink among his coreligionists. These drank wine during fasts, decanting it into "empty and unoccupied veins," something shameful in those "about to pray to God."[11] They are "still

---

[8] "And what do the drinking vessels signify which are discovered in the catacombs? They are of glass, and flat, and engraved or painted in gold with pictures of saints, or short inscriptions, such as the names of these saints or '*bibe in pace*' [drink in peace]" (Lewin, 1964 (1931), p. 161).

[9] "Envyings, murder, drunkenness, revellings, and such like: of which I tell you before, as I have also told [you] in time past, that they which do such things shall not inherit the kingdom of God" (*Epistle to the Galatians*, 5: 21, KJV, blueletterbible.org).

[10] Novatian (c. 200 – 258), anti-pope and founder of the Church of the Pure (*Katharo*), though excommunicated by a synod of sixty bishops, "was able to propagate his church with his own bishops in every sector of the Christian world" (Weyer, P. H. "Novatian and Novatianism," New Catholic Encyclopedia, vol. X, Mas to Pat. New York: McGraw-Hill, 1967, p. 534).

[11] Lewin, 1964 (1931), p. 161; Wallis, R. E., tr. "On the Jewish Meats," Anti-Nicene Fathers: the writings of the Fathers down to A. D. 325, vol. 5, Alexander Roberts and James Donaldson, eds., rev. A. Cleveland Coxe. Grand Rapids, MI: William B. Eerdmans Publishing Company, 1951, American reprint of the Edinburgh edition, p. 649, ch. 6, Epistle 30: "Nor yet are there wanting ... those who ... afford instances and teachings of intemperance; whose vices have come even to that pitch, that while fasting ... they drink in the early morning, not thinking it Christian to drink after meat, unless the wine poured into their empty and unoccupied veins should have gone down directly after sleep: for they seem to have less relish of what they drink if food be mingled with the wine. ... For these things are even greatly [un]becoming ... [in] those who are about to pray to God and to give Him thanks." See also the version at www.ccel.org.

fasting and already drunk, not running to the tavern, but carrying the tavern around with them; and if any one of them offer a salute, he gives not a kiss, but drinks a health."[12] Novatian and the other Fathers repeatedly state that the burning love of one's neighbor induced by ebriety is impious and not in accord with the premises of *caritas*, dangerously close to the "works of the flesh" like "fornication" and "uncleanness."[13]

Figure 79.
Catacombs of the cemetery of San Callisto, Rome, official resting place for the Christians of the city, burial site of nine third century AD Popes. Depiction of the agape – seven commensals seated around a Roman semicircular triclinio (dinner table) with bread, fish and wine.

---

12 Lewin, 1964, p. 161; Wallis, 1951, p. 649.

13 "Now the works of the flesh are manifest, which are [these]: Adultery, fornication, uncleanness, lasciviousness,/ Idolatry, witchcraft, hatred, variance, emulation, wrath, strife, seditions, heresies ..." (*Epistle to the Galatians*, 5: 19-20, KJV, blueletterbible.org).

a. The Entheogenic Promise Betrayed. At the same time, such critiques stumble up against something nuclear in the new cult, precisely the *symposion* or the ritual banquet of the Eucharist. The secret – because inaudible[14] – invocation ('this is my body, this is my blood') that the priest pronounces in order to consecrate the host still guards the promise of the natural religions, clearly based upon an entheogenic reinforcement of a spiritual transformation. The most ancient ceremonies (like the other Hellenistic mysteries) demanded severe fasts beforehand (and under these conditions a glass of wine has the strength of a bottle), suggesting that the consumption of the drug took place afterwards, in its own temple, as Philo of Alexandria (ca. 20 BC – 50 AD)[15] says was the ancestral custom. The greeting, which in the mass follows the receiving of the sacrament (reestablished not long ago in the Catholic liturgy), could be a vestige of the orgy or a

---

[14] Inaudible in the Western Catholic Church but not the Eastern. By the fifth or sixth century, the Western Church had adopted a silent Eucharist prayer, as commanded by Dionysius the Areopagite: "But see to it that you do not betray the holy of holies. ... Keep these things of God unshared and undefiled by the uninitiated. Let your sharing of the sacred befit the sacred things: Let it be by way of sacred enlightenment for sacred men only" (Luibheid, Colm and Paul Rorem, trs. Pseudo-Dionysius The Complete Works. New York: Paulist Press, 1987, p. 195, The Ecclesiastical Hierarchy, ch. 1, 372A); see also scribd.com (134/204), ccel.org and newadvent.org). In contrast, the emperor Justinian, who ruled at Constantinople from 527 to 565, ordered the ritual in the Eastern Orthodox Church performed so the laity could hear it: "We order all bishops and priests to repeat the divine service ... not in an undertone, but in a loud voice which can be heard by the faithful people in such a way that the minds of the listeners may be induced to manifest greater devotion, and a higher appreciation of the praises and blessings of God" (Bernard, L. and T. B. Hodges, eds. Readings in European History. New York: The Macmillan Company, 1958, p. 58, citing Scott, S. P., tr. The Civil Law, vol. XVII. Cincinnati, OH: The Central Trust Company, 1932, pp. 152-156, *Novella* CXXXVII, *De creatione episcoporum et clericum*); see also fordham.edu, constitution.org and //UWACADWEB.uwyo.edu.

[15] See also GHD, vol. I, ch. 3, pp. 112 *ff.*

simulation of the orgy that followed the sacred libations. The Coptic cult was of this type and during the first centuries constituted the most vigorous version of Christianity, spreading itself throughout Egypt, Syria, and Armenia, even showing up in Ethiopia. Its excessively close proximity to the pagan spirit caused it to be split off from the Orthodox trunk, accused of the Monophysite heresy.[16]

In the face of similar interpretations of the evangelical message, some even more infected with the Hellenic spirit, Orthodox Christianity will impose its authority by force to liquidate any examples of relaxed or licentious conduct.[17] We should remember that for paganism relaxation – the alleviation of inflexibility – had been one of the great Dionysian gifts, also allowed for in the Hebrew Bible, while now it would constitute an unconditional synonym for vice. From this attitude proliferated also fanatically abstemious sects, like the Encratites, Tatianites, Marcionites and Aquarians, for whom drinking constituted mortal sin,[18] in accord with Servian traditions that when

---

16 Though a somewhat arcane controversy today, Monophysitism was "the most important of early heresies" producing "a vast and important literature" (Chapman, John. "Monophysites and Monophysitism," The Catholic Encyclopedia, vol. 10, "Mass to Newman," Charles G. Herbermann, et al., eds. New York: Robert Appleton Company, 1911 (GB), p. 489; see also www.ccel.org). **Monophysites** held that Jesus of Galilee had only a single nature, *mia physis*, rejecting the creed of the Council of Chalcedon (451), in contrast with the Orthodox belief in two natures, one human and one divine (Chapman, 1911, p. 490). Their "revolt spread throughout the Orient. ... [They] refused to accept ... the obedience demanded by the Holy See as well as by the orthodox-minded Emperors" (Murphy, F. X. "Monophysitism," New Catholic Encyclopedia, vol. IX, "Ma to Mor." New York: McGraw-Hill, 1967, pp. 1064-1065).

17 "Mortify therefore your members which are upon the earth; fornication, uncleanness, inordinate affection, evil concupiscence, and covetousness, which is idolatry: For which things' sake the wrath of God cometh on the children of disobedience ...." (*Colossians* 3: 5, KJV, blb.org; see also *Epistle to the Galatians* 5: 16-24).

18 Lewin, 1964 (1931), p. 179: "Certain Christian sects, the Encratites, the Tatianists,

Lucifer fell from Heaven, the spot where he first set foot on Earth produced the vine.[19]

---

the Marcionites, and the Water-drinkers, considered the consumption of wine a sin ...." **Encratites**, literally 'abstainers' or 'persons who practiced continence,' "refrained from the use of wine, animal food, and marriage" (Arendeen, J. P. "Encratites," The Catholic Encyclopedia, vol. V, "Diocese – Fathers," Herbermann, et al, eds. New York: Robert Appleton Company, 1909 (GB), p. 412). Paul declares them heretics in 1 Timothy 4: 1-3: "Now the Spirit speaketh expressly, that in the latter times some shall depart from the faith, giving heed to seducing spirits, and doctrines of devils .... Forbidding to marry, [and commanding] to abstain from all meats, which God hath created to be received with thanksgiving ..." (*Letter from Paul to Timothy*, KJV, blb.org). Ireneus says they followed Tatian and "cursed St. Paul and his Epistles. ... In their hatred of marriage they declared woman the work of Satan, and in their hatred of intoxicants they called wine drops of venom from the great Serpent" (Arendeen, 1909, p. 413). **Tatian** was a "second-century apologist born in Assyria and ... trained in Greek philosophy" (Healy, Patrick J. "Tatian," The Catholic Encyclopedia, vol. 14, "Simony – Tournély," eds. Herbermann, et al. New York: Robert Appleton Company, 1912 (GB), p. 464). He "regarded matter as the fountain of all evil; and therefore recommended ... the mortification of the body ... and blended the Christian religion with several other tenets of the Oriental philosophy" (Adams, Hannah. A View of Religion in Two Parts, 3rd ed. Boston, MA: Manning & Loring, 1801 (GB), p. 106). His "followers ... abstained from wine [and his cult] closely resembled, at least in ritual and profession, the vagrant Pagan mysteries (Newman, John Henry Cardinal. An Essay on the Development of Christian Doctrine, 16th ed. New York: Longman, Greene & Company, 1920 (GB), pp. 221-222). **Marcion** "was the son of a bishop of Pontus ... whose followers spread through Italy, Egypt, Syria, Arabia, and Persia ...." Marcionites abstained "from flesh ... [and] had three baptisms or more ... [and dabbled] in magic and astrology" (Newman, 1920, pp. 220-223). The **Aquarians**, "a denomination in the second century ... under pretense of abstinence, made use of water instead of wine, in the Eucharist" (Adams, 1801, p. 49). Indeed, when the reader of Christian history "comes to the second century ... he finds that Gnosticism, under some form or other, was professed in every part of the then civilized world" (Newman, 1920, p. 220, quoting Dr. Burton).

[19] Lewin, 1964 (1931), pp. 179-180: "[T]he *Servians* said that the devil after having been expelled from heaven transformed himself into a snake and mixed with the

The compromise solution to mutually antagonistic positions was a strictly formal Eucharist, reducing the fast to a mere symbol and, somewhat later, reserving the wine only for the priest. Thus, the Eucharist retained the promise of ancient ecstatic religions – the mystic unity with the deity – but changed the very nature of the transformation. Now there was no wine, fast or boisterous celebration of a brotherhood in love, but only a sober faith sustained by an external world freed from any error that might lead one astray.

Commenting on the difference between what a clergyman promises during the preparation for one's first communion and what a believer experiences upon receiving it, Robert Graves remarked that the "disappointment often felt by Protestant adolescents at their first communion is a natural one – the priest promises more than they are able to experience"[20] though not more than could have been felt. If, after that preparation, the aspirant would have received a host impregnated with a visionary drug, his experience might have been converted into a true initiation rite, with sufficient intensity to mold his entire life afterwards.[21] But the originality in the doctrine of

---

earth, the product of this mixture being the vine. The stems, the snake-like arms of the vine proved its diabolic origin." Compare the Vedic tradition in which cannabis sprouted where drops of ambrosia fell from the heavens or that an eagle brought *soma* to the mountains (see for example GHD, vol. I, ch. 4, pp. 150-152).

20 Graves, Robert. "The Universal Paradise," Difficult Questions Easy Answers. New York: Doubleday & Company, Inc., 1973, p. 88.

21 Graves, 1973, pp. 83-93: "The Roman Catholic Church teaches that Paradise cannot be attained except by repentance; and prepares every sinner for the journey of the *viaticum*, a symbolic consumption of Jesus Christ's' body and blood, after asking him to purge his soul by a sincere confession. ... The Christian sacrament of bread and wine was a love-feast in Hellenistic style. ... The Church has indeed banished the Serpent from Paradise. Her sacramental elements give the communicant no visionary foretaste of the new Jerusalem. ... Granted, many Christian mystics and many Jewish mystics have undoubtedly seen Paradisal sights, but always after a life of intense spiritual struggle; and these often alternate with terrifying visions of Hell. ... The love-feast ... strengthens human friendship and at the same time bestows

Christianity in the West – as in that of Brahmanism in the East – was to preserve intact the promise of ecstasy and at the same time carry it over to another life, changing the offer of a very present and real physical transubstantiation for another of an esoteric transmigration deferred until the end of time.

In religions that desire above all to be universal and orthodox, this disillusion is only too well compensated by decisive progress in self-control. The miracle remains in force, and it is *to eat* the god; but instead of falling into a trance, what is required is the will to believe. Though the senses will have noticed no difference whatsoever before and after the communion, to the will of the believer is encumbered the consummation of the miracle. Behold a no doubt brilliant discovery, capable of perpetuating indefinitely the purest liturgy, *so long as any point of comparison is erased.* Without the latter, the former is absolutely nonviable, and, from the very moment when the formality of the Eucharist is consolidated, all communions not based upon the power of autosuggestion are stigmatized as pacts with satanic powers.[22] The

---

spiritual enlightenment: which are the twin purposes of most religions."

[22] The concept of Satan is not independent from the struggle against those kind of powers. *Satan* signifies 'adversary' in Hebrew: "[T]he name 'Satan' comes from the verb *śāṭan*, 'to persecute, be hostile to' and also, more specifically, 'to accuse'" (Kluger, Rivkah Schärf. Satan in the Old Testament, tr. Hildegard Nagel, from the series Studies in Jungian Thought, ed. James Hillman. Evanston, IL: Northwestern University Press, 1967, p. 25). When the word appears in the Jewish Bible it does not indicate anything distinct from Yahweh: "Satan does nothing other than what God himself does in other contexts" (Kluger, 1967, p. 40). Against this position one could cite a verse from *Chronicles*: "And Satan stood up against Israel, and provoked David to number Israel" (I *Chronicles* 21: 1, KJV, blb.org). But this forgets a similar verse in *Samuel*: "And again the anger of the LORD was kindled against Israel, and he moved David against them to say, Go, number Israel and Judah" (II *Samuel* 24: 1, KJV, blb.org). In the Book of Job it is clear that the *satanic* only indicates Yahweh himself in the role of the adversary: "Then said his wife unto him, Dost thou still retain thine integrity? curse God, and die./ But he said unto her, Thou speaketh as one of the foolish women speaketh. What? shall we receive good at the hand of

body is something that stains the spirit, a repugnance. The deity will have nothing to do with the vegetal mystery: He will be one, incorporeal and transcendent, like the authority itself of the Christian faith.

But this repression sets in motion the return of the repressed under different guises. The adversary or Satan will become in fact *the past*, the promise of any mystical union not yet transformed into a formal union. The opposition to the idea of a natural entheogen is so much more severe the more it is born from an entheogenic promise betrayed. This will justify the destruction of the mystery rites around the Mediterranean and in Europe, the indefatigable persecution of witches up into the nineteenth century, and the missionary crusade against the *idolatries* discovered in the Americas and other continents. It will justify, finally, that which distinguishes Christianity from so many of the great religions known: that it is one of the few faiths that never hesitated to impose itself through terror, one in which internal assent often counted for less than coerced signs of an external belief.[23]

God, and shall we not receive evil?" (*Job* 2: 9-10, KJV, blb.org). Though it has few antecedents in the Old Testament, as an autonomous and separate spirit Satan-Lucifer becomes a pre-eminent Christian idol, thought up to discharge the negative from the deity, and later to incriminate any physical miracle not endorsed by the ecclesiastical hierarchy: "The separation of Satan, the dark side of God, is followed by the corresponding release of God's light side. ... This seems to me one of the very great turning points in the Old Testament concept of God" (Kluger, 1967, p. 142). Given that the principal adversaries of the Christian faith in the first centuries were mystery gods linked to orgiastic and ecstatic cults, the *efficacy* of such ceremonies could well have been the principal responsibility of the recently born Satan. In the end we see how for the Encratites, Tatianites, Marcionites and Aquarians that wine was a sin and for the Servians it was born from the conjunction of Satan and the Earth. Lucifer and Dionysus, then, are the same. For more on the conception and evolution of the Devil, see "Satan as Opponent of the mal'āk Yahweh (Zechariah 3: 1 *ff*)" in Kluger (1967), pp. 139-148.

23 The last of the early bishops to make a pronouncement on this subject was the most cultivated, Augustine of Hippo: "I have, then, yielded to the facts suggested to

b. The End of Euphoria. Having established up to what point and why any magical-religious use of drugs attacks the very essence of Christianity, there remains alive the possibility that something identical did not occur with their recreational and therapeutic uses. Notwithstanding, the actual distinction between medical and recreational use was non-existent in antiquity, where conspicuous by its absence is even a single text in which the one thing excludes the other. Euphoria, whether positive (by obtaining contentment) or negative (by alleviating pain), constitutes an end in itself. In other words, euphoria *is* therapeutic. If to a Greek or a Roman it should have been suggested that a certain drug was admissible for medical use but not as a pastime, he would have answered that the distinction between the one and the other was absurd and that, furthermore, it was incumbent only upon the user to decipher the difference.

But that euphoria should be an end in itself is not admissible in Christianity. Only a certain kind of euphoria – the pure or legitimate – can be considered worthy while any other method of obtaining satisfaction incurs sin. The rhetoric of the Apostle Paul is unequivocal: "For the flesh lusteth against the Spirit, and the Spirit against the flesh:

---

me by my colleagues, although my first feeling about it was that no one was to be forced to the unity of Christ, but that we should act by speaking, fight by debating, and prevail by our reasoning, for fear of making pretended Catholics out of those whom we knew as open heretics. But this opinion of mine has been set aside, not because of opposing arguments, but by reason of proved facts" (Parsons, Sister Wilfrid, tr. Saint Augustine Letters, vol. II (83-130), in The Fathers of the Church, vol. 18, ed. Roy Joseph Deferrari. New York: Fathers of the Church, Inc., 1953, pp. 72-73, letter 93, Augustine to his beloved brother, Vincent). See also J. G. Cunningham, tr. Letters of St. Augustine. New York: The Christian Literature Company, 1892 (GB), p. 338, Letter XCIII (A.D. 408) to Vincentius, ch. 5, para 17 or Nicene and Post-Nicene Fathers, vol. I, ed. Philip Schaff, et al. Edinburgh: T&T Clark, 1886, www.ccel.org.

and these are contrary the one to the other: so that ye cannot do the things that ye would ..."[24]

Within the realm of what the Christian desires is a considerable measure of affliction because pain is pleasing to God so long as it constitutes a mortification of the flesh. On the contrary, sensual pleasure offends the Creator in proportion to its intensity.[25] This attitude not only abhors the purposes which from the time of Heraclides of Tarentum[26] were denominated *voluptuous* with regards to

---

24 *Epistle to the Galatians*, 5: 17, KJV, blb.org.

25 "Thus, I muddied the waters of friendship with the filth of concupiscence, and I beclouded its brightness with the scum of lust" (Bourke, Vernon J., tr. Saint Augustine Confessions, in The Fathers of the Church, vol. 21. New York: Fathers of the Church, Inc., 1953, p. 50, book III, ch. 1). See also Pilkington, J. G., tr. Confessions of St. Augustin, Book III, ch. 1, para. 1, in A Select Library of Nicene and Post-Nicene Fathers of the Christian Church, vol. I, ed. Philip Schaff et al. New York: Christian Literature Company, 1892, p. 60.

26 "A physician of Tarentum, a pupil of Mantias, who lived probably in the third or second century B. C. .... He belonged to the sect of the Empirici .. and wrote some works on Materia Medica, which are very frequently quoted by Galen, but of which only a few fragments remain" (Smith, William, ed. A Dictionary of Greek and Roman Biography and Mythology, vol. II. Boston, MA: Little, Brown and Company, 1867, p. 391, //quod.lib.umich.edu); more recent researchers locate him in "the first half of the first century BC. ... All of his writings are lost" (Prioreschi, Plinio. A History of Medicine, vol. II, 2nd ed. Omaha, NE: Horatius Press, 1996, p. 541); see also Sigerist, Henry E. The Great Doctors. Garden City, NY: Doubleday & Co., 1958, p. 31. "Galen says that he wrote On Theriacs and Venomous Animals" and was "disposed to polypharmacy" prescribing "camel's brain and gall, crocodile's dung, the blood of tortoises, and so forth" (Allbutt, T. Clifford. Greek Medicine in Rome. New York: Benjamin Blom, Inc., 1970 (1921), p. 370). Aulus Cornelius Celsus (ca. 25 BC – 50 AD) lists one of his remedies including opium, for example: "If the cough prevent sleep, that catapotia of Heraclides of Tarentum is calculated to mitigate both these complaints: it is composed of saffron, myrrh, long pepper, castum galbanum, ... cinnamon, castor, and poppy tears" (Lee, Alex, tr. Aul. Cor. Celsus on Medicine. London: E. Cox, 1831 (GB), book V, ch. 25, sect. 10, pp. 51-52; see also GHD, vol. I, ch. 6). Heraclides "seems to have first pointed out the

certain drugs, but includes the use of analgesics for prolonged periods (as in theriacal practice), because that which does not alleviate sharp and momentary pathologies hints at an undignified flight before the pain that redeems mankind. The desire to look for pleasure as much as the desire to avoid chronic displeasure by means of drugs is infamous; even if one does not fall into a diabolic plant cult, it is more or less apostasy to veil this vale of tears (*valle lacrimarum*) which – accepted without palliatives – brings one closer to a life of celestial purity. The alteration of the soul through botany incurs the sin of hedonism, which can be considered mortal when it leads to any kind of promiscuity and relaxation, though perhaps it remains on the borderline of venial sin when it merely shuns morally healthy suffering. Officially, any ebriety supposes a guilty weakness.

To these considerations one must add as a fundamental stigma of opium its use *par excelence* in the ancient world, that is, the utility of the drug to achieve a timely death. Christianity considers the life of the believer to be not his own but that of his Creator, that all suicides die

---

great value of opium" (Withington, E. T. Medical History. London: The Scientific Press, 1894 (GB), pp. 66-67). Later writers, like Erasistratus, opposed his use of the drug and "scoffed at theriacs" (Allbutt, 1970, p. 362); Soranus of Ephesus calls his use of drugs "oppressive" and "harmful" and his rejection of bloodletting an "even worse" error (Drabkin, I. E., tr. Caelius Aurelianus: On Acute Diseases and On Chronic Diseases. Chicago, IL: University of Chicago Press, 1950, pp. 110-115, On Acute Diseases, book I, ch. XVII (Reply to Heraclitus), sects. 171-177). Much earlier, the "gloomy, supercilious, and perverse (p. 11)" philosopher Heraclitus of Ephesus (fl. ca. 504-500 BC) condemned the mysteries as "unholy rituals (p. 68)" and the drunken celebrations of Dionysus as "disgraceful exhibitions (p. 69)" (Wheelwright, Philip. Heraclitus. New York: Atheneum, 1964, ch. V, sects. 76, 77); "If it were not Dionysus for whom they march in procession and chant the hymn to the phallus, their action would be most shameless" (Kahn, Charles H. The Art and Thought of Heraclitus. Cambridge, UK: Cambridge University Press, 1979, p. 81, fragment CXVI); "But Hades and Dionysus, for whom they rave and celebrate the festival of the Lenaea, are ‹one and› the same! (Robinson, T. M. Heraclitus Fragments. Toronto, CA: University of Toronto Press, 1987, p. 17)."

in mortal sin. The rejection by the Catholic Church of those who recur to euthanasia will be so ferocious that in many cases not only will it block them from receiving last rites and being interred in a Christian cemetery, but, well into the eighteenth century, the cadavers of these reprobates will "suffer ... a second death," dragged through the streets before going off to a common grave, their worldly goods confiscated and their names crossed out in the parochial registers as infamous.[27]

Eschewing euphoria as an end in itself and declaring that a human life is not that of its holder but only the deity, Christianity caused the traditional realms of drug use to experience a significant decline. In contradistinction to Brahmanism, which limited itself to excluding orgiastic ceremonies, Christianity excluded together with the orgiastic the merely hedonistic, the institution of the good death as well as the chronic and not purely episodic use of drugs. Nothing would be more orthodox than the pronouncement of Bishop C. H. Brent, when from his diocese in Manila in 1909 he made the first call for a planetary

---

[27] *Les lois sont furieuses en Europe contre ceux qui se tuent eux-mêmes: on les fait mourir, pour ainsi dire, une seconde fois; ils sont traînes indignement par les rues; on les note d'infamie; on confisque leurs biens* (Montesquieu, Baron de La Brède et, Charles-Louis de Secondat [1689 – 1755] in "his satirical survey of French conditions [at] the wretched close of the reign of Louis XIV" entitled the *Lettres Persanes*, ed. Robert Loyalty Cru. New York: Oxford University Press, 1914, p. 110, *Lettre 76, Usbek a son ami Ibben, a Smyrne*); see also the version published at Paris: Pierre Didot, 1803 (GB), p. 217). "The laws are furious in Europe against those who commit suicide; these people suffer, as it were, a second death, are dragged ignominiously through the streets, are proclaimed infamous, and, in addition to all this, their goods are confiscated" (Montesquieu, Charles de Secondat. The Persian Letters, tr. C. J. Betts. London: Athenaeum Publishing Company, 1897 (GB), p. 142, Letter LXXVI, "Usbek to His Friend Ibben" at Smyrna). However, before this era (but especially afterwards and even down to our day), the ecclesiastical authorities were inclined toward a method that would permit them to officiate at the funerals, including the sumptuous ones, of suicides. It was expedient to consider that the dead person was mad to conceive of his purpose, being in this way as innocent as a newborn (in reality more so, since he died baptized and free of original sin that affects the newborn).

crusade against drugs, declaring that all non-medical use is immoral.[28] Brent made an exception for clinical use when the therapeutic estate already constituted a power comparable or superior to the ecclesiastic. But the bishops that ruled from the middle of the fourth century felt no need to make such an exception, since for them medicine was suspect for more than one reason. A few innocent uses were very little compared with the general temptation of euphoria as an end in itself, with its danger of idolatries, orgiastic cults, hedonism and euthanasia.

2. The Persecution of Unorthodox Consciousness. It is possible that a rigorous secrecy may have safeguarded some of the entheogenic recipes employed in the mystery cults, disorienting to an ecclesiastical hierarchy not precisely known for its pharmaceutical curiosity. It is also possible that coercion would have yielded its fruits, and that – conveniently interrogated – the mystagogues and pagan believers confessed everything up to and including their final thoughts. In any case the hierarchy gave little publicity to these kinds of interrogations.

a. Theoretical Foundations. An exception was the Bishop of Alexandria, Clement (c. 150 – 216 AD), who, in order to demonstrate the "Absurdity and Impiety of the Heathen mysteries,"

---

[28] Charles Henry Brent (1862 – 1929), "the Protestant Episcopal bishop of the Philippines ... was a world leader against nonmedical uses of narcotics" (Musto, D. F. "The History of Legislative Control over Opium, Cocaine, and their Derivatives," druglibrary.org); "Bishop Brent believes, that the use of opium has no 'unvicious' side" (Devins, J. B. An Observer in the Phillipines. Boston: American Tract Society, 1905, p. 143). Brent began his crusade after being appointed by Philippine governor William Howard Taft to an Opium Investigation Committee when Christian missionaries objected to the continuation of the Spanish government's monopoly on opium, "this moral wrong," after the seizure of the Philippine Islands by the United States at the turn of the twentieth century (Musto, "The History," druglibrary.org).

without fear of the Eleusinian curse revealed: "And the *synthema* [password] of the Eleusinian mysteries is as follows: 'I fasted; I drank the kykeon; I took from the kisté [chest]; having done my task, I placed in the basket [*kalathos*], and from the basket into the kisté.'"[29] Rather than denigrating and prohibiting pagan ceremonies, it may have been more effective to spread mycophobia. Perhaps some of the Fathers intuited something of this nature but they preferred to propagate a generic repugnance than to recognize even indirectly the possibility that the *Amanita muscaria* or analogous agents could have been used in religious contexts. With the express purpose of suppressing any kind of mystery different from the Eucharist, and under pressure from the bishops, the emperors Valentinian and Valens would prohibit (under penalty of death, naturally) any kind of nocturnal sacrifices in their dominions.[30]

---

[29] Mylonas, G. E. Eleusis and the Eleusinian Mysteries. Princeton, NJ: Princeton University Press, 1961, p. 294, *Protreptikos* II, p. 18. See also Wilson, W., tr. The Writings of Clement of Alexandria. Edinburgh: T & T Clark, 1867 (GB), p. 32; Butterworth, G. W. Clement of Alexandria. London: William Heinemann, 1919 (GB), p. 43, "Exhortation to the Greeks," ch. II, sect. 21. Clement (Titus Flavius Clemens), in his attack on pagan rituals (Wilson, William, tr. Clement of Alexandria, in The Ante-Nicene Fathers, vol. II, eds. A. Roberts and J. Donaldson. Grand Rapids, MI: William B. Eerdmans Publishing Co., 1956, p. 174), and other translators often missed the significance of the "cup," the *kykeon*. Arnobius of Sicca (c. 4th century AD) in his Case Against the Pagans, book 5, ch. 26 gives: *ieiunavi atque ebibi cyceonem* (I have fasted, I have drunk the kykeon). See Bryce, Archibald Hamilton and Hugh Campbell. The Seven Books of Arnobius Adversus Gentes. Edinburgh: T. and T. Clark, 1871 (GB), p. 250, Book 5, sections 25, 26, Lenorment, Francois. "The Eleusinian Mysteries," part IV, *Contemporary Review*, vol. 38, July – Dec 1880 (GB), p. 144 and GHD, vol. I, ch. 5, p. 260.

[30] "Emperors Valentinian and Valens Augustuses to Secundus, Praetorian Prefect. Hereafter no person shall attempt during the nighttime to engage in wicked prayers or magic preparations or funereal sacrifices. If he should be detected and convicted of such practices, We decree by Our everlasting authority that he shall be stricken [*mactari*, to be stricken, slaughtered, executed] with a suitable punishment. *Given on the*

The official attitude toward the phenomenon of the entheogenic trance can be illustrated in large measure by a theory of St. Augustine as to the cause of the metamorphosis of Apuleius:

Indeed, we ourselves, when in Italy, heard such things about a certain region there, where landladies of inns, imbued with these wicked arts, were said to be in the habit of giving to such travelers as they chose, or could manage, something in a piece of cheese by which they were changed into beasts of burden, and carried whatever was necessary, and were restored to their own form when the work was done. Yet their mind [sic] did not become bestial, but remained rational and human, just as Apuleius in the books he wrote with the title of The Golden Ass, has told, or feigned, that it happened to his own self that, on taking poison, he became an ass, while retaining his human mind. These things are either false, or so extraordinary as to be with good reason disbelieved. But it is to be most firmly believed that Almighty God can do whatever He pleases, whether in punishing or favoring, and that the demons can accomplish nothing by their natural power .... And indeed the demons, if they really do such things ... do not create real substances, but only change the appearance of things .... I cannot therefore believe that even the body, much less the mind, can really be changed ... by any reason, art or power of the demons.[31]

It is given as a certainty that the phenomena is not due to some natural effect of plants or their mixtures, but that if it exists at all, it can only be due to *demons* who are only able to change the *appearance* of

---

fifth day before the ides of September in the year of the consulship of the sainted Jovian and of Varronianus. – September 9, 364. INTERPRETATION: If any person should celebrate nocturnal sacrifices to the demons or should invoke the demons by incantations, he shall suffer capital punishment" (Pharr, Clyde, tr. The Theodosian Code and Novels and the Sirmondian Constitutions. New York: Greenwood Press, 1952, p. 238, *CTH* 9.16.7).

[31] Dods, Marcus, tr. Basic Writings of Saint Augustine, vol. II, ed. Whitney J. Oates. New York: Random House, 1948, pp. 421-422; see also Wilson, George, tr. The City of God, vol. II, in The Works of Aurelius Augustine, vol. II, Dods, Marcus, ed., tr. Edinburgh: T & T Clark, 1871 (GB), p. 236, book XVIII, ch. 18, entitled "What we should believe concerning the transformations which seem to happen to men through the art of demons" (p. 235).

things. In later centuries we will see it be repeated to the point of exhaustion that the experience of *flight* and the episode of *death-rebirth*, typical of the rapture or ecstatic trance, can only be considered possible by postulating an express intervention by Satan. Given that the *illusion* carries with it a pact with infernal powers, there now exists a theoretical foundation for prosecuting those who should be found in such a state as being guilty of satanic idolatry. They will not be few in number and they will deserve exemplary punishment.

Figure 80.
Hell in the City of God, by Augustine of Hippo (as depicted in a fifteenth century manuscript).

The conflict between the Apostles and Simon the Magician,[32] one of the most well known stories in the gospels (as well as in the

[32] "Then Philip went down to the city of Samaria, and preached Christ unto them. And the people with one accord gave heed unto those things which Philip spake,

hearing and seeing the miracles which he did. For unclean spirits, crying with loud voices, came out of many that were possessed [with them]: and many taken with palsies, and that were lame, were healed. ... And there was a certain man, called Simon, which beforetime in the same city used sorcery, and bewitched the people of Samaria .... Then Simon himself believed also: and when he was baptized, he continued with Philip .... Peter and John ... [and] when they were come down, prayed ... they might receive the Holy Ghost .... And when Simon saw that through laying on of the Apostles' hands the Holy Ghost was given, he offered them money, Saying, Give me also this power .... But Peter said unto him, Thy money perish with thee, because thou hast thought that the gift of God may be purchased with money" (*Acts* 8: 5-24, KJV, blb.org). Hence the word 'simony,' the buying and selling of church offices. In the apocryphal *Acts of Peter* (Coptic fragment, ca. 180 – 190 AD), it is Peter who does the miracles: "On the first day of the week ... on the Lord's day, a multitude gathered together, and they brought unto Peter many sick that he might heal them. And one of the multitude adventured to say unto Peter: Lo, Peter, thou hast made many blind to see and the deaf to hear and the lame to walk, and hast succoured the weak and given them strength" (James, Montague Rhodes, tr. The Apocryphal New Testament. Oxford: At the Clarendon Press, 1955 (1924), p. 300; see also the version at earlychristianwritings.com). In the *Vercelli Acts*, Peter engages in a magical duel with Simon: "[T]here was a great commotion in the midst of the church, for *some* said that they had seen wonderful *works done* by a certain man whose name was Simon .... [Simon] spake to the people with a shrill voice, saying: To-morrow about the seventh hour ye shall see me fly over the gate of the city in the form (habit) wherein ye now see me speaking unto you. ... And when it was the seventh hour, behold suddenly a dust was seen in the sky afar off, like a smoke shining with rays stretching far *from it*" (James, 1955, pp. 306-307, ch. IV). "But the brethren besought Peter to join battle with Simon .... And Peter seeing a great dog bound with a strong chain, went to him and loosed him, and when he was loosed the dog received a man's voice .... And Peter turned and saw a herring (sardine) hung in a window .... And he cast the herring into the bath, and it lived and began to swim ... and ... lest it should be said that it was a delusion (phantom) ... he made it to swim for a long time. ... But Simon the Magician ... in dining chambers he made certain spirits enter in .... [H]e made lame men seem whole for a little space, and blind, likewise, and once he appeared to make many dead to live and move .... And ... a great multitude assembled at the Sacred Way to see him flying ... raised up above all Rome and the temples thereof and the mountains. [And Peter prayed] and he [Simon] fell

Apocrypha and the early writings of the Church Fathers) illustrates the initial struggle between miracles coming from an orthodox deity and miracles derived from other powers. The Old Testament already gives a free hand to those who would strike down the competitors of Yahweh with its command: "Thou shalt not suffer a witch to live."[33] But Israel was a small territory and now this law would have to be imposed universally.

b. Legislative Foundations. Specific legislation for this purpose already existed in the classical era and would serve as a model for the Christians. The GrecoRoman world possessed a legal norm on witchcraft, characterized basically by distinguishing between white and black magic.[34] But with the triumph of Christianity any such distinction is abolished because all magic – even that pretending to be beneficial or white – is reputed to be satanic. Before the Christian faith was converted into a condition for enjoying citizenship – a thing

---

from the height and brake his leg in three places" (James, 1955, pp. 313, 316, 331-332, chs. 9, 13, 31, 32; see also the versions at earlychristianwritings.com and gnosis.org).

[33] *Exodus* 22: 18, KJV, blb.org. By the beginning of the third century, heresy will be "considered to have begun with Simon .... In the Christian reconstruction of the genealogy of error, Simon was the original from whom all heretics descended" (Paño, María Victoria Escribano. "Heretical Texts and *Maleficium* in the *Codex Theodosianus* (*CTH.* 16.5.34)," Magical Practice in the Latin West, eds. R. L. Gordon and F. M. Simón. Leiden: Brill, 2010, p. 135).

[34] "Thus the practice of magic for beneficent purposes was considered legal and even necessary in Greece and Rome. It was commonly practised by a great variety of people, the priests of specific deities on the one hand, and professional people, such as doctors, on the other. ... Even the austerest Roman authors included magic formulae for obtaining useful and beneficial results in their work. ... What of the magic and spells which were intended to cause harm? These were always held to be illegal" (Baroja, Julio Caro. The World of the Witches, tr. O. N. V. Glendinning. Chicago, IL: University of Chicago Press, 1964, pp. 18-19).

established beginning in 380[35] – Roman law already contained a number of prohibitions relative to black magic which became progressively more severe during the Lower Empire.[36]

In the reign of Antoninus Caracalla (211 – 217 AD), for example, those who might consult an astrologer, seer, soothsayer or prophet as to the health of a leader or the head of state, as well as those who answered, were to receive capital punishment.[37] The slave

---

[35] In the so-called Edict of Thessalonica: "It is Our will that all the peoples who are ruled by the administration of Our Clemency shall practice that religion which the divine Peter the Apostle transmitted .... We command that those persons who follow this rule shall embrace the name of Catholic Christians. The rest, however, whom We adjudge demented and insane, shall sustain the infamy of heretical dogmas, their meeting places shall not receive the name of churches, and they shall be smitten first by divine vengeance and secondly by the retribution of Our own initiative, which We shall assume in accordance with the divine judgment" (Pharr, 1952, p. 440, *CTH*, book XVI, title 1, sect. 2). By section 3, dated 381, dissenters were expelled and "denied the right and power to obtain churches" (Pharr, 1952, p. 440).

[36] Black magic was supposedly proscribed as early as the *Lex Duodecim Tabularum* (Law of the Twelve Tables), ca. 450 BC: "A man shall not remove his neighbour's crops to another field by incantations, nor conjure away his corn" (Carpenter, W. S. and P. T. Stafford, eds. Readings in Early Legal Institutions. New York: F. S. Crofts & Co., 1932, p. 79, taken from W. A. Hunter. Roman Law. London: William Maxwell & Son, 1885, pp. 17-22); "And among ourselves, in the Twelve Tables there is the warning: 'No one may make incantations against another's crop'" (Corcoran, Thomas H., tr. *Naturales Quaestiones*, vol. II, in Seneca in Ten Volumes, vol. X. Cambridge, MA: Harvard University Press, 1972 (Loeb), p. 57, book IVB, ch. 7, sect. 2).

[37] *Qui de salute principis vel de summa rei publicae mathematicos, hariolos, haruspices, vaticinatores, consulit, cum eo, qui responderit, capite punitur* (Haenel, Gustavus. Pauli Sententiarum, in Lex Roman Visigothorum. Leipsig: Sumptibus et typis B. G. Teubner, 1849 (GB), p. 434, Book V, Title XXI [XXIII], 3). The *Sententiae* "consists of commentaries ascribed to the jurisconsult Iulius Paulus [2nd – 3rd cent.], an eminent contemporary of Ulpian" (Paño, 2010, p. 129) and "one of the most distinguished of Roman jurists ... perhaps the most fertile of all the Roman law writers" (Smith, W., ed. A Dictionary of Greek and Roman Biography and

who asked about the health of his master was to be crucified; those he consulted, if they responded, were to be sent to the mines or deported to an island.[38] The possession of books of magical formulas also quite early came to be considered a crime against the *salus publica* (public health);[39] not only the practice but the knowledge of black magic was forbidden.[40] But if necromancy found itself prohibited, non-astrological white magic (without threats to Caesar or one's master) enjoyed great prestige, according to the testimony of, among others, Apuleius.[41] What preoccupied the superstitious Roman citizen,

---

Mythology, vol. III. London: John Murray, 1876 (GB), p. 155).

38 *Quod si servi de salute dominiorum consuluerint, summo supplicio, id es, cruce ufficiuntur; consulti autem, si responsa dederint, aut in metallum damnantur aut in insulam deportantur* (Haenel, Pauli Sententiarum, 1849, p. 434, book V, title XXI [XXIII], 4).

39 *Non tantum divinatione quis, sed ipsa scientia eiusque libris melius fecerit abstinere* (Paño, 2010, p. 131, ftnt 120, *Sent.* 5.21.4). At least one scholar argues that "these formulations must date from the early fourth century" (p. 131).

40 Section 5.23.18 of the *Sententiae* provides: "Let no one be permitted to have magic books; those who are discovered in possession of books of this kind shall have their properties confiscated, the books shall be burnt in public, and the offenders shall be deported to an island; if they are *humiliores*, they shall suffer the death penalty. Not only the practice but also the knowledge of the magic arts are forbidden" (Paño, 2010, p. 130); *Libros magicae artis apud neminem habere licet: et si penes quoscumque reperti sint, bonis ademptis ambustis que his publice, in insulam deportantur humiliores capiti puniuntur. Non tantum artis professio, sed etiam scientia prohibita est* (Haenel, 1849, p. 436).

41 Processed for practicing the art of magic, Apuleius did not fight shy of the charge, speaking to the magistrate and his enemies in no uncertain terms: "Do you hear, you who so rashly accuse the art of magic? It is an art acceptable to the immortal gods, full of all knowledge of worship and of prayer, full of piety and wisdom in things divine, full of honour and glory since the day when Zoroaster and Oromazes established it, high priestess of the powers of heaven. Nay, it is one of the first elements of princely instruction, nor do they lightly admit any chance person to be a magician, any more than they would admit him to be a king" (Butler, H. E., tr. The Apology and Florida of Apuleius of Madaura. Oxford: At the Clarendon Press, 1909, p. 56, The Apology, part II, section 26; see also gutenberg.org, //classics.mit.edu); even the supremely rational Stoic, Lucius Annaeus Seneca (4 BC

especially the political power – as an imperial edict from the year 357 makes clear - was "inquisitiveness about future events."[42]

With the enthronement of Christianity, in contrast, to the list of the persecuted an assortment of other characters was added – not only those traditionally associated with white magic like the herbalists, drug makers, faith healers, cathartics, and urban and rural witches but also those newly deemed to be heretics, the shamans, pontiffs of other cults, mystagogues, and theosophists – that did not figure in the classical Roman catalog, much less the Greek. Decrees from the middle to the late fourth century make this clear as every kind of superstition, idol worship and sacrifice was to be abolished[43] as was any

---

– 65 AD), while ridiculing earlier superstitions that supposed sacrifices to darkening clouds could "make a bargain with hail or buy off a storm with little gifts," admits that "presents do win over even the gods" (Corcoran, 1972, p. 55, book IVB, "Hail and Snow," ch. 6, sects. 2, 3, ch. 7, sect. 1).

[42] "Emperor Constantius Augustus to the People. No person shall consult a soothsayer [*haruspex*] or an astrologer [*matematicus*, astrologer, "numerologist"] or a diviner [*hariolus*]. The wicked doctrines of augurs and seers [*vates*] shall become silent. The Chaldeans and wizards [*magi*] and all the rest whom the common people call magicians [*malefici*, workers of evil], because of the magnitude of their crimes, shall not attempt anything in this direction. The inquisitiveness of all men for divination shall cease forever. For if any person should deny obedience to these orders, he shall suffer capital punishment, felled by the avenging sword. *Given on the eighth day before the kalends of February at Milan in the year of the ninth consulship of Constantius Augustus and the second consulship of Julian Caesar. – January 25, 357.* INTERPRETATION: When anyone, because of inquisitiveness about future events, consults either an invoker of demons or prophets, whom they call diviners, or soothsayers, who collect auguries, he shall suffer capital punishment" (Pharr, 1952, p. 237, *CTH* 9.16.4).

[43] "Let superstition cease and the insanity of sacrifices be abolished. ... It is decreed that in all places and all cities the temples should be closed at once .... We decree also that we shall cease from making sacrifices. And if anyone has committed such a crime, let him be striken with the avenging sword. And we decree that the property of the one executed shall be claimed by the city ... We order that all found guilty of attending sacrifices or of worshipping idols shall suffer capital punishment. ..." (Thatcher, Oliver J., ed. <u>The Library of Original Sources</u>. Milwaukee, WI:

kind of white magic.[44] As a legal principle, this extension to the list of the persecuted grew out of the elimination of the differences between

---

University Research Extension Company, 1901, pp. 70-71, *Codex Theodosianus*, 16.10.2, 16.10.4, 16.10.6, dated 341, 356). "All heresies are forbidden by both divine and imperial laws and shall forever cease" (Pharr, 1952, p. 450, *CTH* 16.5.5, dated 379). "We forbid all heretics to hold unlawful assemblies within the towns" (Pharr, 1952, p. 451, *CTH* 16.5.6.3, dated 381).

[44] Ammianus Marcellinus (325 – ca. 391 AD), a Syrian Antioch Greek and member of the imperial bodyguard, noted the change of policy in his *Res Gestae*. Under Constantius, in the years 356-7, for example, "[I]f anyone consulted a soothsayer about the squeaking of a shrew-mouse, the meeting of a weasel on the way, or any like portent, or used some old wife's charm to relieve pain (a thing which medical authority allows), he was indicted (from what source he could not guess), was haled into court, and suffered death as the penalty" (Rolfe, John C., tr. Ammianus Marcellinus, vol. I. Cambridge, MA: Harvard University Press, 1963 (Loeb), p. 233, book XVI, ch. 8, sect. 1). Under Valens, in the years 371-372, many are "condemned, are put to death, some justly, others unjustly ... on the ground of having stained themselves with the knowledge of magic" (Rolfe, 1963, vol. III, p. 215, book XXIX, ch. 2, sect. 2). As for their property, "men were immediately sent to put the seal on the houses, and during the examination of the furniture of the householder who had been condemned, to introduce privily old-wive's incantations or unbecoming love-potions, contrived for the ruin of innocent people. And when these were read in a court where there was no law or scruple or justice to distinguish truth from falsehood, without opportunity for defence young and old without discrimination were robbed of their goods and, although they were found stained by no fault, after being maimed in all their limbs were carried off in litters to execution" (Rolfe, 1963, vol. III, pp. 215-217, book XXIX, ch. 2, sect. 3). "After this, innumerable quantities of papers, and many heaps of volumes were collected, and burnt under the eyes of the judges, having been taken out of various houses as unlawful books ... though in fact, the greater part of them were books teaching various kinds of liberal accomplishments or books of law" (Yonge, C. D., tr. The Roman History of Ammianus Marcellinus. London: George Bell & Sons, 1894 (Bohn), p. 513). "As a result, throughout the oriental provinces owners of books through fear of a like fate, burned their entire libraries; so great was the terror that had seized upon all" (Rolfe, 1963, vol. III, p. 217, book XXIX, ch. 2, sect. 4). "There was a simple-minded old woman who was in the habit of curing intermittent fevers

white and black magic as well as those between magic and heresy.[45] It also represented an effective means of persecuting the centers of pharmacological culture, as much at the level of producer as that of investigator or consumer.

Legal norms adapted for this purpose were not slow in appearing during the "transition from the GrecoRoman social order to

---

with a harmless charm. [Valens] caused her to be put to death as a criminal, after she had been called in with his own knowledge and treated his daughter" (Rolfe, 1963, vol. III, pp. 231-233, book XXIX, ch. 2, sect. 26).

45 The religious dissident and the witch were often classified together in the law codes of the early Christian emperors. Those guilty of "sacrilege ... crimes against the dead, the sorcerer [*venefici*], or magician, the adulterer, ravisher, or homicide" were excluded from the traditional Easter pardoning of criminals under sections 9.38.3, 9.38.4, and 9.38.7 of the *Codex Theodosianus* as was anyone "who has compounded poisons for mind and body, poisons sought from noxious herbs and murmured over with incantations in dread secrecy" by 9.38.6 (Pharr, 1952, pp. 253-254, dated 367, 369, 370, 381, 384 from the reigns of Valentinian, Valens, Gratian and Theodosius). But section 16.5.34 may be "the first explicit association in a legal context between magic and heresy" (Paño, 2010, p. 108). In 398, the emperor Arcadius signed a law making the writings of religious dissidents "legally equivalent with magical codices," i. e., the crime of *maleficium* (Paño, 2010, p. 107). The statute uses section 5.23.18 of the Pauline *Sententiae* against the possession and even knowledge of magical books as a model: "We order ... that the codices that contain the doctrine [of the Eunomians and Montanists] and subject matter of all their crimes be searched for thoroughly and handed over for them to be burnt immediately under the supervision of the judges. In the event that anyone is convicted for having hidden and not surrendered any of these works for whatever reason, or with criminal intent, he should know that he shall be put to death for possessing harmful codices classed as criminal *maleficium*" (Paño, 2010, p. 108). Pharr, 1952, p. 456 gives: "If perchance any person should be convicted of having hidden any of these books [of heresy] under any pretext or fraud whatever and of having failed to deliver them, he shall know that he himself shall suffer capital punishment, as a retainer of noxious books [*codices*] and writings and as guilty of the crime of magic [*maleficium*. Or: as a retainer of books that are noxious and that were written by the crime of magic. That is, the composition of the books constituted the crime of magic]."

that of the new barbarian emperors."[46] In the year 424 AD the Salic Law contemplates the extermination of witches and those who give deadly herbs generally, though it also includes fines for those who accuse others of these crimes without being able to prove them;[47] this exception deserves to be taken into account because when the great persecutions begin (starting around the XIV century) denunciations will be made freely and in secret, without any risk either for informants or Inquisitors. In the year 506 the Council of Agde (*Agathense*), in its Canon 42, expressly excommunicates both clergy and laity who practice divination using sacred lots.[48] Five years later, in 511 the

---

46 Shehan, T. J. "Council of Agde," The Catholic Encyclopedia, vol. I, Aachen – Assize, ed. Herbermann, C. G. New York: Robert Appleton, 1907 (GB), p. 206.

47 "Title XIX – Concerning Magicians. 1. If any one have given herbs to another so that he die, he shall be sentenced to 200 shillings (or shall surely be given over to fire). 2. If any person have bewitched another, and he who was thus treated shall escape, the author of the crime, who is proved to have committed it, shall be sentenced to 2500 dinars, which make 63 shillings" (Carpenter, W. S. and P. T. Stafford, eds. Readings in Early Legal Institutions. New York: F. S. Crofts & Co., 1932, p. 122, taken from Henderson, Ernest F., ed. Select Historical Documents of the Middle Ages. London: G. Bell and Sons, Ltd., 1912, pp. 176-189). "The Salic Law is the most ancient as well as the most important of the Germanic law codes known as the *Leges Barbarorum.* Compiled under Clovis towards the close of the fifth century, ... (t)he procedure of the Salic Law is not a system of proof but a process of coercion" (Carpenter, 1932, pp. 115-116). Accusation without proof could be expensive: "If any person call a free woman *stria* (or *stiria*) or evil one, and fail to prove it, they shall themselves be arraigned and fined seventy-five hundred *denarii*, which are sixty-two (187 in some texts) *solidi* and a half" (Baroja, Julio Caro. The World of the Witches, tr. O. N. V. Glendinning. Chicago, IL: University of Chicago Press, 1964, p. 59, citing Cancioni, P. *Barbarorum Leges Antiquae* (ed. Venice 1781-92), II, pp. 107-8, 153, *Pactus Legis Salical Antiquior.*, LXVII, 1-3).

48 "*[Q]uod aliquanti clerici, sive laici, student auguriis, & sub nomine fictae religionis, per ea quas sanctorum sortes vocant, divinationis scientiam profitentur: aut quarumcunque scripturarum inspectione futura promittunt; hoc quicunque clericus vel laicus detectus fuerit vel consulere vel docere, ab ecclesia habeatur extraneus*" (Mansi, Johannes Dominicus. *Sacrorum Conciliorum Nova et Amplissima Collectivo*, vol. VIII. Florentiae: Expensis Antonii Zatta Veneti, 1762, p.

Council of Orleans [*Aurelianense*] adds monks to the list and "repeats the decree with very little variation. But the practice continued for all this ..."[49] After a rebellion in 588, in the year 589 Canon 14 of the Council of Narbonne (*Narbonense*) orders excommunication for "those who kept conjurers in their houses; these latter were to be publicly beaten and then sold [with their women, children and servants] and their price given to the poor."[50]

In the Fuero Juzgo, a list of the decrees of the Visigoth monarchy, there appear various dispositions of Chindasuinth (c. 563 – 653) which also prefigure the later crusade against the infamous covens

---

332, 172/623, documentcatholicomnia.eu; //gallica.bnf.fr). "[T]hat some of the clergy and laity followed after soothsaying, to the great detriment of the Catholic religion: and under the name of feigned religion, professed the art of divination, by what they call the lots of the saints, making use of a casual inspection of the Scriptures to divine futurities by ... that whoever of the clergy or laity should be detected in the practice of this art, either as consulting or teaching it, should be cast out of the communion of the church" (Bingham, R., ed. The Antiquities of the Christian Church, Book XVI, in The Works of the Rev. Joseph Bingham, vol. VI. Oxford: At the University Press, 1855, p. 245). The practice of foretelling the future by opening a page of the Bible at random, done "out of a base spirit, and love of filthy lucre" (Bingham, 1855, p. 245) seems to have been popular in the southern French towns of Languedoc. Indeed, the "practice of magic in fourth-century Christian circles, even within Church administration, was common" (Paño, 2010, p. 124).

49 Bingham, 1855, p. 245; *Si quis clericus, monachus, secularis, divinationem vel auguria crediderit observanda, vel sortes, quas mentiuntur esse sanctorum, quibuscunque putaverint intimandas, cum bis, qui eis crediderint, ab ecclesiae communione pellantur* (Mansi, 1762, p. 356, 182/623).

50 Urban, Sylvanus. "Curiousities of the Old Church Canons No. 11," *The Gentlemen's Magazine*, vol. XXXVI, New Series, July – Dec. London: John Bouvyer Nichols and Son, 1851 (GB), p. 123, August); [*I*]*n cujulcumque domo Gothli, Romani, Syri, Craeci, vei Judzi fuerint inventi ... Illi vero qui tali iniquitate repleti sunt, & sortes, & divinationes faciunt, & populum praevaricando seducunt: ubi inventi vel inventae fuerint, seu liberi, seu servi vel ancillae sint, gravissime publice tiestigentur, venundentur, & pretia ipsorum pauperibus erogentur* (Mansi, *Sacrorum*, vol. 9, 1763, pp. 1013 – 1017, 513-515/627, //gallica.bnf.fr).

of witches. In the second title of Book VI, the condemnation of those who consult "fortune tellers, spell casters or seers" was enlarged to include "those who give herbs,"[51] without distinguishing between poisons properly said, philters and drugs. But to superimpose the crime of the necromant and the religious dissident, the spell caster and the apostate, is also to erase the distinction between different kinds of drugs. Although the upper classes probably continued to use without any danger the traditional plants of the Celtic and GrecoRoman pharmacopeias, among the lower classes those remedies were

---

[51] *Quien toma conseio de muerte ó de vida del rey ó de otro omne con los adevinos, ó con los encantadores, ó con los provizeros, é los qui les responden, si fueren libres, con todas sus cosas sean siervos de la corte, ó de quien mandare el rey. ... Los que fazen pecados de muchas maneras deven ser penados de nuchas maneras. E primeramientre aquellos que dan yerbas deven aver tal pena, que si aquel á quien dieran las yerbas murier, manamano deven seer penados los que ie las diéron, é morir mala mientre. E si por ventura escapar de muerte aquel que las bevier, el que ie las dió deve ser metudo en su poder, que faga dél lo que quisiere* (Real Academia Española. *Fuero Juzgo, en latín y castellano, cotejado con los más antiguos y preciosos códices*. Madrid: Ibarra, 1815, pp. 104-105, Indice 8, Book VI, Title 2, sections 1, 2 //bib.cervantesvirtual.com). The Latin is available at Indice 2, Libro VI, Titulo II, p. 81. "Those who consult as to the death or life of the king or of another noble with fortune tellers, spell casters or seers, and those who answer them, if they are free, with all their possessions they should serve the court, or whomever the king commands. ... Those who sin in many ways must be punished in many ways. And firstly, those who give herbs must have such punishment, that if the one to whom was given the herbs should die, he who gave them must be beaten with violent blows until he die badly. And if by chance the one that drank [the herbs] should escape death, the one who gave them should be put into his power, to do with what he wishes" (tr. gwr). The king of the Visigoths, Chindasuinth, fused the Brevarian and Roman law "into one, and formally abolished Roman law; there was from that time but one code, and one nation. ... The law of the Visigoths ... is a universal code, a code of political, civil, and criminal law ... but it is also a system of philosophy, a doctrine .... [Principally] the work of the clergy ... it emanated from the councils of Toledo ... [and] has the vices and merits of their spirit" (Guizot, F. The History of Civilization: the Book of Judges, vol. II, tr. William Hazlitt. New York: D. Appleton & Company, 1864, pp. 217-219). Later, it will become the basis for medieval Spanish law.

contaminated with paganism and represented something *impure*. Any use of *diabolic plants*, ordered an edict of 743 AD from the last king of the Merovingian dynasty, Childeric III (c. 717 – 754), was to be repressed as being *superstitionesque gentilium*.[52]

A later cascade of laws in the domains of the Frankish emperors punished those who exercised the *diabolic arts* as well as those who believed in them. Various chapters of the legal code of Charlemagne – whose coronation also marked the ascension of the Bishop of Rome to the Papacy – urged his subjects "to forsake their superstitious beliefs. When mere exhortation proved useless, he resorted to edicts which laid down sentences appropriate to these crimes. ... [T]hose who practised the arts of the Devil would be dishonoured and treated like murderers, poisoners and thieves."[53]

---

52 "Superstition and paganism," signifying all enemies of the Catholic Church, including "heretics, schismatics and astrologers" (Paño, 2010, p. 112, and ftnt 26); "Childeric III published an edict condemning pagan and magical practices as if they were much the same thing" (Baroja, 1964, pp. 53-54, citing Baluze. Baluzius, 1780, vol. I, cols. 150-152, under the heading *Indiculus Superstinionem et paganiarum* lists a chapter XIV against *divinis vel sortilegis* (diviners and soothsayers). "*Maleficium*, in fourth-century legal parlance, fundamentally denoted malign magic, in other words, a specialized ritual directed against the well-being, physical or mental, of one or more victims. The pre-398 *constitutiones* of *CTH*. 9.16, *de maleficis et mathematicis et ceteris similibus*, understand *artes magicae* as the use of spoken *sortilegia* – recited from *dira carmina* – and material *sortilegia* – the preparation of philtres, potions, *venenum*, *medicamenta* – or casting spells, curses, performing exorcisms or making predictions based on numerology or observation of the stars" (Paño, 2010, p. 122). *Sortilegis* is said to be derived from "the Latin *sors-sortis* (French *sort*, Spanish *suerte*, and English 'fate'" (Baroja, 1964, p. 150).

53 Baroja, 1964, p. 54: "These edicts specifically condemned all kinds of witchcraft, such as the making of wax figures, summoning devils and using love philtres, disturbing the atmosphere and raising storms, putting curses on people and causing the fruits of the earth to wither away, drying up the milk of some people's domestic animals to give it to others, practising astrology or making talismen. ... [T]hose who consulted them [witches] and made use of them would be given a similar sentence,

Curiously, one from the year 800 lists some eighty-nine plants, most of them medicinal (including *pavot*, identified as either the garden or the opium poppy, and hemlock, both occasionally employed in the "arts of the Devil"), which Charlemagne demanded be grown on his imperial estates.[54] A statute from 801 prohibits the clergy from "drinking or inducing others to drink."[55] From 812 another chapter extends to soldiers the previous statute.[56] Together, it's evident that to be around

---

and in some cases that meant death" (citing Baluze, vol. I, cols. 220, 518, 707, 837, 929, 962, 999, 1104). Statute XVIII from the year 789 forbids consulting with witches and sorcerers (*malefici, incantadores, & incantarrices*), statute XL from the year 814 condemns those who inquire of fortune tellers, witches, sorcerers or seers (*qui ariolos sciscitetur ... malefici, nec incantatores, nec phitones ... damnentur*), and later statutes condemn them (*quos in Simone mago Dominus terribiliter damnavit*) as was Simon the Magician (Baluzius, Stephanus. Capitularia Regum Francorum, vol. I. Paris: Ex Typis Francisci-Augustine QUILLAU, Typographi Serenissimi Principis CONTII, via vulgo dicta, du Fouarre, 1780 (1677), cols. 220, 518, 707, 837).

54 *Volumus quod in horto omnes herbas habeant: id est lilium, rosas ... febrefugiam, papaver [Papaver somniferum], betas ... sclareiam* (Boretius, Alfredus, ed. Capitularia Regum Francorum, vol. I, in Monumenta Germaniae Historica, ed. Societas Aperiendis Fontibus, Legum Sectio II. Hannover: Bibliopolii Hahniani, 1883, p. 90, Capitulare de Villis, sect. 70, 102/474, gallica.bnf.fr); "We desire that each steward shall make an annual statement of all our income, giving an account of our lands ... of the gardens .... We want that in the garden they have all sorts of plants, that is ... lilies, roses ... hemlock ... [opium poppy], beets ...." (Buli, Jean Marc, tr. "Of Imperial Lands and Imperial Courts," Readings in European History, vol. I, ed. James H. Robinson. Boston, MA: Ginn & Co., 1904, pp. 137-139; Baluzius, 1780, vol. I, pp. 330, 341, chapter 70; see also archive.org and baudelet.net). "This capitulary of Charlemagne, A. D. 764-814, gives the best description of the villa and its organization in the ninth century. Since land was the primary source of income it was worthy of great attention, and no detail was too minute to be neglected" (Cave, Roy C. and H. H. Coulson. A Source Book for Medieval Economic History. NY: Biblio and Tannen, 1965, p. 17).

55 "Whoever disobeyed this law was to be excommunicated or corporally chastised [... *a communione statuimus submovendum aut corporali subdendum esse suplicio*]" (Lewin, 1964, p. 191, citing Balusius, *Capitularia regum Francorum*, Venetiis, 1722, pp. 257, 177, 782).

56 "[I]f one of them were discovered in a state of drunkenness he was to be

any *diabolic plant* not grown on the imperial estates was incomparably more serious than to frequent the wine seller. Somewhat later (873) is a chapter from the reign of Charles the Bald proposing to drive out from his kingdom the "godless and those who made philtres and poisons."[57]

Figure 81.
One of the Councils that met between 590 and 691 in the city of Seville, Spain, which appears defended by archers and lancers, symbol of the unification of civil and religious power.

excommunicated and sentenced to live on water until he had repented of his evil behaviour. In spite of interdictions of this kind, reinforced by those of Church councils, drinking continued even in sacred places" (Lewin, 1964, p. 191).

57 "We therefore expressly recommend the lords of the realm to seek out and apprehend with the greatest possible diligence those who are guilty of these crimes in their respective countries. If they are convicted ... they must perish ..." (Baroja, 1964, p. 54, citing Baluze, II, cols. 230-1, sect. VII).

It cannot be established with any certainty which drugs were considered to be impious and perhaps even for the judges and bailiffs charged with applying the law there never came to be anything so precise as a list of forbidden substances. But it is instructive the degree of what is being attempted, as this does not deal so much with repression as it is with making all knowledge disappear about such things:

If they are under suspicion or accused without being convicted, and if the testimony against them is not sufficient to prove their guilt, they shall be submitted to the will of God. This shall decide whether they are to be pardoned or condemned. But the associates and accomplices of those who are really guilty, both men and women, shall be put to death, so that all knowledge of such a heinous crime may vanish from our dominions.[58]

---

[58] Baroja, 1964, p. 54, citing Baluze, vol. II, cols. 230-1 (sect. VII). The 'will of God' was trial by ordeal used "to prove the innocence or guilt of a sorcerer or a witch from the darker period of the Middle Ages onwards" (Baroja, 1964, p. 203). Five were common: (1) the Duel, in which a man "bringing the accusation of witchcraft against a freedwoman ... should be compelled to make good his charge in single fight" (Smith, W. and S. Cheetham, eds. A Dictionary of Christian Antiquities, vol. II. London: John Murray, 1880 (GB), p. 1467); (2) the Ordeal of Hot or Cold Water, where either the accused would be forced to lift a "heavy stone from the vessel containing the [boiling] water" and if his hands "exhibited marks of injury ... he was to put to death" or the accused "was only held guilty if he or she floated on the surface" of the cold water (Smith, 1880, p. 1468); (3) the *Judicium Crucis*, in which both "accused and accuser lifted their arms to a horizontal position ... and he who, from fatigue, was first compelled to let fall his arms was held to be defeated (Smith, 1880, p. 1468); (4) the Ordeal of Hot Iron, in which the accused was made to draw a "bar of hot iron from a furnace with the naked hand" or to walk "over heated ploughshares with naked feet" (Smith, 1880, p. 1468); and (5) the Ordeal of Swallowing Food, in which bread and cheese force-fed to the accused "would infallibly choke him if he knowingly perjured himself" (Smith, 1880, p. 1469). "In Spain there were also many varieties, commonly called *salvas*" (Baroja, 1964, p. 203).

c. ***The War on the Past.*** Certain crimes can be punished by standardizing them in codes and castigating their commission. Certain others are so intrinsically abominable that the mere fact of listing them might suggest their commission to the perverse and would gravely offend the decency of the just. The latter are the crimes against the grace of redemption – against the Holy Spirit itself – that traditionally were considered to be the only ones that were unpardonable. Without prejudice toward condemning the culprits for these acts, the acts themselves are so odious that the policy to be followed is to expel them from the symbolic order, excluding them completely from the written word.

To this order of things belongs of course, for Orthodox Christianity, the pharmacological alteration of consciousness. It must, then, be affirmed that the prohibition of drugs is already completely defined from the moment when the Pauline interpretation of Christian doctrine triumphs. The first Christians did not call the abominable *to take drugs* as we say today, but rather *to sign a pact with the devil*; instead of suggesting that the chemical modulation of the soul leads to *madness* or an *abyss of depravity*, they called it *apostasy* and *idolatry*. Apostasy is to deprecate one's own salvation: to expose the infinite gift of blind faith, laboriously constructed, to those horizons of ecstasy the more terrifying the more liberated they are from the emotional and mental routine. Idolatry is to venerate a physical nature animated by different *spirits*, who once were the patrons of each particular drug and now have been converted into *demons*, the entheogenic become the enechthrogenic.[59]

But the repugnance toward entering into the details of such apostasies and idolatries not only led to the condemnation in a very vague manner of *malevolent herbs* and *diabolic plants* but also to the use of a more refined method of combat, the same which would be employed in the struggle against the direct attacks by pagan thinkers and

---

[59] See GHD, vol. I, 2010, ch. 7, p. 394.

philosophers on the cult of Christianity. By the reign of Marcus Aurelius there was a certain tolerance of magical practices and free speech[60] as well as libraries in the principal cities of the empire.[61] Upon

---

60 "From my grandfather Verus I learned good morals and the government of my temper. ... From Diognetius, not to busy myself about trifling things, and not to give credit to what was said by miracle-workers and jugglers about incantations and the driving away of daemons and such things ... and to endure freedom of speech" (Aurelius, Marcus Lucius. The Meditations, tr. George Lang, book one, //classics.mit.edu). Said tolerance did not often extend to treasonous atheists: "The Christians had been branded atheists for their refusal to pay homage to the recognized gods of the state ... and refusing to recognize the divinity of the emperor" (Hoffmann, R. Joseph, tr. "Introduction," Celsus On the True Doctrine A Discourse Against the Christians. Oxford: Oxford University Press, 1987, pp. 22-23) in an "age when religious traditions were widely held to express a people's continuity with the past and their national allegiance to constituted authority" (Hoffman, 1987, p. 34).

61 As early as the second century BC, Polybius of Megalopolis (c. 203 – 121 BC) notes that the study "of documents involves no danger or fatigue, if one only takes care to lodge in a city rich in such records, or to have a library in one's neighbourhood. You may then investigate any question while reclining on your couch, and compare the mistakes of former historians without any fatigue to yourself" (Shuckburgh, Evelyn S., tr. The Histories of Polybius, vol. II. London: Macmillan and Co., 1889, p. 113, book XII, sect. 27). By the beginning of the first century AD, Seneca decries the private collecting of books not for knowledge but for show: "What is the use of having countless books and libraries, whose titles their owners can scarcely read through in a whole lifetime? ... What excuse have you to offer for a man ... who ... sits yawning in the midst of so many thousand books? ... [F]or by now among cold baths and hot baths a library also is equipped as a necessary ornament of a great house" (Basore, John W., tr. Seneca Moral Essays, vol. II. Cambridge, MA: Harvard University Press, 1965 (Loeb), book IX, *De Tranquillitate Animi* ("On Tranquility of Mind"), pp. 247-249, ch. IX, sects. 4, 6). Two centuries later, educational "institutions expanded at all levels, from the village schools to the provincial and metropolitan universities. Perhaps never until recent times was education so general, so universal as in the Roman Empire of the third century. ... The Emperors accompanied their generosity with an increasingly close supervision over all professorial appointments. One might hope to find that these expenditures

the institutionalization of the Christian faith, incendiary mobs were charged with converting these projects of illumination into smoke and ash. The last pagan emperor, Julian (r. 361 – 363), installed an "excellent collection of books including philosophy of every school, history and Christian writings" at Antioch in a "small and graceful" temple built by "Hadrian in honor of the deified Trajan"; his Christian successor, the emperor Jovian, "at the instigation of his wife ... allowed a mob to burn" it a short time later.[62] Archbishop Theophilus (Patriarch of Alexandria from 385 to 412) personally directed the believers who in the year 391 destroyed the *impious* paintings and sculptures of the museum of art in Alexandria, in whose flames also perished part of the library.[63] In the fifth century, a fire purified the

---

in education had led to intelligent criticism and stimulating suggestions for imperial policies. Unfortunately, the opposite occurred; the professors seemed most interested in championing the Emperors and their system" (Williams, C. Dickerman. "Introduction," in Pharr, Clyde, tr. The Theodosian Code and Novels and the Sirmondian Constitutions. New York: Greenwood Press, 1952, pp. xix, xxi).

62 Downey, Glanville. A History of Antioch in Syria. Princeton, NJ: Princeton University Press, 1961, pp. 395-6, 398).

63 "At the solicitation of Theophilus bishop of Alexandria the emperor issued an order at this time for the demolition of the heathen temples in that city; commanding also that it should be put in execution under the direction of Theophilus. ... These were therefore razed to the ground, and the images of their gods molten into pots and other convenient utensils for the use of the Alexandrine Church; for the emperor had instructed Theophilus to distribute them for the relief of the poor" (Zenos, A. C., tr., ed. Socrates, Sozomen: Church Histories. New York: The Christian Literature Company, 1890 (GB), p. 126, book V, ch. XVI; see also ccel.org). The library had been burned before, once in 47 BC by accident by Julius Caesar who, "when the enemy endeavoured to cut off his communication by sea, ... was forced to divert that danger by setting fire to his own ships, which, after burning the docks, thence spread on and destroyed the great library" (Clough, A. H., ed., rev. Plutarch's Lives, vol. 2. London: J. M. Dent & Sons, Ltd., 1910, p. 566); Seneca writes that some "forty thousand books were burned" (Basore, John W., tr. Seneca Moral Essays, vol. II. Cambridge, MA: Harvard University Press, 1965 (Loeb), p. 247, book IX, *De Tranquillitate Animi*, ch. IX, sect. 5). The last and completely devastating

Basilica of Julius (Caesar) at Rome and a library of some 36,500 volumes was lost including an "ancient manuscript of Homer, on a roll of parchment one hundred and twenty feet in length, the intestines, as it was fabled, of a prodigious serpent."[64] For the *greater glory of God* the emperor Leo III (c. 675 – 741), "the Iconoclast," ordered the Library of Constantinople burned including the Basilica of the Emperors, enlarged by Julian to contain some 120,000 volumes, among them the oldest rolls of parchment containing the Homeric poems, written in gold letters.[65] The number of temples, schools and pagan libraries consumed by the flames is still incalculable.

---

fire in the mistreated library of Alexandria, principal deposit of ancient knowledge, was decreed by Caliph Omar (ruled 634-644), a leader animated by another monotheism with a vocation for universal empire: "Omar bn-Al Hattab, the second Halif ... ordered [the destruction of] the library on the ground that if the books were in accord with the Kurân, the Kurân alone was sufficient, and if at variance with it, there was no need of them" (Joseph, Isya. "Bar Hebraeus and the Alexandrine Library," *The American Journal of Semitic Languages and Literatures*, vol. XXVII, October 1910-July 1911. Chicago, IL: University of Chicago Press, 1911, p. 335). Supposedly, the books and scrolls fueled the public baths for six months. Others dispute the story: "Critical scholarship has shown the story to be completely unfounded" (Lewis, Bernard. The Arabs in History. Oxford: Oxford University Press, 2002, p. 53).

[64] Gibbon, Edward. History of the Decline and Fall of the Roman Empire, vol. III. New York: Modern Library, 1932, p. 296.

[65] "[M]ore than half were burned ... by the command of the Emperor Leo III, who thus sought to destroy all the monuments that might impede his opposition to the worship of images" (E. E. "Libraries," Encyclopedia Britannica, vol. XIII, 8th ed. Edinburgh: Adam and Charles Black, 1857 (GB), p. 385). The number of volumes lost to the fire varies with the citation, at least one author disputing the event entirely (see Beeton, Samuel Orchard. Beeton's Science, Art and Literature, vol. II. London: Ward, Lock & Tyler, 1870 (GB), p. 262; Edwards, Edward. Memoirs of Libraries, vol. I. London: Trubner & Company, 1859 (GB), p. 72-73).

Figure 82.
Leo III (c. 675 – 741), "the Iconoclast," directs the melting of the pagan images of the city of Constantinople (from a Byzantine hymnal).

Certainly, in the last days of the Lower Roman Empire there were already hundreds of functionaries dedicated to blocking the diffusion of thought and even simple news, to censoring correspondence, to creating an artificial climate of opinion, to falsifying facts, defaming political adversaries with accusations capable of exciting their lynching at the hands of tumultuous crowds already maddened by oppression and misery.[66] But the Christian hierarchy inherited the bureaucratic apparatus of the censor and then invented techniques for modifying the *past.* Thus, they not only destroyed the works of Celsus, Proclus, Porphyry and Julian opposed to the Christian

[66] "[T]here was an exceedingly numerous secret police, the *agentes in rebus*, to report disobedience. In addition there was a special 'super' secret police, the *curiosi*, appointed to watch the *agentes in rebus* and other government departments whose work was regarded as of particular importance, such as the public post" (Williams, C. Dickerman. "Introduction," in Pharr, 1952, p. xix, citing sections 6.27-29 of the *CTH*).

concept of the world, but the titles of these specific books were erased from the catalog of their authors as well, leaving the rest intact; if not for luck, some Arab translation and commentary, a little scholarly plagiarism and disobedience, and the attacks of Christian polemicists, they would be for posterity something more than lost: they would never even have existed.[67]

---

[67] "Practically nothing is known of [Aulus Cornelius **Celsus**] ... a learned and experienced medical practitioner [possibly of the second century AD]. ... [He] probably lived in Narbonensis" (Spencer, W. G., tr. Celsus: De Medicina, vol. I. Cambridge, MA: Harvard University Press, 1971 (Loeb), pp. vii-xi). "He is accessible because his eloquent opponent, Origen of Alexandria, quotes from Celsus' On the True Doctrine in generous measure; hence it is possible to reconstruct the main lines of the philosopher's argument in detail" (Hoffmann, R. Joseph, tr. Celsus: On the True Doctrine. Oxford: Oxford University Press, 1987, p. 29). His attacks on the cult practically demanded a response from the early Christian fathers: "The cult of Christ is a secret society .... As to their doctrine, it was originally barbarian. ... There is nothing new or impressive about their ethical teaching .... Jesus himself was thought to work wonders by the use of magic and incantations. ... This savior ... deceived many and caused them to accept a form of belief harmful to the wellbeing of mankind. Taking its root in the lower classes, the religion continues to spread among the vulgar: nay, one can even say it spreads because of its vulgarity and the illiteracy of its adherents" (Hoffman, 1987, pp. 53-57). The life of the "spokesman of mature Neo-Platonism," **Proclus** (ca. 411 – 485), roughly coincided with the "collapse of the western frontiers of the Roman Empire (406 – 410), the great barbarian migrations, the invasion of Attila the Hun (440 – 52) and the sack of Rome, first by the Visigoths (410) and then by the Vandals (455). Finally came the end of the Western empire itself (476)" (Siorvanes, Lucas. Proclus Neo-Platonic Philosophy and Science. New Haven, CT: Yale University Press, 1996, pp. x, 6). His "support for the worship of the Greek pagan gods led to conflict with the Christian authorities" (Gregory, John. The NeoPlatonists: A Reader. London: Routledge, 1999, p. 155). The "hostile ideological climate ... forced Proclus to go [from Athens] to Lydia for one year" (Steel, Carlos. "Proclus," The Cambridge History of Philosophy in Late Antiquity, vol. II, ed. Lloyd P. Gerson. Cambridge, UK: Cambridge University Press, 2010, p. 630). Yet, he "systematised Neo-Platonism" as "head of the school of philosophy at Athens, the 'Academy,' from the

age of 25 until his death at 75" (Siorvanes, 1996, pp. ix – x). His "*Commentary on the Timaeus* is arguably the most important text of ancient Neoplatonism" (Tarrant, Harold, tr. Proclus' Commentary on Plato's Timaeus, vol. I. Cambridge, UK: Cambridge University Press, 2007, p. 1). But his argument in On the Eternity of the World that the universe must have "had no beginning" invited an attack "on behalf of Christianity [by] Philoponus in Alexandria" (Share, Michael, tr. Philoponus Against Proclus's "On the Eternity of the World 1 – 5." Ithaca, NY: Cornell University Press, 2005, p. vii) who believed "Proclus had aimed his proofs specifically at the Christians" (p. 5). After his death, in "the Islamic world, Proclus, or *Buruklus* as he was called by the Arabs, was read extensively .... Some fragments are still extant solely as Arabic translations. ... [His] works contributed to the birth of Islamic philosophy and science" (Siorvanes, 1996, pp. 31-2). A Christian writer using the pseudonym Dionysius the Areopagite "took Proclus' philosophical system, joined God the creator with the transcendent, adapted it to Christian doctrine, and made it the first coherent Christian theology of the divine Being and the spiritual worlds" (Siorvanes, 1996, p. 31). The Neoplatonist **Porphyry** (c. 232 – c. 306 AD) "was born at Tyre in Syria ... educated in Syria and Athens ... and died in Rome" (Warren, Edward W., tr. Porphyry the Phoenician. Toronto, CA: Pontifical Institute of Medieval Studies, 1975, p. 9). His fifteen book opus Against the Christians survives only in "quotations, paraphrases, or references in various Christian authors, chiefly Eusebius, Jerome, and Augustine. ... [V]arious imperial edicts ordered the destruction of Porphyry's anti-Christian work. The first was issued by Constantine in 325 ... it mentions that Porphyry's works – as well as his reputation – were to be destroyed. ... In 448, Theodosius II and Valentinian III jointly issued another edict .... [T]he philosopher's anti-Christian writings were condemned to be burnt, as they may cause God's wrath and be harmful to men's souls. ... Against the Christians was meant to disappear for good when it was burned on the orders of Christian emperors .... Some copies must have survived, but the principal sources for Porphyry's treatise are Christian apologists who aimed at defending their dogmas against future threats of persecution ... or against ridicule" (Magny, Ariane. "Poetry in Fragments: Jerome, Harnack, and the Problem of Reconstruction," *Journal of Early Christian Studies*, 18. 4 (Winter 2010), pp. 516, 517 ftnt 5, 529, 536). The emperor Constantine used the actions against Porphyry as the model for his attacks on the Arian heresy: "Victor Constantine Maximus Augustus, to the bishops and people. ... Wherefore as Porphyry, that enemy of piety, for having composed licentious treatises against religion, found a suitable recompence, and such as thenceforth branded him with

It is extremely likely that the same policy was followed with regards to drugs and pharmacological cults. Around 1560 Fray Bernardo de Sahagún watched in pain as his Prior destroyed the first version of his *Historia general de las cosas de Nueva España* containing apostasies and idolatries with magical plants; though already very old

---

infamy, overwhelmed him with deserved reproach, his impious writings also having been destroyed; so now it seems fit both that Arius and such as hold his sentiments should be denounced as Porphyrians" (Zenos, A. C., tr., rev. The Ecclesiastical History of Socrates Scholasticus, in A Select Library of Nicene and Post-Nicene Fathers, vol. II, second series, Socrates, Sozomenus: Church Histories, eds. Philip Schaff, Henry Wace. Grand Rapids, MI: William B. Eerdmans Publishing Co., 1952, p. 14, book I, ch. 9). See also Zenos, A. C., tr. The Ecclesiastical History of Socrates, surnamed Scholasticus. London: George Bell and Sons, 1874 (GB), p. 31, book I, ch. 9). The emperor Flavius Claudius Julianus (331/2 – 363 AD), aka **Julian** the Apostate, nephew of the first Christian emperor, Constantine I, felt "that his destiny was to restore the religion of his forefathers to Rome" (Hoffman, R. Joseph, tr., ed. Julian's Against the Galileans. New York: Prometheus Books, 2004, pp. 11, 27). He attempted to isolate the Christians by limiting their rights, creating a "pagan church" and writing a "philosophical polemic designed to prove the unoriginality of the faith" (Hoffman, 2004, p. 32). "For it is a disgrace to us that no Jew has to beg, and that every Galilean is ready to provide support for our poor as well as their own, while men laugh that we cannot muster aid for our people" (Hoffman, 2004, p. 516, "Epistle XXII, Letter to Arsacius, A High Priest of Galatia"). "Among pagan collectors, Libanius, Aristophanes of Corinth, and Zosimus (450 – 501) had key roles to play in the preservation of the epistles and in deciding which were safe for keeping [and which were] too dangerous for circulation" (Hoffman, 2004, p. 88). Bishop Gregory Naziazen wrote "tirelessly against him" and much of Against the Galileans survives in the refutation of Cyril of Alexandria (Hoffman, 2004, pp. 11, 87). Ironically, the very provocative nature of his polemic may have helped it to survive: "I am persuaded that the fraudulent machination of the Galileans ... is the fiction of men, composed with an evil intention; and that it possesses indeed nothing divine, but employing that part of the soul which delights in the fabulous, which is puerile and stupid, adduces monstrous narrations in order to a belief of the truth" (Taylor, Thomas, tr. The Arguments of the Emperor Julian Against the Christians. Chicago, IL: Ares Publishing Inc., 1930 (1809), p. 13).

he rewrote it but this copy of the work disappeared again for another three centuries – practically speaking hidden away – in the Franciscan convent of Tolosa.[68] The sixteenth century Spanish translator and annotator of Dioscorides, Andrés Fernandez de Laguna only avoided persecution due to fame and Church patronage[69] while other men of the Renaissance like Cardano[70] was imprisoned and forbidden to

---

68 "On account of the fear of encouraging the educated natives to dwell upon their heathen past – a very real danger at the time – and on account of the author's strictures upon the methods of the *Conquistadores*, it was not published, but was consulted in manuscript, being sent from one to the another college of the order, until finally carried to Spain and deposited in the convent of Tolosa, where it was found, and a copy made, by the archivist Muñoz shortly before 1800. It was published under the title *Historia general de las cosas de Nueva España* in three volumes at Mexico in 1829" (Mooney, James. "Sahagún, Bernadino de," The Catholic Encyclopedia, vol. 13, Revelation – Simon Stock, Herbermann, C. G., ed. et al. New York: Robert Appleton Company, 1912 (GB), p. 325); "*Hoy sale á luz, despues de haber estado occulta por mas de dos siglos en el convento de S. Francisco de Tolosa de Navard*" (Sahagún, Bernadino de. *Historia general de las cosas de Nueva España*, vol. I, Carlos Maria de Bustamente, ed. Mexico: Alejandro Valdés, 1829 (GB), p. i).

69 In 1545 Andrés Fernandez de Laguna (1499 – 1559), humanist, military surgeon, pioneer in anatomy and urology, journeyed to Italy to become personal physician to an important Cardinal in the Church hierarchy, receiving in return security and protection from the Inquisition: *Il parvint à devenir le médecin personnel du cardinal Francisco Bobadilla y Mendoza. Sans doute cherchait-il, par ces relations, protection et sécurité, pour ne pas être l'objet de persécutions de la part de l'Inquisitiòn* (Causape, Maria del Carmen Frances. "*Dioscoride, Andrés Laguna et la Pharmacie*," *Revue d'histoire de la pharmacie*, vol. 79, Issue 291 (1991), p. 424, www.persee.fr).

70 Girolamo Cardano (1501 – 1576). His "searching intellect brought him encyclopedic learning, and he wrote more than 200 works on medicine, mathematics, physics, music, religion, and philosophy" (Baigrúe, Brian S., ed. The Renaissance and the Scientific Revolution: Biographic Portraits, vol. I. New York: Charles Scribner's Sons, 2001, pp. 26-27). "[W]hen Cardano wrote, Inquisitors and Spaniards were already busy in Italy, either hindering the production of such natures, or, where they existed, by some means or other putting them out of the way" (Burkhardt, J. The Civilization of the Renaissance in Italy, Middlemore, S. G. C., tr. London: S.

publish and the intellectual society of Porta was forced to disband by the Inquisition.[71]

Somenschien, 1904 (GB), p. 335). "[I]n 1570 he was imprisoned for several months by the Inquisition, which accused him of heresy against the Roman Catholic Church" (Baigrúe, 2001, pp. 26-27). "No details of the charges are known .... If the Inquisition officials put their minds to it, they could certainly discover clandestine heretical statements in the works Cardano had published over the past twenty years. In *De Subtilitate* he put Christianity, Judaism, and Islam side by side and objectively compared them. ... He had, after all, cast Jesus' horoscope and published it in his commentary on Ptolemy" (Fierz, Marcus. Girolamo Cardano (1501 – 1576), tr. Helga Niman. Boston: Birkhäuser, 1983, pp. 28-29). "After his imprisonment at Bologna he was again prohibited from teaching, and was also finally prohibited from publishing his works" though he continued to write in secret until his death five years later (Morley, Henry. Jerome Cardano: The Life of Girolamo Cardano, Physician, vol. II. London: Chapman and Hall, 1854, p. 297, archive.org).

[71] Giambattista della Porta (1535 – 1615), polymath, mycologist and founder of *Academia dei Segreti* (*Accademia Secretorum Naturae*) "the first scientific society of modern times, progenitor of the *Accademia dei Lincei* (Academy of the Lynxes) [of which Galileo was a member], the *Accademia del Cimento*, [and] the Royal Society of London" (Price, Derek J., ed. Natural Magick: John Baptista Porta. New York: Basic Books, Inc., 1957 (1658), p. v, "Introduction"). The original society "came to its end very characteristically because Della Porta was accused of meddling with witchcraft, having made a 'witches' salve'" (Bronfenbrenner, Martha Ornstein. The Rôle of Scientific Societies in the Seventeenth Century. Chicago, IL: University of Chicago Press, 1975 (1928), p. 74). The record of their investigations survives in the twenty books of Natural Magick, first published in Naples in 1558, that "treats the wonders and marvels of the natural world as phenomena underlain by a rational order that can be divined and manipulated by the natural philosopher through theoretical speculation and practical experiment" (Safra, Jacob E, chmn. The New Encyclopedia Britannica, vol. 9, 15th ed. Chicago, IL: Encyclopedia Britannica, 2005, p. 624, "Porta, Giambattista della"). The seventh book treats "Of the Wonders of the Lode-stone," the tenth "Of Distillation" in which is described how one may obtain "Oyl of Poppy-Seed" that is "useful in dormitive Medicines" (Price, 1957, p. 259), the seventeenth book speaks of "Burning-glasses, and the wonderful sights to be seen with them" (p. 355) and describes the camera obscura by which one may "see all things in the dark, that are outwardly alone in the Sun, with the colour of

I do not see a valid reason to suppose that something common in the sixteenth century, when the culture of the cleric was more elevated, should not have been practiced during the epoch of the great library burnings, when one of the Christian pretensions was to rewrite ancient history so as to present it as an anxious awaiting of Christ. It seems a very weak objection to say that in the sixteenth century there was a crusade against witchcraft, because from the end of the fourth century there was a war even more widespread and uncertain of outcome against the Hellenistic religions and other pagan cults. In reality, the sudden collapse of news and opinion regarding pharmacology from the fifth century onwards ought to be attributed not only to the Orthodox Christian attitude toward drugs but also to its general policy with regards to the subject of books.

Along with the direct and indirect repression of what were then habitual customs, the new Christian era presupposed – in my opinion – a destruction as deliberate as it was casual of uncountable ancient documents related to the matter. Consequently, instead of saying that the use of psychoactive drugs has always sought the shameful shadows – as Lewin intimates – we might be better off saying that from the triumph of Christianity said use of persecuted drugs wished to be veiled by shadows, shameful or otherwise.[72] Together with the evident

---

them" (p. 363), while the third book, chapter twenty details how to "make that kind of Wine which is called Phthorium, and kills children in their mother's wombes" (p. 107) and book twenty, chapter eight suggests that "a Lamp ... filled with Hares fat ... when it burns in the middle of womens company, it constrains them all to cast off their clothes .... I believe this effect can come from nothing but the Hares fat, the force whereof perhaps is venemous" (p. 407).

[72] An effect understood implicitly by Lewin if not the underlying cause: "In the solitude of isolated and inaccessible mountains far from the world, in places to which Chinese authority and its agents penetrate rarely and with difficulty, these ... tribes cultivate the poppy and introduce its juice surreptitiously into China" (p. 43). "Pharmacologist, toxicologist, medical historian ...," Louis Lewin (1850 – 1929) writes with the scientific observation of a physician, the thundering damnation of the

advantage of historical exactitude, this correction has the added advantage of explaining why nothing similar to this obscuration was recorded in other parts of the planet and why the return of laicism to Europe will involve a rapid accumulation of news and discoveries, in a field until then empty of both.

B. The Preparation for an Internal Crusade

From the middle of the seventh century only the territories that today comprise France, Spain and Italy retained their loyalty to the Bishop of Rome. The practices of the clergy exhibited features of unheard of corruption, attempting to counter and stop monastic movements of reform arising in Ireland and Palestine. Evangelical jealousy pronounced an anathema against the ancient knowledge and

---

moralizer and as a sadder but wiser prohibitionist. In the admittedly brilliant Phantastica (1964) these contradictions abound. On the one hand, we hear the experienced medical doctor explaining: "There is no formula or rule which affords a definite standard, for general limits are overpassed by the individual constitution. ... Consequently there are no psychological constants common to all individuals" (pp. 9-10). On the other hand, "We may take it as a fact that negroes have greater recuperative powers than white people. This is not due to climatic conditions but to certain innate qualities possessed by them" (p. 9) and "The Indians of South America are said to have an intuitive appreciation of their own defectiveness ..." (p. 2). He never hesitates to apply morality to insensate substances: "The use of opium and its ingredients as a soothing and euphoric remedy has developed into a grave menace to the life of nations" (p. 32); "[T]he sketch of Hogarth representing a party of punch drinkers ... cannot equal in horror the picture of degradation presented by an assembly in the throes of cocaine" (pp. 80-81); [For chlorodyne] women sell their husbands' property and steal in order to obtain the drug, and spend large sums on their morbid craving" (p. 75). But of the prohibition of alcohol in the United States, he penned: "I fancy that this fanatical prohibition has roused adverse forces which will one day be able to restore things to a reasonable level. No! The idea that the world can be improved by innovations of this kind is destitute of all reasonable foundation" (p. 187).

Figure 83.
Christ burns the pagan books, preserving only the gospels on the shelves that appear on the left (mosaic in the Mausoleum of Gala Placida).

did not hesitate to say – from the mouth of the Bishop of Hippo, Augustine – that the aim of the sciences was to develop an unhealthy curiosity.[73] In a few centuries Europe fell back economically and

[73] "For even when we have a knowledge of these worldly matters, it is folly to make a profession of them; but confession to Thee is piety" (Pilkington, 1892, p. 81, book V, ch. 5, para. 8); "Whatever was written either on rhetoric or logic, geometry, music, or arithmetic, did I, without any great difficulty, and without the teaching of any man, understand, as Thou knowest, O Lord my God, because both quickness of comprehension and acuteness of perception are Thy gifts. Yet did I not thereupon sacrifice to Thee. So, then, it served not to my use, but rather to my destruction" (p. 77, book IV, ch. 16, para. 30).

spiritually a millennium. Plagues of field and shack, natural catastrophes, social chaos, privilege, barbarities, continuous plundering and all manner of things previously remedied in larger or smaller measure by civil law, experience and knowledge were combined with invasions of Vikings, Magyars and Saracens to produce a rapid feudalization. Many villages were abandoned, others subjected to isolation, the forests took over the great plantations, agriculture and animal husbandry did not produce excesses capable of sustaining a true commerce, the mining, metallurgy and food industries suffered a collapse, and communications became impossible or simply too dangerous.

Without foreseeing that it would only convert simple unbelievers into potential heretics, Rome solicited the support of nobles and kings to baptize by force Saxons, Danes, Prussians, Lombards, slaves, Jews and Moors who fell under its zone of influence. Yet with all that the general cantonalization conspired against the purity of the faith. From all sides the orthodox ritual appeared to be plagued by polytheistic echoes, borrowed from each newly *converted* region, while this fusion of ignorance and intolerance unceasingly produced new missionary conflicts. The catechism during the High Middle Ages found itself in a phase of open reception to believers, not yet in that of its spiritual perfection properly said.

From here onwards magic is to be prohibited, any kind of magic. The type of medicine recommended by Hippocrates and Galen is suspected of heathenism, and as that of the witches is even more objectionable, the only legitimate therapy is the counsel of the clergy. Masses, offerings, bribes and devout prayers remedy all kinds of illnesses within a general return to the cure by prayer that only demands that faith healers dress in the habit of some recognized order. After emptying the old pagan temples of their sacred offerings, relics, icons and mummies, allowing the clerics to sell eternal life in exchange for precious metals and other fungible goods, Christianity insists upon placing outside the law any kind of *superstition.*

But superstition has gathered a formidable momentum. On the one hand, it is the poorest and most isolated communities who recover their traditions of shamanism and witchcraft, trusting more in those older therapies than in the blessed water, branches, candles and holy oils. On the other hand, the well thought of classes tend to look for the reasons for the reigning disastrous situation and begin to find them in the witches who are causing the hail storms, droughts and epidemics. From the ninth century these accusations begin to become an epidemic in themselves, at the very moment a general theory of Satan is developing – *demonology* – which enjoys favor among the principal theologians. It could be said that the equilibrium between model A and model B of the sacrifice had already disappeared from the fifth century on, and that the hope of collective salvation through the immolation of sacrificial lambs is rapidly gaining ground.

1. The Classical Witch. The classical witch (*striga*) is someone who "practised a trade, and needed for it money, and, above all, sense."[74] She is an urban character, perfectly well known in ancient Rome. The older poets like Laevius mention their arts in combining substances[75] and in the imperial epoch the witch is alluded to with a mixture of fear and ridicule by Virgil,[76] Horace,[77] Ovid,[78]

---

[74] Burkhardt, 1904, p. 529, part V, ch. IV.

[75] Baroja, 1964, p. 29. Laevius (c. 80 BC). Only some sixty lines of his poetry remains, mostly in the citations of other writers. "Those who have read Laevius will recognize his lines: Philtres are brought out from everywhere:/ they look for love-charms, magic wheels and nails,/ ribbons, rootlets, herbs and twigs, and then/ the neighing animals' *hippomanes*" (Harrison, Stephen et al., trs. Apuleius Rhetorical Works. Oxford: Oxford University Press, 2001, p. 56, Apology (*Pro Se De Magia*), sect. 30); see also perseus.tufts.edu.

[76] **Virgil** (70 BC – 19 BC). His Alphesiboeus makes love charms: "Bring out water and wreathe these shrines with soft wool; and burn rich herbs and male frankincense, that I may try with magic rites to turn to fire my lover's coldness of mood" (Fairclough, H. Rushton, tr. Virgil, vol. I, rev. ed. Cambridge, MA: Harvard

Petronius[79] and Apuleius.[80] Theocritus describes one of these women – Simaetha – in a poem titled exactly *Pharmakeutriai* ("Incantation,"

University Press, 1974, p. 61, *Eclogue* VIII, lines 64-67).

77 **Horace**'s Canidia prepares a love potion for Varus but something goes wrong: "Why are the dreadful drugs of the savage Medea failing to work? ... And yet no herb or root has escaped me .... The bed he sleeps in has been smeared with a substance designed to make him forget all his other lady loves. Ah *that's* it! He walks free because of the spells of a *cleverer* witch [*solutus ambulat veneficae scientioris carmine*]. Well, Varus, you wretch, you will bitterly regret all this; draughts of quite abnormal power will bring you running back to me" (Rudd, Niall, tr., ed. Horace Odes and Epodes. Cambridge, MA: Harvard University Press, 2004 (Loeb), pp. 284-287, *Epode* V); see also Baroja, 1964, pp. 25-26, 33.

78 Publius **Ovidus** Naso (43 BC – 18 AD). His Circe arouses sympathy for her feelings and admiration for her knowledge even while her acts are reprehensible: "Offended, hurt, she crushed together herbs/ Whose juices had a dreadful power, and, singing/ Spells she had learned from Hecate, she mixed them. ... Sorting out plants, arranging, from confusion,/ In separate baskets, the bright-colored flowers,/ The different herbs. She told them what to do,/ Knew what each leaf was for, which ones would blend,/ Weighing her simples. ... She gave us welcome .../ Gave us all we asked for .../ All in a sweetish brew, and in the sweetness,/ Were hidden drugs" (Humphries, Rolfe, tr. Ovid Metamorphoses. Bloomington, IN: Indiana University Press, 1967, pp. 339, 346-347, book XIV, lines 20-51, 240-275). His Dipsas is an old bawd but with magical powers: "There is a certain – whoso wishes to know of a bawd, let him hear! – a certain old dame there is by the name of Dipsas. Her name ["thirsty"] accords with the fact .... She knows the ways of magic, and Aeaean incantations, and by her art turns back the liquid waters upon their source; she knows well what the herb can do, what the thread set in motion by the whirling magic wheel, what the poison of the mare in heat" (Showerman, Grant, tr. Ovid in Six Volumes, vol. I.: Heroides and Amores. Cambridge, MA: Harvard University Press, 1971, pp. 346-347, *Amores* I, ch. 8, lines 1-8); see also Baroja, 1964, pp. 25, 34.

79 **Petronius** Arbiter was the "judge of taste" under the emperor Nero: "Nero thought nothing elegant or exquisitely sensual unless Petronius had approved it" (Ruden, Sarah. Petronius Satyricon. Indianapolis, IN: Hackett Publishing Co., Inc., 2000, p. 129 quoting Tacitus, *Annals*, book 16, ch. 18). For Petronius witches are simply more oddball characters in a witty, crude and irreverent farce: "[Trimalcho:] ... suddenly the witches began to screech but to tell the honest truth we did ... not see

"Sorceress," "Spellbinder");[81] Lucan's Erichthro may be the exception that proves the rule.[82] The interventions of the classical witch have

---

the witches themselves. ... Ah! yes, I would beg you to believe there are wise women, and night-riders, who can turn the whole world upside down" (Heseltine, Michael, tr. Petronius, rev. E. H. Warmington. Cambridge, MA: Harvard University Press, 1969 (Loeb), pp. 139, 141, *Satyricon*, sect. 63); see also Baroja, 1964, p. 36.

[80] **Apuleius**' Pamphile sparks fear but in the context of a ribald farce: "[Pamphile] gathered together all her accustomed substance for fumigations (*omne genus aromatis*), she brought forth plates of metal carved with strange characters, she prepared the bones of birds of ill-omen, she made ready the members of dead men brought from their tombs. ... [B]eware I say, beware of the evil arts and wicked allurements of that Pamphile – for she is accounted the most chief and principal enchantress of every necromantic spell (*maga primis nominis et omnis carminis sepulchralis magistra creditur*)" (Adlington, W., tr. Apuleius: The Golden Ass. London: W. Heinemann, 1924, pp. 56-57, 126-127, book II, sect. 5, book III, sect. 17); see also Baroja, 1964, p. 38.

[81] **Theocritus** (ca. 300 BC). His Simaetha is described by one scholar as "a suburbanite of the lower middle class, whose sights are set on the 'station above her,' but whose respectable aim is marriage" (Rist, Anna. The Poems of Theocritus. Chapel Hill, NC: University of North Carolina Press, 1978, p. 34). For another, Simaetha represents "self-assertive women retaliating against traditional male acts that threaten their sense of self" (Burton, Joan B. Theocritus's Urban Mimes: Mobility, Gender, and Patronage. Berkeley, CA: University of California Press, 1995, p. 63). "Simaetha's extravagant exhibition of the full range of desperate emotions ..." (Halperin, David M. Before Pastoral: Theocritus and the Ancient Tradition of Bucolic Poetry. New Haven, CN: Yale University Press, 1983, p. 221) "[unfolds in] a series of magic incantations and prayers to the feminine divinities of the night, magic, and love ... designed to make her lover [Delphis] return" (Walker, Stephen F. Theocritus. Boston, MA: Twayne Publishers, 1980, p. 95). "Now with my love-magic will I bind him, but if he vex me still, so help me Fates, he shall beat upon the gate of Hades, such evil drugs, I vow, I keep for him in my box .... Coltsfoot is an Acadian weed, and for it all the foals, all the swift mares run mad upon the hills. So may I see Delphis, and so like one maddened may he come to this house from the bright wrestling-school. ... I will bray a lizard, and bring him an ill-draught to-morrow. ... My magic wheel, draw to my house the man I love" (Gow, A. S. F., tr. The Greek Bucolic Poets. Cambridge: At the University Press, 1953, pp. 11, 14, Idyll II); see also Baroja, 1964, p. 26.

much of a theatrical effect, but she possesses a laboratory or something analogous where she prepares a variety of articles. She made feminine cosmetics, as well as philters related with carnal love in its widest sense; she elaborates products that cause erotic passion and also others capable of inciting hatred, an abortion of undesired

---

[82] Marcus Annaeus **Lucanus** (39 – 65 AD). His Ericthro may be the first example of a medieval witch, a rural Thessalian crone meant to evoke fear, horror and disgust to whom Pompey comes to consult about the future of a battle: "[T]he camp was near the habitation of those Thessalian witches, whom no boldness of imaginary horror can outdo, and who practise all that is deemed impossible. ... By their spells love steals into insensible hearts against the decree of destiny ... [and] men's minds are destroyed by incantations. ... Every creature that has power to kill and was born to do mischief dreads the Thessalian witches .... These criminal rites and malpractises of an accursed race fierce Ericthro had scouted as not wicked enough .... [S]he inhabited deserted tombs, and haunted graves from which the ghosts had been driven. ... Her tread blights the seeds of the fertile cornfield, and her breath poisons air that before was harmless. ... Haggard and loathly with age is the face of the witch, her awful countenance, overcast with a hellish pallor and weighed down by uncombed locks .... At last she chose a corpse [from the battlefield] and drew it along with the neck noosed .... Then she began by piercing the breast of the corpse with fresh wounds, which she filled with hot blood; she washed the inward parts clean of clotted gore; she poured in lavishly the poison that the moon supplies. ... The froth of dogs that dread water was not wanting ... eyes of dragons were there .... Then she went on to speak plainly in a Thessalian spell .... 'I invoke the Furies, the horror of Hell ... and Chaos, ... the Ruler of the world below ... to Styx ... to Persephone ... our patron Hecate ....' [The corpse speaks to Pompey:] 'Let not short-lived glory trouble you: the hour will soon come that makes all the leaders equal .... By whose grave shall flow the Nile, and by whose the Tiber – that is the question; and the battle of rivals settles nothing but their place of burial. ... Ill-fated house! you must fear Europe and Africa and Asia; Fortune divides your graves among the lands you have triumphed over; you shall find no place in all the world less dangerous than Pharsalia'" (Duff, J. D., tr. Lucan The Civil War (Pharsalia). London: W. Heinemann Ltd., 1969, pp. 337-365, book VI, lines 435-820); see also Baroja, 1964, pp. 20, 31-32.

children, etc.[83] While she understands operations abominable to a good Christian, she has to be an intelligent and able character, with much experience, like Celestina,[84] a renaissance witch in the classical

---

[83] "The business of the 'Strega' was to provide for other people's pleasure. ... By far the most important field of activity of the 'Strega' lay, as has been said, in love-affairs; and included the stirring up of love and of hatred, the producing of abortion, the pretended murder of the unfaithful man or woman by magical arts, and even the manufacture of poisons ..." (Burkhardt, 1904, p. 529, part V, ch. IV, quoting Maccaroneide, *Phant.* xvi, xxi).

[84] A character in the *Tragicke-Comedy of Calisto and Melibea* by Fernando de Rojas, "one of the most extraordinary creators of imaginary life ever to exist .... [H]e is a peer of Shakespeare – it is impossible to overestimate the unconventionality of his art" (Gilman, Stephen. The Spain of Fernando de Rojas. Princeton, NJ: Princeton University Press, 1972, p. 357). The work is a "product of a mind vigorous, grave, lucid, shackled by few prejudices or opinions, alert to impression, stored with a large experience of life and of men, their occasions, foibles, and pitfalls" (Fitzmaurice-Kelly, James. "Introduction," Celestina or the Tragicke-Comedy of Calisto and Melibea Englished from the Spanish of Fernando de Rojas by James Mabbe, 1681. London: David Nutt, 1894 (GB), pp. xv-xvi). "So preeminent is [Celestina] among her compeers that the original title ... has been supplanted by the name of the great wise Bawd" (Fitzmaurice-Kelly, 1894, pp. xvii-xviii). Calisto woos Melibea but she spurns him: "How durst such a one as thou hazard thy selfe on the vertue of such a one as I? Goe wretch, be gone out of my sight ..." (Fitzmaurice-Kelly, 1894, p. 22, Act I); *y el intento de tus palabras calisto ha seydo: de ingentio de tal hōbre como tu hauer de salir para se perder en la virtud de tal muger como yo. Vete vete d'ay torpe: que no puede mi paciencia tollerar* ... (Rojas, Fernando de. *La Celestina*. -----------: Archer M. Huntington, 1909, p. a ii). Calisto's servant suggests he go see Celestina: "For a long time I have known a bearded old crone who lives in the outlying parts of our district here. Her name is Celestina. She's a witch, and she's shrewd and instructed in every evil that exists. I have heard that she has destroyed and repaired more than five thousand maidenheads in this city. If she wishes, she can cause rocks and crags to melt with lust" (Singleton, M. H., tr. Celestina: A Play in twenty-one acts attributed to Fernando de Rojas. Madison, WI: University of Wisconsin Press, 1958, p. 28); *Días ha grandes que conozco en fin desta vecindad una vieja barbuda, que se dice Celestina, hechiceria, astuta, sagaz en cuantas maldades hay. Entiendo que pasan de cinco mil virgos los que se han hecho y deshecho por su autoridad en esta ciudad. A las duras peñas promoverá y provocará a*

style. Her services are demanded by every social class, especially by the rich.

2. The Medieval Witch. A curious ambivalence shows up in the medieval laws on witchcraft from the earliest times. On the one hand it is necessary to eliminate the *belief* in any kind of witchcraft, punishing even with the death penalty those who admitted the efficacy of the spells cast by the witches (*strigae*); thus, a chapter written for Saxony in 789 – when the tribes of the country were being passed under the knife if they did not agree to be baptized and recite the Creed – ordered the execution of those who believed in the existence of such characters, including those who questioned the salutary effect of burning them. [85] It was understood that only the witches and wizards could have faith in themselves.

On the other hand, a number of laws prohibited the *practice* of magic, presupposing that it was effective thanks to the collaboration of the Devil. There was, then, the crime of believing in something decreed impossible or unreal, and along with it, the crime of doing the impossible and unreal. The witch was accused of believing in – vainly – the existence of (satanic) *spirits* and, at the same time, of having command over them. But little by little both things will become fused

---

lujuria, si quiere (Rojas, Fernando de. *La Celestina*, first edition. Buenos Aires, AR: Editorial Sopena, 1941, p. 21). Adds Parmeno: "When the French ambassador was here she sold him as a virgin three times over the same one of her servants" (Singleton, 1958, pp. 35-36); see also Baroja, 1964, p. 40.

[85] "[The statute] refers to Saxony and condemns belief in *strigae* and their ability to eat men, expressing the view that they ought to be burned for it. The same act prescribes capital punishment for all who believe such things" (Baroja, 1964, p. 56 citing Baluze, vol. I, cols. 251-252): *Si quis á diabolo deceptus crediderit, secundúm morem paganorum, virum aliquem aut feminam strigam esse & homines comedere, & propter hoc ipsam incenderit, vel carmen ejus ad comedendum dederit, vel ipsam comederit, capitis sententiâ punietur* (Baluzius, 1780, cols. 251-252, vol. I, ch. VI, *De magis & strigas occisis*); see also Boretius, 1883 (GB), pp. 68-69, *Capitulatio de Partibus Saxoniae*, sect. 26, subsect. VI).

together, given the advantages of isolating and concentrating evil into certain symbols, presenting a secret world society as responsible for all of the ills of society.

In contrast with the classical urban witch, as timeless as the courtesan, there begins to appear in the High Middle Ages a very different rural witch. She too is found linked to drugs, but more than concocting cosmetics, philters and remedies, she uses unguents to induce magical flights and other operations typical of shamanism and the sorcery of possession. In fact, she officiates as a minister in religious ceremonies that are understood by those foreign to her circle as rites of adoration to Lucifer, though they belong to cults dedicated to much earlier goddesses, especially those to Artemis/Diana. The classical urban *striga* is essentially a nondenominational character while the medieval rural *striga* serves as a channel for an amalgam of purposes, including celebrations of the orgiastic type.[86] The attendees at these acts – which in time will be called *sabbats* – appear to be mostly women, similar in spirit to the bacchantes described by Euripides. The entheogenic vehicles employed are the pomades or *unguents* of great psychoactivity which in the Renaissance – when for the first time they are investigated – will be composed basically of opium, cannabis and certain solanaceas.

---

[86] Burkhardt classifies witches by race. In contradistinction to the German witch, the "Italian witch has a job and wants to earn money. Above all she must have a good deal of sang-froid and act rationally. Not for her the hysterical visions of the witches of the North, belief in long rides through the air and so forth" (Baroja, 1971, p. 100). In contrast, Baroja classifies them by sociology: "The typical witch is above all found in *country* areas; the sorceress of classical extraction, however, is more usually found in *urban* districts, or in areas where an urban-type culture exists" (Baroja, 1971, p. 100, italics Baroja). As can be observed by comparing Ovid's Dipsas with Lucan's Erichthro or De Rojas' Celestina with those of the Basque Aquelares, both kinds of witches were found "in Europe at the time of the Renaissance and perhaps also before as well as after that period" (Baroja, 1971, p. 100), though it appears that one or the other predominates in a particular locale in a given epoch.

Here the pharmacological aspects come back into play. The resurgence of witchcraft can be linked to various factors, among these being the ruin of Hippocratic medicine, the inutility of the ecclesiastic therapies, and the passive resistance of many communities to the Christian catechism. Upon witchcraft fell the added stigma of treating with malevolent herbs, diabolic plants and infernal potions. However, now one can see important transformations.

These rural witches (most frequently female, though also sometimes male) clearly represent the only *drug manufacturers* there are in the High Middle Ages, and enough of their recipes ended up being passed along to the herbalists as respectable medicines. The news about them comes from the Christians, so we cannot be sure of who they really were or how they thought of themselves in the beginning, before the great persecutions.[87] Among scholars there is no shortage of those who believe, like Burkhardt, that the personality of the witch was practically invented by the Inquisition.[88] Others think the witch is a character "slightly mad, weird, but not wholly improbable ... [who] finds consolation in the dream world which certain European herbs can give her."[89] Still others, the realists, think that they represented the

---

87 "Unfortunately, we know less about what the sorcerers and witches themselves believed than what was believed about them. Possibly witches and sorcerers had more complicated emotions and systems of beliefs than those who believed in them" (Baroja, 1971, p. 243).

88 "The illusion was now added that by means of magical arts it was possible to enter into relations with the evil ones, and use their help to further the purposes of greed, ambition, and sensuality. ... [W]hen the so-called magicians and witches began to be burned, the deliberate practise of the black art *became more frequent.* With the smoke of the fires in which the suspected victims were sacrificed, were spread the narcotic fumes by which numbers of ruined characters were drugged into magic; and with them many calculating impostors became associated" (Burkhardt, 1904, p. 524).

89 *De otro, a un ser raro, alocado, estrambótico, al que no podemos negar toda realidad, pero cuya personalidad acaso hay que aminorar considerablemente. ... y que acaso busca el consuelo en los paraísos artificiales que la flora europea le puede suministrar* (Baroja, Julio Caro. Las brujas y su mundo. Madrid: Alianza Editorial, 1966, pp. 314-315); "Sometimes, an altogether

old religion of Western Europe, basically Celtic, practiced by many sectors of a medieval community, in particular those populating the geographically less dense regions.[90]

All these positions have important support, and they can be made compatible if we calculate that the phenomenon lasted some eight hundred years, being deformed and exacerbated progressively with the persecutions. In the beginning they would been simply non-Christians, with alternative systems of therapy and culture, who tended to the entheogenic use of drugs without renouncing the mystery inherent in plants. Though caricaturized by the inquisitors, their ceremonies show important parallels with both primitive and classical rites, which will not pass unperceived by certain cultivated men. In the opinion solicited by the ecclesiastical authority regarding the Basque Aquelares,[91] already in the seventeenth century the humanist Pedro de Valencia (1555 – 1620) is comparing these ceremonies with certain pagan mysteries. But he believes that their ultimate purpose is to periodically suspend – with pharmacological support – the restrictions imposed upon sexual liberty:

---

stranger type of person emerges, slightly mad, weird, but not wholly improbable, and perhaps nothing like so fantastic as she is made out to be. ... She foretells the future from time to time, and maybe finds consolation in the dream world which certain European herbs can give her" (Baroja, Julio Caro. The World of the Witches, tr. O. N. V. Glendinning. Chicago, IL: University of Chicago Press, 1971, p. 254).

[90] "The evidence proves that underlying the Christian religion was a cult practised by many classes of the community, chiefly, however, by the more ignorant or those in the less thickly inhabited parts of the country. It can be traced back to pre-Christian times, and appears to be the ancient religion of Western Europe" (Murray, Margaret Alice. The Witch-Cult in Western Europe. Oxford: At the Clarendon Press, 1921, p. 4, hermetics. org); see also sacred-texts.com.

[91] Named for their meeting place, the *akelarre*, meaning the "field or plain of the he-goat (from *akerr*: he-goat, and *larre*, *larra*: a field. ... The Devil usually appeared at these meetings in the form of a he-goat" (Baroja, 1964, pp. 147, 160).

The evidence of all my senses leads me to feel that the meetings have been between men and women who have come together for the same reasons they have always come together; to commit sins of the flesh ... [and the Devil] is only a vision that occurs in dreams brought on by ointments, poisons and other substances.[92]

The repression will provoke a growing identification with the aggressor in these characters and their acolytes, who will finally end up accepting the thesis of demonology to the detriment of their original system of beliefs, far removed from "the ancient religion of Western Europe"[93] or better still a GrecoRoman paganism with Eastern elements. Already in the High Middle Ages, the ideological conditions exist for the arising of an internal crusade, directed at the decontamination of the social body. Nevertheless, there is still lacking

---

92 Baroja, 1966, pp. 232-233; *pero en cuentos de tiempos y autoridades, y particularmente en estos de Logroño, todo mi sentimiento y afecto se inclina á entender que aquellas hayan sido y sean juntoas de hombres y mugeres que tienen por fin el que han tenido y tendrán todos los tales en todos los siglos, que es torpeza carnal* (Valencia, Pedro de. "*Segundo discurso de Pedro de Valencia acerca de los brujos y de sus maleficios,*" *Revista de Archivos, Bibliiotecas y Museos.* Madrid: Tip. de la Revista de Archivos, Bibliotecas y Museos, 1906, pp. 454, //ab.dip-caceres.org); Baroja, 1971, p. 183, referring to the first discourse, *Discurso de Pedro de Valencia â cerca [sic] de los quentos de las/ Brujas y cosas tocantes a Magia dirigido al Illmº. Sr. D. Berdº. de Sandobal y Roxas Cardenal Arcpoº de Toledo Inquisidor/ General de España.* Department of Manuscripts, Biblioteca Nacional, Madrid, MSS 9087, fols. 260v-276r, Simancas – Lib. 939, and Manuel Serrano y Sanz, Revista de Extremadura, año segundo (1900), pp. 289-303, 337-347. "Valencia even reaches the conclusion that parts of the visions may simply be due to the natural powers of ointments 'without the Devil's intervention at al'" (Baroja, 1964, p. 183).

93 "Ritual Witchcraft – or, as I propose to call it, the Dianic cult – embraces the religious beliefs and ritual of the people, known in late medieval times as 'witches.' ... It is now a commonplace of anthropologists that the tales of fairies and elves preserve the tradition of a dwarf race which once inhabited Northern and Western Europe. Successive invasions drove them to the less fertile parts of each country which they inhabited. ... The dwarf race obtained the reputation of wizards and magicians and their god was identified by the conquerers with the Principle of Evil" (Murray, 1921, pp. 4-6).

the smallest degree of administrative flexibility, a more effective organization of the services, and a better enrooting of ecclesiastical power in all parts. In the year 936 Pope Leo VII suggests to the Archbishop of Lorch, Gerhard, that he should not burn those guilty of witchcraft without offering them the possibility of converting to the true faith.[94] The catechism is still new in many zones; only much later will the Church demand perfect orthodoxy. The great hunt will arrive when papal power becomes consolidated and the balance of power begins to shift in the monolithic societies created out of the accord between Church and State.

Drugs, lust and Satanism have begun to be complementary phenomenon in Europe.

---

[94] Baroja, 1964, p. 57. "This *Gerard* came afterwards to *Rome*, and consulted with the Pope about several Questions .... The first of these Questions is concerning Necromancers, Magicians, and Wizards, whether they ought to be admitted to Penitence: The Pope reply'd, that the Bishops ought to bring them over to repentence by their exhortations, that so they might live like Penitents rather than dye like Criminals. He adds, that if they slighted the censures of the Bishops, they ought to be punish'd according to the Rigor of the civil laws" (Du Pin, Lewis Ellies. A New Ecclesiastical History, vol. X. London: Abel Sibal & Timothy Child, 1698 (GB), p. 19). "Although by the old law such people were condemned to death, ecclesiastical law spared their lives so that they could repent" (Regino, Abbot. "A Warning to Bishops," *Libri duo de synodalibus*, //bibleapologetics.wordpress.com). Antecedents exist in the statutes of the later Roman Empire regarding the treatment of repentant heretics: "[E]ven though such heretics have nourished a deep-rooted evil by long and continued meditation ... it shall suffice for annulment that they should condemn their false doctrine by their own judgment and should embrace the name of Almighty God, which they may call upon even in the midst of their perils [tortures and imminent dangers of death at trial]" (Pharr, 1952, p. 457, *CTH* 16.5.41, dated 407).

Figure 84.
Two witches provoke a storm
(De lamiis, 1489, Ulrich Molitor).

9
Islam and Ebriety

The Grape that can with Logic absolute
The Two-and-Seventy jarring Sects confute:
The subtle Alchemist that in a Trice
Life's leaden Metal into Gold transmute.[1]
-- Omar Khayyam

A. Alcohol
B. Opium
C. Cannabis
1. The Diversity of Arab Use
2. The Fundamentalist Reaction
D. Coffee
E. Tobacco

---

[1] Fitzgerald, Edward, tr. Rubáiyát of Omar Khayyám / Six Plays of Calderon. London: J. M. Dent & Son Ltd., 1948, p. 17, Quatrain XLIII, first edition, 1859. FitzGerald (1809 – 1883), an "easy-going amateur Orientalist who constructed a mid-Victorian poem of his own from an ill-understood classical Persian text," produced a "literary metempsychosis," a "transmogrification" of the stanzas of Khayaam (Graves, Robert and Omar Ali-Shah, trs. The Original Rubaiyyat of Omar Khayaam. Garden City, NY: Doubleday & Company, Inc., 1968, pp. 2, 16). "Muhammad said, 'My people shall be divided into seventy-three sects, all of which, save one, shall have their portion in the fire'" (Whinfield, E. H., tr. "The Quatrains of Omar Khayyam," in Arnot, Robert, ed. The Sufistic Quatrains of Omar Khayyam. New York: M. Walter Dunne, 1903, p. 189).

Figure 85.
Fabric from Musulman Granada depicting two poets improvising verses, stimulated by wine.

CHAPTER NINE -- ISLAM AND EBRIETY

Although the world was ripe for monotheistic religion, the Catholic Church would never become catholic. The Papacy took centuries to conquer by force of arms what another monotheism – less burdened with bureaucracy, idolatry and the condemnation of the flesh – conquered by conviction, beginning its spread out of Arabia in the middle of the seventh century. The European continent will owe a debt to Islam ('submission to the will of God') for its intellectual recuperation, acting as a repository of many Greek and Latin works as well as much of the culture of India and the Far East.

But Islam will act as much more than a passive receptacle or inanimate transmitter. From its start until the thirteenth century, the religion preached by Mohammed will be one of the most dynamic factors in world history, making contributions to nearly all the arts and sciences. Influenced by and indebted to Judaism, and to a lesser extent the evangelical gospels, Islam's relations with Christianity will turn sour beginning with the Crusades to the Holy Land, a business very much in agreement with the other ideals then in effect in Medieval Europe.

As a monotheism, Islam also trespasses upon the terrain of subjective intimacy, always avoided by pagan religions, permitting itself to pontificate on food, daily and weekly schedules, and drugs. However, over the course of its history, it will show signs of a considerable devolution, especially with regards to intoxicants. This fact is often poorly known and interpreted by the West.

A. Alcohol

It's often maintained that Mohammed severely prohibited all alcoholic drinks, inaugurating a repressive paternalism with regards to fermentation. In reality, both the Koran and the Hadiths ('sayings') are ambivalent on the subject. The original impetus for such a total prohibition is rooted in a conspicuously simplistic misreading of certain verses of the Koran itself.

For example, chapter two [*al-Baquarah*, "The Cow"], verse 219, notices sin but also utility in wine: "They will ask thee concerning wine and lots: Answer, In both there is great sin, and *also some* things of use unto men; but their sinfulness is greater than their *use.*"[2] Or consider chapter sixteen [*an-Nahl*, "The Bee"], verse 67, distinguishing between inebriation and food: "And of the fruits of palm-trees, and of grapes, ye obtain an inebriating liquor, and also good nourishment. Verily herein is a sign unto people who understand."[3]

Two other verses are less prohibitionist than admonitory. Chapter five [*al-ma'idah,* "The Table"], verse 90 reads: "O true believers, surely wine, and lots, and images, and divining arrows are an abomination of the work of Satan; therefore avoid them, that ye may prosper."[4] Verse 91 continues in the same tone: "Satan seeketh to sow dissension and hatred among you, by means of wine and lots, and to divert you from remembering God, and from prayer: will ye not therefore abstain *from them*?"[5]

It is a considerable distance from ambiguity and admonition to a total ban. Sale, the translator of the Koran used by Jefferson, notices

---

2 Sale, George, tr. The Koran, commonly called the Alcoran of Mohammed. London: C. Ackers, 1734, p. 25, posner.library.cmu.edu; Sale adds a footnote: "Under the name of *wine* all sorts of strong and intoxicating liquors are comprehended" (p. 25). The arabic word used, *al-khamri*, is generally translated as strong drink, intoxicants, alcoholic drinks as well as most commonly, simply wine (islamawakened.com).

3 Sale, p. 219. Here the Arabic word is *sakaran* or intoxicant (islamawakened.com). Graves writes that "only the drinking of date-liquor, which caused a great deal of bloodshed and disorder in seventh-century Arabia, came under the Prophet's ban. Wine had long been used for religious purposes by the Hebrews (many of whose doctrines Mohammed accepted) .... Nevertheless, puritanical theologians of Khayyam's day had attempted to put a *syeg*, or hedge, around the use of date-liquor by banning all other intoxicants ...." (Graves, Ali-Shah, 1968, p. 4).

4 Sale, p. 94.

5 Sale, p. 94.

the contradiction between the actual words of the Koran and their harsher official interpretation:

From these words some suppose that only drinking to excess, and too frequent gaming are prohibited. And the moderate use of wine they also think is allowed .... But the more received opinion is, that both drinking wine or other strong liquors in any quantity, and playing at any game of chance, are absolutely forbidden.[6]

Even the Hadiths, generally more fundamentalist than the Koran itself, are ambivalent. One verse, for example, supposes that Mohammed, on one occasion at least, prescribed no punishment for drinking wine, even for a staggering drunk:

Ibn 'Abbas [619 – 687, one of the original followers of Mohammed] said: The Prophet (may peace be upon him) did not prescribe any punishment for drinking wine. ... A man who had drunk wine and become intoxicated was found staggering on the road, so he was taken to the Prophet (may peace be upon him). When he was opposite al-'Abbas's house, he escaped and going into al-'Abbas, he grasped hold of him. When that was mentioned to the Prophet (may peace be upon him), he laughed and said: Did he do that? and he gave no command regarding him.[7]

---

[6] Sale, p. 25, footnote c.

[7] Hasan, Ahmad, tr. _Sunan Abu Dawud_, eleventh edition, vol. III (chapters 1338 – 1890). New Delhi: Kitab Bhavan, 2012, book XXXIII, ch. 1639 ("Prescribed Punishment for drinking wine"), p. 1250, archive.org. Abu Dawud [817 – 889] "widely traveled throughout the world for collecting *Hadith*. ... [_Sunan Abu Dawud_] is one of the six canonical collections of Traditions of the Prophet (*Sihah Sittah*). It contains 4800 select Traditions. ... The distinctive quality of this book is that Imam Abu Dawud collected only legal traditions (*ahkam*) in it and omitted others. ... No other book contains such a large number of traditions as it contains on law" (vol. 1, pp. iii-v).

Abu Dawud adds a footnote, explaining: "The Prophet (may peace be upon him) did not inflict punishment on him as the evidence of drinking against him could not be established."[8]

Otherwise, the punishments for drinking varied from a simple beating to too many lashings and even death. On another occasion Mohammed only prescribed a brief impromptu beating and afterwards social condemnation and mercy:

> Abu Hurairah [603 – 681] said: When a man who had drunk wine was brought to the Apostle of Allah (may peace be upon him), he said: Beat him. Abu Hurairah said: Some struck him with their hands, some with their garments. ... The Apostle of Allah (may peace be upon him) then said to his Companions: Reproach him, and they faced him and said: You have not respected Allah, you have not feared Allah and you have not shown shame before the Apostle of Allah (may peace be upon him). Then they released him. At the end he said: But say: O Allah, forgive him, O Allah, show mercy to him.[9]

In another tradition, the punishment could vary between forty and eighty lashes: "Anas b. Malik [d. 709, companion of Mohammed] said: The Prophet (may peace be upon him) gave a beating with palm-branches and sandals for drinking wine and Abu Bakr gave forty lashes. ... When 'Umar [ibn al-Khattab, 584 – 644, senior companion and second caliph after Abu Bakr] came to power ... he fixed eighty lashes for it."[10] Asked for the reason for eighty lashes, "'Ali [ibn Abi Talib, 601 – 666] said: When a man drinks wine, he makes up lies. I, therefore, think that he should prescribe it like the prescribed punishment for making up lies."[11]

---

[8] Hasan, v. III, book XXXIII, p. 1250, footnote 3897.

[9] Hasan, v. III, book XXXIII, ch. 1639, 4462, 4463, p. 1250.

[10] Hasan, v. III, book XXXIII, ch. 1639, 4464, pp. 1250 - 51.

[11] Hasan, v. III, book XXXIII, ch. 1640, 4474, p. 1255. Abu Dawud adds, "By this he means the prescribed punishment of slandering (*qadhf*) which is eighty lashes" (footnote 3908).

In still another tradition, death was the prescribed penalty for repeated indulgence: "Mu'awiyah b. Abi Sufyan [602 – 680] reported the Apostle of Allah (may peace be upon him) as saying: If they (the people) drink wine, flog them, again if they drink it, flog them. Again if they drink it, kill them."[12] But Abu Dawud adds a footnote that this punishment was no longer in effect in his own time: "This tradition which suggests the killing of a drunkard after a third time has been abrogated. Al-Tirmidhi [824 – 892, Persian scholar and collector of hadith] said in his *Kitab al-'Ilal*: The people are agreed on the abandonment of this punishment, that is, it has been repealed."[13]

The prohibition of wine did not come down all at once. Nor did everyone accept it all at once. Even some of the companions of the Prophet were known to repeatedly indulge in drinking wine.[14] There was some initial resistance to the ban and at least one senior companion repeatedly called for a satisfactory explanation:

> 'Umar b. al-Khattab said that when the prohibition of wine came down, he said: O Allah, give us about wine a satisfactory explanation. So the following verse of Surat al-Baqarah came down; "They ask thee concerning wine and gambling. Say: In them is great sin ...." 'Umar was then called and it was recited to him. He said: O Allah, give us about wine a satisfactory explanation. Then the following verse of Surat al-Nisa' came down: "O ye who believe! approach not prayers with a mind befogged ...." ... 'Umar was again called .... He said: O Allah, give us about wine a satisfactory explanation. This verse was revealed: "Will ye not abstain?" 'Umar said: We abstained.[15]

Yet one could certainly argue that the Koran would hardly include an "abomination of the work of Satan" in the paradise promised to the upright found in chapter 47 [*Muhammed*], verse 15:

---

[12] Hasan, v. III, book XXXIII, ch. 1640 ("Of a Man Who Drinks Repeatedly"), 4467, p. 1252.

[13] Hasan, v. III, book XXXIII, ch. 1640, p. 1252, footnote 3903.

[14] Hasan, v. III, book XXXIII, ch. 1640, p. 1252, footnote 3903.

[15] Hasan, v. III, book XX, ch. 1382 ("Prohibition of Wine"), p. 1041.

The description of paradise, which is promised unto the pious: therein *are* rivers of incorruptible water; and rivers of milk, the taste whereof changeth not; and rivers of wine, pleasant unto those who drink; and rivers of clarified honey: and therein shall they have *plenty* of all *kinds of* fruits; and pardon from their Lord.[16]

Asceticism "is scarcely a Koranic aspiration; since its Paradise offers among other delights pure water, clarified honey, milk that has not turned sour, and wine that is a pleasure to drink, administered by fair cupbearers, it evidently does not despise these good things."[17]

The Arabist D. S. Margoliouth [1858 – 1940] also notices:

The prohibition of wine was made in the Medinah period, and though it is thought to extend to all intoxicants, there is some difference of opinion. The violation of this rule has been common during all periods of Islam, even some of the Prophet's companions having yielded to the temptation. The Arabic language has as fine a collection of wine-lays as the Greeks once possessed.[18]

In the eleventh century, considered the moment of maximum spiritual splendor for the Islamic world, the Persian mathematician and philosopher Omar Khayyam (ca. 1050 – ca. 1125)[19] composes a powerful apology for intoxication[20] in the quartets of the *Rubaiyyat*:

---

[16] Sale, p. 410.

[17] Margoliouth, D.S. The Hibbert Lectures (Second Series), The Early Development of Mohammedanism, Lecture V. London: Williams and Norgate, 1914, p. 135, muhammadism.org; "But as for the sincere servants of God, they shall have a certain provision in paradise, namely ... a cup shall be carried round unto them, filled from a limpid fountain, for the delight of those who drink ..." (Sale, ch. 37, p. 367).

[18] Margoliouth, D. S. Mohammedism. London: Williams and Norgate, 1920, p. 130, archive.org.

[19] "Omar Khayyam was born at Naishapur in Khorassan in the latter half of our eleventh, and died within the first quarter of our twelfth century" (FitzGerald, 1948, p. 3). "Not many years after the Norman Conquest of England, this middle-aged Persian University professor broke away from his academic colleagues at the College of Nishapur and returned to the Sufic way of thought .... He was at that time not only a famous orthodox Moslem philosopher, but also an inventive mathematician

Yesterday This Day's Madness did prepare;
To-morrow's Silence, Triumph, or Despair:
Drink! for you know not whence you came, nor why:
Drink! for you know not why you go, nor where.[21]

---

whose treatise on algebra is still highly regarded, and an outstanding astronomer. He had also played an important part in reforming the Moslem calendar, some five centuries before the Christian calendar was similarly taken in hand" (Graves, Ali-Shah, 1968, p. 3).

[20] "Khayaam treats wine in Sufic fashion as a metaphor of the ecstasy excited by divine love: a simple concept not readily grasped by Westerners, if only because they are convinced that wine-drinking was forbidden by Mohammed in the Koran" (Graves, Ali-Shah, 1968, p. 4). His "mystical poem has been erroneously accepted throughout the West as a drunkard's rambling profession of the hedonistic creed" (Graves, Ali-Shah, 1968, p. 2). On the other hand, "Khayaam may well have privately mocked at the 'painted' or false Sufis, very much as Jesus denounced the 'painted' Pharisees" (Graves, Ali-Shah, 1968, p. 18), "renouncing puritanical theology and allowing the divine warmth of love free vent" (pp. 25-26), while refusing "to recognize as valid any condition short of drunkenness – meaning any loveless religious concept" (p. 26). Though FitzGerald never completely accepted a less-than-literal interpretation for wine for his *Rubáiyát* (Arberry, 1959, p. 18), it "has been for more than eight hundred years an integral part of the Sufis' poetic heritage" (Graves, Ali-Shah, 1968, p. 26). Perhaps only those familiar with *both* kinds of intoxication will have ever truly understood his mystical verse.

[21] Haight, Gordon S., ed. The Rubaiyat of Omar Khayyam, rendered into English quatrains by Edward FitzGerald, the five authorized versions. New York: Walter J. Black, 1942, p. 90, quatrain 80, second edition, 1868. "Of Edward FitzGerald's quatrains ... [f]orty-four are traceable to more than one quatrain, and therefore may be termed 'composite' quatrains" (Heron-Allen, Edward. "An Analysis of Edward FitzGerald's Translation of the Quatrains of Omar Khayyam," in Arnot, 1903, p. 40); such is the case here: the first two lines come from one quatrain and the last two lines from another. Heron-Allen renders them more literally: "Live happily, for without any importunity on thy part yesterday, / They appointed with certainty what thou wilt do tomorrow – yesterday! / Be happy! – thou knowest not whence thou hast come: / Drink wine! – thou knowest not whither thou shalt go" (Heron-Allen, in Arnot, 1903, p. 90).

Also:

And this I know: whether the one True Light,
Kindle to Love, or Wrath consume me quite,
One Glimpse of It within the Tavern caught
Better than in the Temple lost outright.[22]

In the Tale of the Jewish Doctor in the Thousand Nights and a Night, wine is both medicine and boon:

The stream is rippled by the hands of clouds;
We too, a-rippling, on our rugs recline,
Passing pure wine, and whoso leaves us there
Shall ne'er arise from fall his woes design:
Draining long draughts from large and brimming bowls,
Administ'ring thirst's only medicine – wine.[23]

Also:

How dear is our day and how lucky our lot,
When the cynic's away with his tongue malign!
When love and delight and the swimming of head
Send cleverness trotting, – the best boon of wine.[24]

---

[22] Haight, 1942, p. 38, quatrain 56, first edition, 1859. The French translation by J. B. Nicolas is said to read, in English prose: "Better to be with Thee in the tavern, and there tell Thee my secret thoughts, than to go without Thee and make a prayer in the mosque. Yea, O Creator of all that was and all that is! such is my faith, whether Thou burnest me, or accordest me thy favor" (----------. "The Quatrains of Omar Khayyam, translated into prose from the French version of Monsieur J. B. Nicolas," in Arnot, 1903, p. 334, quatrain 222).

[23] Burton, Richard F. The Book of the Thousand Nights and a Night, vol. I. Teheran Edition, Number 738: Printed by the Burton Club for Private Subscribers Only, 1885, p. 291.

[24] Burton, 1885, p. 293.

Somewhat later but in the same tradition with Omar Khayyam is the mathematician and philosopher Shemsuddin Mahommad Hafiz, born in Shiraz and writing in the fourteenth century, whose *Divan* is said to be the heighth of Arab lyricism:

Arise, oh Cup-bearer, rise! and bring
To lips that are thirsting the bowl they praise ...
Hear the Tavern-keeper who counsels you:
"With wine, with red wine your prayer carpet dye!"
... Of all the treasures the earth can boast,
A brimming cup of wine I prize the most –
This is enough for me!

But when the Day of Reckoning is here,
I fancy little will be the gain
That accrues to the Sheikh for his lawful cheer,
Or to me for the draught forbidden I drain.

All you that misconstrue my words' intent,
I lie on the bricks of the tavern floor,
And a brick shall serve me for argument.[25]

In Iraq Ibn al-Marzubān collected anecdotes about "drink, drinking-companions, deceit and treachery" in the tenth century:

A Baron called Muhammad b. Bakr was a friend of mine; he was always with me, sharing my meals and drinking date wine .... We stopped at a certain spot to eat and drink. When I began to feel tipsy, he attacked me .... He threw me in a wadi, taking all I had, left me there and made off. I gave up all hope of survival. Now this dog sat down with me, then he left too and went off. But he soon returned to me, bringing a loaf of bread and putting it in front of me. ... To me he is dearer than any family or relation.[26]

---

[25] Bell, Gertrude L. Poems from the Divan of Hafiz. London: William Heineman, 1897, archive. org.

[26] Smith, G. R. and M. A. S. Abdel Haleem, trs. The Book of the Superiority of

In Baghdad Ibn at-Tilmīd, the foremost physician of his day , could pen these verses in the 12th century:

I broke my life in these two glasses,
And this is how my lifetime passes:
One glass is filled with writing-ink,
The other one with wine to drink –
The former makes my wisdom stay,
The latter puts my grief away.

One glass of wine to cool the chest,
A second one to help digest,
A third one, then, just to unwind,
Another one will shift your mind![27]

At the other end of the empire, in al-Andalus, images "of both thirst and drinking abound"[28] in the poetry of Ibn Khafajah [1058 – 1138]: "I tripped on the tail of drunkenness that evening while the wind was entangled in the waves of the gulf."[29] In his poetry, nature "serves ... as a background for love, drinking, and festivities"[30] as when with delightful irony he describes a "wine which the grapevine reared, so it is noble and it did not commit adultery with the son of the clouds [water], so it is chaste."[31]

Dogs over many of Those who wear Clothes by Ibn al-Marzubān. Warminster, UK: Aris & Philips, Ltd., 1978, pp. 22-23. The translators add a note that the Arabic word "*nabidh* could refer in a more general sense to any intoxicating drink (p. 37)."

[27] Kahl, Oliver. The Dispensatory of Ibn at-Tilmīd. Leiden: Brill, 2007, p. 18.

[28] Jayyusi, Salma Khadra. "Nature Poetry in Al-Andalus and the Rise of Ibn Khafaja" in The Legacy of Muslim Spain, S. K. Jayyusi, ed. Leiden: E. J. Brill, 1992, p. 385.

[29] Jayyusi, p. 385.

[30] Al-Nowaihi, Magda M. The Poetry of Ibn Khafaja: A Literary Analysis. Leiden: E. J. Brill, 1993, p. 2.

[31] Al-Nowaihi, p. 94.

He particularly enjoys mixing the themes of intoxication and sexuality:

The snow had put a veil over the face of the earth, ...
So when I headed to a wine-house,
I rode a white horse [i.e. the snow]
To a red horse [i.e. the wine],
And I saluted her tavern, coming at night,
And she said responding: oh welcome,
And got up with a long-necked wine-glass,
To a short-necked hunchback earthern jug,
And she came back with a flaming red one,
Blazing in its cup like a star.[32]

In the same Bacchic vein is Al-Qushayri's [b. 986] Epistle on Sufism, written about 1045:

There are two kinds of drunkenness;
The drunkenness of passion and
The drunkenness of wine.
How can a man who has
Tasted either of them
Ever come to his senses.

Know that one's sobriety
Corresponds to one's drunkenness.
He who experiences true drunkenness,
Enjoys true sobriety.[33]

In the newly conquered regions of Al-Andalus, tolerance of the customs of the conquered was required from sheer practicality:

---

[32] Al-Nowaihi, p. 148.

[33] Knysh, A. D., tr. Al-Qushayri's Epistle on Sufism. Reading, UK: Garnet Publishing Ltd., 2007, p. 94.

Tolerance occurred synchronically in Al-Ãndalus and in the Christian kingdoms. Although the Koran did not suggest benevolence of the Musulmans toward «the people of the book» – Jews and Christians – who accepted the rule of Islam, the handful of Islamic conquerors of Spain would have had to resign to co-live peacefully with the millions of Spaniards whom they could not convert nor exterminate overnight.[34]

According to the medieval historian Aljoxaní [d. 971] in his Kitáb al-quda' bi-Qurtaba [History of the Judges of Cordoba], instead of punishing drunkards with the required eighty lashes, Cordoban judges preferred to not see them whenever possible.[35] In part, this is because they believed there was no strict prohibition in the Koran and no admitted and secure tradition from the Prophet who died without deciding how one ought to punish drunkenness. Traditionalists recall that Abu Bakr, when he was dying, said: "The only thing that worries me is the question of how to punish those who drink wine, one of those things unresolved since the death of Mahommed."[36]

---

[34] Sanchez-Albornoz, Claudio. Spain: A Historical Enigma, vol. I, trs. C. J. Dees, D. S. Rehen. Madrid: Fundacion universitaria española, 1975, p. 291: *La tolerancia nacio sincrónicamente en Al-Ãndalus y en los reinos cristianos. Aunque el Alcorán no hubiera aconsejado a los musulmanes benevolencia para con "las gentes del libro" – judias y cristianos – que aceptaban el señorío del Islam, el puñado de conquistadores islamitas de España habría tenido que resignarse a convivir pacificamente con los milliones de españoles trinitarios que no podían convertir ni exterminar en abrir y cerrar de ojos* (Sanchez-Albornez, Claudio. España: Un Enigma Histórico, tomo I. Barcelona: Edhasa, 1973, p. 294).

[35] Ribera, J., tr. *Historia de los Jueces de Córdoba por Aljoxaní*. Madrid: Imprenta Iberica, 1914, p. 126: *Lo que se cuenta de la conducta de los jueces andaluces en esta materia, es decir, el que los jueces cerraran los ojos para no ver a los borrachos* [The conduct of Andalusian judges in this matter shows that the judges would close their eyes so as not to see the drunkards (tr. gwr)].

[36] Ribera, J., tr., pp. 126-127: *[L]a pena que ha de aplicarse al borracho es, entre todas las del derecho musulmán, aquella que no está marcada taxativamente en el libro revelado; ni siquiera hay una tradición mahomética, admitida y segura .... Murió el Profeta y no señaló concretamente que debiera castigarse al borracho .... Los tradicionistas recuerdan que Abubéquer, al tiempo de morir, dijo: lo unico que me preocupa es una cosa: la pena del que bebe vino, por ser cuestion que dejó sin*

In one tradition, the judge Muhammad ben Salma espied a drunk in the street and told his aide to arrest him so he could be punished. The drunk told the judge to come arrest him himself and if he touched him he would give him a beating he would not soon forget. The judge, seeing he had a fight on his hands, turned away, saying: "Did you hear what that drunkard said? I think he was capable of doing it. Thanks be to Allah that we left him alone."[37]

On the one hand it was important to be seen doing one's duty but on the other hand any excuse would do to ignore it. Judge Mohammed ben Ziad one day was walking in the company of Mohammed ben Isa Elaxa, when they encountered a wandering, unsteady drunkard. The judge ordered his aides to arrest him so he could punished according to the law. Soon they came to a place so narrow that the judge went forward and left behind Elaxa, who told the aides that the judge had said to release the drunkard. The judge later asked about the drunk and aides replied that they had been ordered to let him go. "And did you let him go?" asked the judge. "Yes," they replied. "Well, good," answered the judge.[38]

---

resolver el Profeta ....

[37] Sanchez-Albornez, Claudio. La España Musulmana según los autores islamitas y cristianos medievales, third edition, vol. I. Madrid: Espasa-Calpe, 1973, p. 349, quoting *Kitab Qudat Qurtuba* de Al-Jusani: *Dice Ahmad ben Ubayda que un hombre que estuvo al servicio de Muhammad ben Salma y le solía acompañar cuando iba por la calle, le refirió lo siguiente: Un día andando por la calle, el juez vio a un borracho y me dijo: - Préndelo para aplicarle la pena con que la ley castiga la borrachera. -¡Senor juez! – exclamó el borracho al oír esa orden -. Ven tu mismo y préndeme. ¡Rediez!, si me tocas, te voy a arrear un sopapo que te sentará muy bien. El juez, al ver el cariz que la cosa presentaba, se desvió del camino o dirección que el borracho llevaba, yéndose por otra parte. El juez me dijo luego: -¿Has oído lo que decía el borracho? ¡Pardiez!, yo creo que es capaz de hacerlo. Gracias a Dios que nos hemos librado;* Ribera, J., tr., pp. 208-209.

[38] Ribera, J., tr., pp. 125-126: *Iba Mohámed ben Ziad cierto dia andando en compañía de Mohámed ben Isa Elaxa, cuando se encontraron con un borracho que caminaba vacilante e inseguro por efecto de su borrachera. El juez Mohámed ben Ziad mandó prenderlo para aplicarle el castigo que la ley religiosa impone al borracho. Los sayones del juez lo prendieron. Luego anduvo un poco*

Aljoxaní records two stories about judge Ahmed ben Baki, both told by his friend Asbag ben Isa el Zacac. One day they were riding on horseback through the streets of the city when before them they came upon a drunkard. The judge pulled up on the reins of his horse to allow the drunk to avoid him or escape. But the drunk did neither. The judge, however, simply turned to Asbag and said: "Look at that unhappy fellow. He has lost his mind." "Yes," I answered him, "It's a grand disgrace." The judge felt sorry for him and asked Allah to cure him of his madness and pardon his sins."[39]

In a second story about the same judge, a drunk smelling of wine was brought before him. The judge asked his secretary to smell the drunk. "Yes," said the secretary, "he smells of wine." Then the judge asked Asbag to smell the drunk. But Asbag said, "Yes, he smells of something but I'm not sure that he smells of drink." A smile of gratitude illuminated the face of the judge who declared: "Let him be set free; it is not proved that a crime has been committed."[40]

---

y llegó a un sitio tan estrecho que tuvo que adelantarse el juez y quedar detrás Elaxa. Al rezagarse e ir tras del juez, Elaxa se volvió hacia aquel sayón que había cogido al borracho y le dijo: - El juez me ha dicho que sueltes a ese borracho. El sayón lo soltó entonces. Luege se separon ambos, tomando cada uno su dirección. Al acabar su paseo y entrar en su casa, el juez preguntó por el borracho y le contestaron: - El faquí Abuabdala nos dijo que usted había ordenado que lo soltáramos. – ¿Y lo habéis soltado? – preguntó el juez. – Sí – le contestaron. – Bueno, bien – repuso el juez.

[39] Sanchez-Albornoz, Claudio. "*El vino y los borrachos en la España mora hace mil años,*" in Ensayos Sobre Historia de España, first edition. Madrid: Siglo XXI de España Editores, 1973, p. 35: *El cadí Ahmed ben Baki cabalga por las calles de la ciudad con un amigo. Delante va un borracho. El juez lo ha visto. Lejos de apresurarse a ordenar su dentención, el cadí, comprensivo ante la flaqueza del ebrio cordobés, tira de las riendas de su cabalgadura, para dar tiempo, a fin de que el borracho al notar la presencia del juez, le evite y se largue. Pero cuanto más lentamente cabalga el cadí Ahmed, más se para el borracho. Hasta que el juez no puede menos de toparse con él. ... Pero el juez ... dice, como complacido: «Mira ese desdichado transeúnte; ha debido de perder la razón; pidamos a Alá por que le vuelva el seso»*; Ribera, pp. 243-244.

[40] Sanchez-Albornez, C. Ensayos (1973), pp. 35-6: *El almotacén trae ante él un hombre al que acusa de borracho. ... Y aunque el borracho huele a vino a cien leguas, el juez dice a su*

In Islam drinking to excess is not deplored by suspecting the drunk had signed a pact with Satanic powers or for sinking into infernal concupiscience, but simply for making a person lie and do stupid things. In this context, it is of the greatest interest that from the fourteenth century – the beginning of the Islamic decadency – theological discussions and juridic treatises against ebriety using one or another agent begin to appear, each time defending a thesis more and more fundamentalist. This occurs with the new drugs (coffee, tobacco) as well as with the old (opium, wine, cannabis).

Figure 86. An herbalist doing a medicinal plant extraction (from the Arabic translation of De Materia Medica of Dioscorides, a codex of Abd Allah ibn al-Fazl, 1222, Baghdad.

---

secretario: «Huélele» .... Pero el secretario ... responde: «Sí, huele a vino.» ... Pero está rodeado de los jurisconsultos de su Curia y entre estos se halla Asbag, su amigo, y con un rostro incapaz de dejar duda alguna sobre sus intenciones, se vuelve hacia el jurista y le dice: «Asbag, huélele tu.» Y Asbag ... dice al juez: «Sí, huele a algo, pero no estoy seguro de que huela a bebida que pueda emborrachar.» Una sonrisa de gratitud ilumina al punto la cara del cadí y, con alegría sin disimulo alguno, dice inmediatamente a los sayones: «Que le pongan en libertad; no está probado que haya realmente cometido falta»; Ribera, p. 244.

B. Opium

The Arabs in large part assimilated the cultures of classical Greece and Rome by way of the Byzantine Empire. This fact takes on comparative value remembering that in the same period the Holy Roman-Germanic Empire viewed this drug – and others, confusingly grouped together as 'malevolent herbs' – as a vehicle of Satan, used only by his most unconditional admirers. The Arabs will imitate the Eastern Roman Empire more than the Western in their use of opium. It will be a medicine for the young and a panacea for the old.

The most noteworthy medieval Islamic physicians followed and deviated from the Galenic and Hippocratic models. Both Rhazes and Avicenna were advocates for the theriacal tradition and both recommended recipes calling for either poppies or opium as did Ibn at-Tilmīd, who marks the apogee of Arab clinical pharmacology.

Abū Bakr Muhammad ibn Zakariyyā al-Rāzī (865 – 925), "known to the Latin world as Rhazes – was so called after the place where he was born and died – Rayy, near Teheran."[41] He came to medicine through music:

> In his youth, he played on the lute and cultivated vocal music, but, on reaching the age of manhood, he renounced these occupations .... Having then applied himself to the study of medicine and philosophy, he read the works on these subjects with the attention of a man who seeks to follow the author's reasonings step by step; and he thus acquired a perfect acquaintance with the depths of these sciences and appropriated to himself whatever truths were contained in the treatises which he perused. He then commenced attending the sick and composed a great number of books on medicine.[42]

---

[41] Tibi, Selma. "Al-Razi and Islamic medicine in the 9th century," *Journal of the Royal Society of Medicine* (*JRSM*), 2006 Apr; 99(4): 206-207, ncbi.nlm.nih.gov.

[42] Slane, Baron Mac Guckin De, tr. Ibn Khallikan's Biographical Dictionary, vol. III. Paris: Oriental Translation Fund of Great Britain and Ireland, 1868, p. 312, archive.org.

He became "one of the greatest physicians of the medieval period, writing over 200 works; half of them on medicine, but others on topics that included philosophy, theology, mathematics, astronomy and alchemy."[43] His medical works include the twenty-three volume *Kitab al-Hawi fi al-tibb* (The Comprehensive Book of Medicine, translated into Latin as *Liber Continens*), the *Kitab al-Mansuri* (*Liber ad Almansorem*, dedicated to prince Abû Salîh Mansûr) and *Man la Yahduruhu Teb* (For One without a Physician) among many others. Aphorisms attributed to him include, 'The physician, even though he has his doubts, must always make the patient believe that he will recover, for the state of the body is linked to the state of the mind'[44] as well as:

> "When you can cure by a regimen, avoid having recourse to medicine; and when you can effect a cure with a simple medicine, avoid employing a compound one." He said again: "With a learned physician and an obedient patient, sickness soon disappears." And again: "Treat an incipient malady with remedies which will not prostrate the strength." Till the end of his life, he continued at the head of his profession.[45]

In his Treatise on the Small-Pox and Measles, he recommends concoctions using poppies as well as opium. In chapter five he suggests "those things which by their nature thicken the blood, such as jujubes, lentiles, cabbage, coriander, lettuce, poppy, endive, black night-shade, tabasheer, the seeds of fleawort, and common camphor."[46] Opium was prescribed in cases of high fever:

---

[43] Tibi (*JRSM*, 2006), p. 206.

[44] Tibi (*JRSM*, 2006), p. 206.

[45] Slane, vol. III, p. 312.

[46] Greenhill, W. A., tr. A Treatise on the Small-Pox and Measles by Abú Becr Mohammed ibn Zacaríyá ar-Rází. London: Printed for the Sydenham Society, 1848, p. 41, archive.org.

[W]hen the fever arises which is accompanied by the symptoms of the Small-Pox, this regimen is not to be used, except after much observation, inquiry, and caution. ... Nor is it possible for the ebullition, if it be vehement, to be checked but by remedies in which there is great danger, and which do in a manner greatly congeal and coagulate the blood, (such as opium, hemlock, a great quantity of the expressed juice of lettuce, black night-shade, and the like,) and by the constant and excessive use of the regimen which we have just mentioned.[47]

In the *Liber Continens*, he offers a recipe using poppies for pustules on the eyelids:

Those pustules which appear in a circular form with their summit concealed are of a bad and mortal kind. When pustules come out on the eyelids wash them with a collyrium composed of red horn poppy, rusot, aloes, and saffron; and drop into the eyes rose-water with sumach.[48]

In the same work he offers treatments for gout and rheumatism that employ opium and colchicum, the latter still used today:

Al-Razi gives four recipes for 'gout and the joints' in *Kitab al-Hawi*. ... Opium occurs in all of them, henbane in one and hemlock in two – one of which also has mandrake. ... Three of al-Razi's four remedies for gout and the joints include colchicum, which had been used for treating gout since at least the second millennium BCE. Indeed, it active ingredient, colchicine, is still used to treat acute attacks of the condition today. ... Where gout is accompanied by high fever, the recipe contains seeds ... of white colchicum, water melon and cucumber. These, in equal parts, are mixed with one third of a part of opium, and an oral dose of four dirhams (12g) of the mixture with the same amount of sugar is analgesic and effective within the hour. ... Where there is no high fever, the ingredients, in an oral remedy, are: colchicum, opium, borax, colocynth, ammi, aristolochia, and mountain thyme.'[49]

---

[47] Greenhill, p. 44.

[48] Greenhill, p. 120, citing book xviii, ch. 8.

[49] Tibi (*JRSM*), p. 207.

In one story, at the end of a long life al-Razi went blind and later died after prince Mansur struck him on the head with a whip when he could not transmute lead into gold: "That stroke caused a descent of humour into ar-Râzi's eyes, but he would not permit them to be lanced, declaring that he had seen enough of the world."[50]

Al-Shaikh Al-Ra'īs (*the chief*) Abu 'Alī al-Husain Ibn 'Abd Allāh Ibn Sīnā or Avicenna [980 – 1037] was a native of Bokhara [modern Bukhara, Uzbekistan]. He appears to have been a quick study:

> At the age of ten years, he was a perfect master of the Koran and general literature, and had attained a certain degree of information in dogmatic theology, the Indian calculus (*arithmetic*), and algebra. ... [He] mastered the art of logic, the Elements of Euclid, and the Almagest .... Besides these studies ... he learned jurisprudence ... laboured in the acquisition of natural philosophy, divinity and other sciences; he read the texts with the commentaries, and God opened for him the gates of knowledge.[51]

His Canon of Medicine (*Al-Qānūn Fi'l-Tibb*) "was translated into Latin by Gerard of Cremona (d. 1187) and formed the bedrock of medical curricula in universities around the world, from Baghdad to Montpellier and Leuven, for over six hundred years."[52]

For his theriaca, Avicenna recommended following the formula of Andromachus, not that of Galen:

> *[El] recommande de suivre fidèlement la formule d'Andromaque, et non pas celle de Galien, décrit sa préparation, et celle des trochisques de vipères, indique la manière d'en faire usage, et déclare qu'elle est le meilleur des médicaments composés, à cause du grand nombre de cas où elle peut rendre service: hac theriaca est sumlimior medicinarum compositarum, et melior earum, propter multitudinem sui juvamenti.*[53]

---

[50] Slane, v. III, p. 313.

[51] Slane, tr. Ibn Khallikan's Biographical Dictionary, vol. I (1842), p. 440.

[52] Mustafa, Yassar. "Avicenna the Anaesthetist," aagbi.org, p. 3.

[53] Bernhard, J. *Le Thériaque: Étude historique et pharmacologique*. Paris: *J.-B. Baillière et Fils*, 1893, p. 48, gallica.bnf.fr; "[He] recommends following faithfully the formula of Andromachus, and not that of Galen, describes its preparation, and that of the

Avicenna used opium both as an analgesic (*taksin*, "to make silent") and as an anaesthetic (*mukhaddar*), citing it as "the most powerful stupefacient, while those less powerful include mandrake (mandragora), poppy, hemlock (henbane), hyoscyamus and lettuce-seed."[54] In Book Two of the Canon can be found the entry for opium:

49 *Ufyūn* Opium

Nature: *Ufyūn* is the sun-dried extract of black poppy. Its dose should not exceed 2 *dāniq* (1 gm.). It is used along with *Khas barrī* (wild lettuce) which itself is a weak sedative. Opium is fried on [sic] hot iron plate till it becomes red.

Choice: The best variety of opium is that which is sedative, has strong smell, is brittle, dissolves in water easily and once dissolved is not condensed. It melts under sun shine [sic] and if it is used as a fuel of a lamp, the latter remains lighted. The yellow variety of opium gives colour to water. The rough variety has a feeble smell. The opium which is bright in colour, is an adulterated one. It is adulterated wtih *māmithā* (horned poppy). It is also adultered with *Khas barrī* (wild lettuce) but such opium possesses a weak smell. When adulterated with gum it becomes extremely bright.

Temperament: Opium is cold and dry in fourth degree.

Actions and properties: Opium whether administred orally or used as a paint, is sedative and soothing for all types of pains. The dose is equal to the weight of a big grain of lentil.

Swellings and pimples: It is useful in hot swellings.

Wounds and ulcers: It dries up wounds.

Joints: Opium gives relief to the patient of gout when it is mixed with the fried yellow of the egg and painted over the affected parts, especially with milk.

---

troches of vipers, indicates the manner of using it, and declares that it is the best of composite medicines, because of the great number of cases where it can be of service [tr. gwr];" Andromachus (physician to Nero) wrote a poem describing his theriaca, whose main ingredients were opium and pills made of viper flesh [see for example, Maviglia, A. "*Une lettre de Valerius Cordus sur les trochisques de vipère et sur quelques simples*," *Revue d'histoire de la pharmacie*, 58e *année*, no. 205, 1970, pp. 83-92].

54 Mustafa, p. 9.

Organs of the head: It induces sleep even if it is used with wicks or without wick. It gives relief to earache when it is dropped in the ear in liquid form along with myrrh and dissolved in rose-oil. It is useful in chronic headache also. It disturbs understanding and intellect.

Ocular organs: It relieves conjunctivitis and swelling of the eyes when mixed with human milk and painted over the eyes. Ancient physicians did not use opium in conjunctivitis since it is harmful to the sight.

Respiratory organs and the chest: It gives relief in cough and the patients who are severely affected with persistent cough.

Alimentary organs: It promotes gastric coction because it produces relaxation in the stomach. In most cases when used without *Jundbĭdastar* (Castoreum) it either corrupts or completely blunts the digestion.

Excretory organs: It stops diarrhoea and helps in curing abrasions and ulcers of intestines.

Poisons: It kills by hardening the organs (of the user) and *Jundbĭdastar* (Castoreum) is its antidote.

Substitutes: *Bazr al-banj* (henbane seeds) three times of the quantity of opium and double quantity of mandrake seeds are its substitutes.[55]

The pentultimate section shows he certainly was aware that opium could be employed as a euthanist but there is no evidence he ever used it as such. In Islam, as in Catholicism, one's body is not one's own property but rather the property of one's deity. The Koran forbids euthanasia: "No soul can die unless by the permission of God,

[55] Ibn-Sina, Hakim. Al-Qānūn Fi'l-Tibb, Book II (*Materia Medica*), supervising translator Hakeem Abdul Hameed. New Delhi: Department of Islamic Studies, *Jamia Hamdard* (Hamdard University), 1998, pp. 69-70, naimh.com; also, Mustapha, pp. 10-11; *Opium quid est: Est succus papaveris nigri Aegyptiaci exiccati sub sole* ("What is opium: It is the juice of the black poppy of Egypt dried up under the sun"); *Papaver. Natura. Hortulanum est frigidum & siccum in secundo, & nigurm in tertio* ("Poppy. Nature. The cultivated variety is cold and dry in the second degree, the black in the third"), according to the commentary and supplement by Alpago, Andrea (1450 – 1522) on the translation of Gerard de Cremona (1114 – 1187) entitled *Avicennae Liber canonis de medicinis cordialibus et cantica*. Venice: Apud Juntas, 1555, book II, cap. 526, p. 150, cap. 570, p. 157 (GB).

according to what is written in the book containing the determinations of things."[56]

On the other hand, then as now, the difference between active and passive euthanasia was well understood to be a matter of intention. A physician was and is forbidden to deliberately terminate life. But a physician has a duty to relieve pain, if at all possible. A physician who prescribes a painkiller that might also kill a terminally ill patient depending on the dosage has not administered a euthanist if this was not her intent.

Of Avicenna's own death, there are two stories. In the first he contracted a severe colic on a military campaign: "A great quantity of opium was also thrown into one of his medicines by his boys who had deceived him in some manner, and were apprehensive of being punished by him if he recovered."[57] In the second, "the prince in whose service Avicenna was employed, having been irritated against him, caused him to be imprisoned till he died."[58]

Benefitting from a "translation movement which took place between the middle of the 2nd/8th and the end of the 4th/10th centuries in Baghdad,"[59] Ibn at-Tilmīd became acquainted with the

> medico-pharmacological practices notably of the Greeks and Indians, either through direct translations from Greek and Sanskrit or through Syriac and Pahlavi intermediates; the translation movement also played a major role in the formation of a professional language, that is in developing Arabic into a language of scientific and philosophical discourse.[60]

---

[56] Sale (1734), ch. 3, p. 52.

[57] Mustapha, p. 442.

[58] Mustapha, p. 444.

[59] Kahl (2007), p. 1.

[60] Kahl (2007), p. 1.

His *al-Agrābāadīn* ["The Dispensatory"] "thus already stands near the end of a relatively long chain of inventive pharmacological development in the Arab world ...."[61]

Muwaffaqalmulk Amīnaddaula Abū l-Hasan Hibatallāh ibn Sā'id ibn Hibatallāh ibn Ibrāhīm ibn 'Alī Ibn at-Tilmīd [1074 – 1165] followed his grandfather and father into the medical profession. He was trained by the physician to the Abbasid palace, travelled extensively in Persia, then returned to Baghdad and set up a medical practice: "His reputation as a physician and teacher spread, and so it is no surprise that a few years later he was appointed head physician (*sā'ūr*) of the famous 'Adudī hospital, a post for life."[62] He sponsored impoverished scholars, treated the poor for free and was appointed court physician, where he served the Caliph for more than twenty years until his death.[63]

In his recipes, poppy and opium are some of the ingredients that show up most frequently. For example, his recipe called the *sumach* pastille for the treatment of dysentery and haemorrhage is made from the "fruit of the tarfa, Syrian sumach, myrtle seeds, gum-arabic, pomegranate flowers, grains of paradise, and Egyptian opium one part of each. (This) is kneaded with apple-water, formed into pastilles of one *dirham*, (and) a potion (may be made by using) just one pastille."[64] His "cooling pastille with camphor which is useful against flaming sensations, remnants of fevers, thirst, and gastric debility" calls for "light-coloured and dark-coloured poppy seven *dirham* of each."[65] For hepatic fever, his poppy pastilles were made of

> [l]ight-coloured and dark-coloured poppy four *dirham* of each; the peeled seeds of serpent melon, cucumber, gourd, and purslane, and starch and gum-arabic one part

---

61 Kahl (2007), p. 5.

62 Kahl (2007), pp. 7-9.

63 Kahl (2007), pp. 8, 10-11.

64 Kahl (2007), p. 179.

65 Kahl (2007), p. 180.

of each. (This) is pounded, kneaded with water, formed into pastilles of one *mitqāl*, and drunk with seed-water, and with the *pomegranate* beverage and its oxymel.[66]

He uses poppy and opium in recipes against bleeding, urinating sensations, blood and purulent matter, bloody expectoration, hyperaemia, ischuria, headache, insomnia, abrasions, weak stomach, chronic cough, fevers, bleeding gums, toothache, hiccups, vomiting, black-bilious palpitations, colical pain, a lax constitution and for protection of the unborn.[67]

Therapeutic botany and rational medicine also found a congenial center in Cordoba, especially in the reign of Abd ar-Rahman III [r. 912 – 961]. The HispanoArab philosophers/physicians, led by the Zaragozan Avempace [Ibn Bâjja, c. 1085 – 1138] and the Cordoban Averroës [Ibn Rushd, 1126 – 1198], made some of the most significant scientific investigations realized in many centuries. Both were well acquainted with the use of opium.

Of Abu Bakr Muhammad Ibn Yahyà ibn as-Sa'igh at-Tujibi Ibn Bâjja [Avempace, in Latin] little is known and of that much comes from his enemies, who concede he studied music, poetry, philosophy, astronomy and medicine while decrying him as "infidel and an atheist."[68] He fled Zaragoza after that city was taken by the Franks in 1119, was briefly vizier of the governor of Murcia and died in Fez, Morocco from eating a poisoned eggplant.[69] His *Tadbir al-Mutawahhid* [Rule of the Solitary] draws parallels between the human body and the perfect city, using opium as metaphor for both poison and medicine: "[B]read and meat are healthy nutriment by nature, while opium and

---

66 Kahl (2007), p. 181.

67 Kahl (2007), in recipes 13, 15, 16, 20, 21, 22, 24, 37, 38, 48, 105, 119, 120, found on pages 182, 183, 184, 185, 186, 190, 193, 210, 215, 216.

68 Slane, Baron Mac Guckin de, tr. Ibn Khallikan's Biographical Dictionary, vol. III. Paris: Oriental Translation Fund of Great Britain and Ireland, 1848, archive.org, p. 131.

69 Slane, pp. 132-133.

colocynth are deadly poison; but the body may be in unnatural states where these latter two can be useful and must be used, and natural diets harmful and must be avoided."[70]

Averroës [Ibn Rushd] was born and lived in Cordoba

> in the midst of intense philosophical and cultural activity. Spain was then a pluralistic society in which three great religions subsisted side by side. Coming from a family of distinguished jurists, Ibn Rushd was commissioned by Caliph Abu Yugub Yusuf to comment on and interpret Aristotle's works. ... Nearing the end of his life, however, the attitude toward Ibn Rushd's work changed, a prohibition against his studies was issued, his books were burned, and he was insulted by a mob.[71]

He was at the end of his life exiled for two years to a small town in Andalucia, Lucena. The reason for this sanction was both political and religious. He died at Marrakesh barely a year after his return to the good graces of the Caliph.[72] The best known of his medical treatises is "*al-Kulliyāt fi'l-Tibb* (General Principles of Medicine), written around 1162. ... Al-Kulliyāt was translated into Latin as *Colliget*, and was used as a medical textbook in Europe for centuries."[73]

---

[70] Ziyadah, Ma'am. "Ibn Bajja's Book Tadbir al-Mutawahhid: An Edition, Translation and Commentary." Institute of Islamic Studies, MA Thesis, McGill University, 1968, p. 136; Salomon Munk translates it as "meat and wine" in *Mélanges de Philosophie Juive et Arabe*. Paris: Chez A. Franck, 1857, gallica.bnf.fr., p. 403: *Ainsi, par example, la viande et le vin sont des aliments qui conviennent à l'homme, tandis que la coloquinte et l'opium tuent; et neánmoins il peut arriver quelqufois que ces derniers soient salutaires, et que les aliments naturels tuent.*

[71] Kurtz, Paul. "Intellectual Freedom, Rationality and Enlightenment: The Contribution of Averroës," in Averroës and the Enlightenment, eds. M. Wahba, M. Abousenna. Amherst, NY: Prometheus Books, 1996, p. 30.

[72] Ricordel, Joëlle. "*Le traité sur la thériaque d'Ibn Rushd (Averroes)*," *Revue d'histoire de la pharmacie*, 88e année, no. 325, 2000, p. 84: *Les raisons de ces sanctions sont vraisemblablement d'abord d'ordre politique et religieux. Ibn Rushd est mort à Marrakech, à peine un an après son retour en grace.*

[73] Fakhry, Majid. Averroes (Ibn Rushd): His Life, Works and Influence. Oxford:

Ibn Rushd's 'Treatise on Theriac' is theoretical in nature. We do not find in this text a recipe, a formula for making a theriac. The list of ingredients, the quantities of each of them, the means of preparation are considered as already known.[74] This is because he was working from a long tradition of Greek and Arab manuscripts including the *Theriaca* and *Alexipharmaca* (using, among other ingredients, bull's blood and opium) of Nicandros of Colophon (second century BC), the *Antidotum Mithridaticum* (myrrh, darnel and opium) of Mithridates (120 – 60 BC), the 'Poem on Theriac' (opium and the flesh of poisonous serpents) of Andromachus (first century BC), the *De Theriaka ad Pison* (opium, rhubarb and castoreum) of Galen 131 – 201 AD), the *Kāmil al-sinā'a al-tibbiyya* (serpent pills, opium, cardamum) of Al-Majūsī (d. 994), and *De la Theriaka al-Fārūq* of Avicenna, who recommends the formula of Andromachus.[75]

Averroës does not list ingredients in his *Tractatus de Theriaca* but he notices that "in every part of it, you will find for example the power of opium and euphorbia and other medicines of which it is composed," that "it relieves and takes away a cough from one who has it because of the opium" and he recommends that "whom a mad dog has bitten, the weight of one penny should be given to him of euphorbium in drink and opium."[76]

Oneworld Publications Ltd., 2001, p. 124.

[74] Ricordel (2000), pp. 84-85: *Ibn Rushd se place donc sur un plan théorique. Nous ne trouverons pas dans ce texte une recette, une formule pour composer une thériaque. La liste des ingrédients, les quantités de chachun d'eux, le mode de préparation sont considérés comme des données connues. Ibn Rushd n'y revient pas.*

[75] Anawati, Georges C. "*Le Traite D'Averroes sur la Theriaque et ses Antecedents Grecs et Arabes*," *Quaderni Di Studi Arabi*, 5/6, 1987, pp. 26 – 44.

[76] Alpago, Andrea, ed. *Tractatus de Theriaca*, in Averrois Cordubensis Colliget, Libri VII, tr. Armegando Blasio. Venice: Apud Juntas, 1552, archive.org., pp. 139, 140, 141: *in qualibet parte eius, inuenies, verbi gra, virtutem opii & euforbii, & aliarum medicinarum, ex quibus est ipsa compositio; ... sedat & tollit tussim illi, qui habet ea propter opium, quid est in ea; ... quem canis rabidus momordir, cum pondere unius denarii de pinguedine picis, detur & illi qui*

It may seem odd and slightly out of place to include in a discussion of medieval Islamic medicine the celebrated "Al-Ra'īs Abū 'Imrān Mūsā ibn Maimūn al-Qurtubī [a native of Cordoba], a Jew learned in the traditions of the Jews and one of their religious authorities and greatest scholars,"[77] known to us as Maimonides. Yet the medical writings of this quintessential Jewish philosopher ("A Guide for the Perplexed") encapsulate the best of the healing arts in the twelfth century Muslim empire. He was in the vanguard of the many Jewish physicians practicing in Cairo.

Rambam was born "on Passover Eve, 1135" at Cordoba, Spain when that city was still the 'Bride of Andalusia' where

> 'the rarest flowers and trees of other countries were carefully cultivated, and the Arabs introduced their system of irrigation, which the Spaniards, both before and since, have never equalled.' ... The Moors were the spiritual heirs of the Hellenists; in their scheme of life all the faculties of body and soul were organically united. ... The medieval Jewish poets write of the cities of Spain with an enthusiasm and tenderness such as no other city than Jerusalem ever evoked from the Hebraic muse. ... The origin of this love is simple. The Moor was Hebraic in his pure monotheism, his stern purpose, his devotion to the righteous ideals of life; he was Hellenic in his graces, in his culture. His Hellenism made him tolerant, his Hebraism imparted to him profundity.[78]

---

sumpsit euphorbium in potu, & opium; Euphorbia obtusifolia ssp. regis-jubae, named after Euphorbos, greek physician to Juba II of Numidia (ca. 50 BC – 23 AD) contains a poisonous milky sap used as a powerful laxative: "And I have read in the discourse of Juba that elephants assist one another when they are being hunted, and that they will defend one that is exhausted, and if they can remove him out of danger, they anoint his wounds with the tears of the aloe tree, standing round him like physicians" (Conybeare, F. C., tr. Philostratus: The Life of Apollonius of Tyana, vol. I, book 2. London: William Heinemann, 1912, p. 161).

[77] Kopf, L. tr. The English Translation of the History of Physicians by Ibn Abi Usaybi'ah. Bethesda, MD: National Library of Medicine, MS C 294, 1971, (tertullian.org), ch. xiv: "On the Classes of Famous Egyptian Physicians."

[78] Yellin, D. and I. Abrahams. Maimonides. Philadephia, PA: The Jewish Publication Society of America, 1903 (archive.org), pp. 1-4, quoting S. Lane-Poole.

When he was only 13, Cordoba was taken by the Almohades. The Jewish community, "which had existed for centuries, was totally destroyed by the Berbers. The synagogues and houses of study were burned, the inhabitants scattered to the four winds."[79] The Rabbi Maimon fled with his family to Almería, and in 1157, when the Almohades conquered Almería, to Fez, North Africa "which had always been a refuge for Jews fleeing from religious persecution in Spain."[80] Even in Fez, his precocious son had already studied medicine and associated with prominent physicians where he would have read the Greek works of Hippocrates, Galen and Aristotle in Arabic but also those of Rhazes, Avicenna and Ibn Zuhr.[81]

Eventually, Maimonides made his way to Egypt and settled in Fustat, today's Old Cairo where he was appointed court physician to Saladin's vizier, Al Fadil.[82]

> His medical writings, all of which are composed in Arabic, are for the most part summaries or elaborations of Galen .... Yet, this does incomplete justice to our hero. Maimonides certainly used experience as well as precedent as his guide; he tested his remedies by actual experiment; he recognised how deeply physical conditions are affected by psychic causes, and maintained, with a strong touch of modernity, that the aim of the doctor is to prevent illness more than to cure it.[83]

In July 1198, Al Fadil commissioned Maimonides "to write a treatise ... offering popular instruction on first aid, in the absence of a physician, for poisonings."[84] In his 'Treatise on Poisons' he

---

[79] Heschel, A. Maimonides: A Biography, tr. J. Neugroschel. NY: Farrar, Strauss, Giroux, 1982 (archive.org), pp. 15-16.

[80] Heschel (1982), p. 16.

[81] Heschel (1982), pp. 16, 18, 22.

[82] Heschel (1982), pp. 71, 181, 183.

[83] Yellin, D. et al., pp. 154-155.

[84] Heschel (1982), pp. 231-232.

recommends that one immediately tie a tourniquet above the place of a poisonous bite:

This tourniquet should be very tight to halt the course of the poison, and to block it from spreading throughout the body. At the same time as one person is tying the tourniquet, another person should open the site by means of an incision, and with his mouth make a suction as strongly as possible, and spit out all that he sucks. Beforehand, he should rinse out his mouth with olive oil or oil mixed with wine. He should also wipe his lips with oil of violets or if that is lacking with olive oil, and take care that he has not in his mouth sores or rotten teeth.[85]

He distinguishes between hot and cold poisonings:

In my opinion, I would counsel him who has been stung or bitten by an animal of which he does not know the species, to carefully observe the symptoms which manifest. If he feels a great heat similar to that which occurs in one who has been bitten by a viper, he should prefer remedies taken in milk, vinagre or water. If on the contrary, he feels a strong cold as with the sting of a scorpion, he should prefer remedies administered in wine. Those who lack wine can employ a decoction of anise, because all physicians are unanimous on the effectiveness of anise against any of the animal poisons.[86]

---

[85] Rabbinowicz, I.-M., tr. Traité des Poisons de Maimonide. Paris: Adrien Delahaye, 1865 (archive.org), ch. 1, p. 21: *Aussitôt qu'un individu a été piqué ou mordu, ou doit se hâter de pratiquer une ligature au-dessus de la plaie. Cette ligature doit être très-serrée pour arrêter la marche du poison, et l'empêcher de se répandre dans le corps. En même temps qu'on fera cette ligature, une autre personne devra élargir la plaie au moyen d'une incision, et avec sa bouche faire une succion aussi forte que possible, et cracher tout ce qu'elle pourrait absorber. Avant de la faire, rincer sa bouche avec de l'huile d'olive ou seule on mêlée de vin. Il faut aussi frotter ses lèvres avec de l'huile de violette ou si on en manque avec de l'huile d'olive, et bien prendre garde qu'on ait dans la bouche quelque ulcération ou dent gâtée.*

[86] Rabbinowicz (1865), ch. 3, pp. 26-27: *Quant à moi, je conseillerai à celui qui a été mordu ou piqué par un animal dont il ne connaît pas l'espèce, de bien observer les symptômes qui se manifestent. S'il ressent une grande chaleur pareille à celle qu'éprouve celui que a éte [sic] mordu par une vipère, il doit accorder la préférence aux médicaments qui se prennent avec du lait, du vinaigre ou bien de l'eau. Si au contraitre, il ressent un froid vif comme celui causé par la piqûre*

Of the various theriacs he mentions as remedies against the stings and bites of venemous animals, many of them call for, among other ingredients, opium, including the 'onion theriac' of Abu Mervan Aben-Zohar (peeled onion, white and black pepper, ginger, agaric, lavender and two drachms of opium dissolved in wine), that of Galen (castoreum, white pepper, myrrh, and a mitskal of opium pulverized in sweet wine) and one recommended by Galen especially for scorpion stings and spider bites (pepper, a mitskal of opium, *anthemis pyrethrum* kneaded altogether in honey into pills the size of an Egyptian bean and taken with three ounces of pure wine).[87]

In September 1199, in a letter to a friend and translator, Samuel ibn Tibbon, he describes his busy practice at the end of his life:

I dwell at Misr (Fostat) and the Sultan resides at Kahira (Cairo) .... My duties to the Sultan are very heavy. I am obliged to visit him every day, early in the morning; and when he or any of his children, or any of the inmates of his harem, are indisposed, I dare not quit Kahira, but must stay during the greater part of the day in the palace. ... Hence, as a rule, I repair to Kahira very early in the day, and even if nothing unusual

---

d'un scorpion, il donnera la préférence aux médicaments qu'on administre dans du vin. Celui qui manque de vin peut employer une décoction d'anis, parce que tous les médecins sont unanimes sur l'efficacité de l'anis contre tous les poisons animaux.

[87] Rabbinowicz, chs. 4, 5, pp. 32-35: *Abou-Mervan Aben-Zohar (Dieu lui fasse miséricorde) dit avoir vérifié par l'expérience la thériaque de l'oignon, et avoir constaté son efficacité dans les piqûres et les morsures d'animaux venimeux. Voice sa composition: oignon pelé, 4 onces; feuilles d'arbousier, gentiane, poivre noir et blanc, poivre long, gingembre, 1 once de chaque; agaric femelle, lavandula staechas une demi-once de chaque; opium, 2 drachmes qu'on fait dissoudre dans du vin. ... Galien fait mention d'un remède très-utile contre la morsure de toute espèce d'animal venimeux, contre les douleurs opiniâtres et la suffocation hystérique. On le compose de la manière suivante: suc de ciguë et de jusquiame de chacun 4 mitskals; du castoréum, du poivre blanc, du costus, de la myrrhe, de l'opium, de chacun 1 mitskal: on pulvérise le tout, on verse dessus 3 onces de vin doux. ... Galien a indiqué une thériaque particulière pour la piqûre du scorpion et la morsure de l'araignée (phalangium, tarentule). Voici sa recette: aristoloche, 4 mitskals; poivre, 2 mitskals; opium, un; anthemis pyrethrum, 3 mitskals; on pétrit le tout ensemble dans du miel, et on en fait des pilules de la frosseur d'une fève d'Égypte; on la prend ensuite en deux pilules avec 3 onces de vin pur.*

happens, I do not return to Misr until the afternoon. Then I am almost dying of hunger. I find the ante-chambers filled with people, both Jews and Gentiles, nobles and common people, judges and baliffs, friends and foes – a mixed multitude, who await the time of my return. I dismount from my animal, wash my hands, go forth to my patients, and entreat them to bear with me while I partake of some slight refreshment, the only meal I take in the twenty-four hours. Then I attend to my patients, write prescriptions and directions for their various ailments. Patients go in and out until nightfall, and sometimes even, I solemnly assure you, until two hours and more in the night. I converse with and prescribe for them while lying down from sheer fatigue, and when night falls I am so exhausted that I can scarcely speak. In consequence of this, no Israelite can have any private interview with me except on the Sabbath.[88]

One of the most often recited tales is that Richard Lionheart sought from Saladin the medical services of Maimonides but that the latter refused because he "felt safer in Cairo than in London."[89] What is true is that Saladin "has been rightly held to be the type and pattern of Saracen chivalry."[90] Equally asserted is that "Sultan al-Malik al-Nāsir Salāh al-Dīn put his trust in him [Maimonides] and availed himself of his medical services, as did his son, al-Malik al-Afdal 'Alī."[91] That the Franks "respected the superior medical knowledge of the East and at times consulted Eastern physicians is in general known from other sources," but this romantic story "derives from a single source – the *Tar'ïkh al Hukamā'*, or History of Physicians, of the Egyptian Muslim writer Jamāl al-Dīn Abul'l-Hasan 'Alī ibn Yūsuf al-Qiftī (1172 – 1248)."[92] The original text is lost, only an abridgment survives, the Frankish king is not named, and the dates make the intersection of the three men improbable.

---

88 Yellin, D. et al., pp. 202-203.

89 Yellin, D. et al., p. 153.

90 Yellin, D. et al., pp. 57-58.

91 Kopf, L. tr., MS C 294 (1971), (tertullian.org), ch. xiv.

92 Lewis, Bernard. "Maimonides, Lionheart, and Saladin," *Eretz-Israel: Archeological, Historical and Geographical Studies* (1964), p. 70 (jstor).

Yet his reputation as a healer was secure even among his critics. A contemporary Arab physician from Baghdad came to Cairo especially to meet him. Even though he thought the 'Guide' was "a bad book, because it perverts the fundamental dogmas of religions by the very means which seem destined to strengthen them," he also "recognized in him a man of very superior merit."[93]

The poet and judge Qādī al-Sa'īd ibn Sana' al-Mulk wrote of him in verse:

I see that Galen's medicine is for the body alone,
While the medicine of Abū 'Imrān is for both
mind and body.
If he were to treat the world with his vast learning,
He would restore it from the disease of ignorance
to knowledge.[94]

He died at age 70 in 1204 and was buried in Tiberias.

Another who made the journey from Spain to Egypt was Abenalbeitar. His 'Treatise on Simples' not only brought up to date the ancient catalog of medicinal plants but also added hundreds more. Abou Mohammed Abd Allah ben Ahmed [Ibn el-Baytār, 1197 – 1248], also surnamed *El-Malaky*, after his native city, Malaga, Spain, was the son of a veterinarian and developed a taste for botany while working with his father. He studied in Seville, traveled in Morocco, Tunis and Egypt where he was named inspector of herborists at Cairo. In his works he frequently gives the names of the localities where he discovered new plants as well as those of the herborists who helped him.

His most important work is the *Djami el-Moufridat* in which he cites Dioscorides, Galen, Hippocrates and Aristotle as well as Arab,

---

[93] De Sacy, Silvestre, tr. Relation de L'Égypte, par Abd-Allatif, Médecin Arabe de Bagdad. Paris: De L'Imprimerie Impériale, 1810 (archive.org), pp. 465-466 [tr. gwr].

[94] Kopf, L. tr., MS C 294 (1971), (tertullian.org), ch. xiv; see also Yellin et al., p. 156.

Persian, Syrian, Chaldean and Indian authors.[95] Of opium, he quotes Dioscorides as saying in a small dose it calms pain and is useful against chronic cough while at a high dose it provokes a deep sleep, lethargy and then death. He quotes Diagoras saying that Erasistratus would not use it against ophthalmia nor ear infections because it weakened the sight and provoked a coma.[96]

The number of new plants introduced by Ibn el-Baytār is often exaggerated, sometimes put at some two thousand plants unknown to Dioscorides.[97] For example, *Peganum harmala* (*Ruta graveolens* L.), also known as harmel, wild rue or Syrian Rue, is often supposed to be a new addition. But in fact Ibn el-Baytār quotes Dioscorides on harmel[98] and Dioscorides lists it twice, saying that mixed in vinegar, "the seed (taken as a drink in wine) is an antidote for deadly medicines."[99] Again,

---

95 Leclerc, L. Traité des Simples par Ibn El-Beïthâr, vol. 1, in *Notices et Extraits des Manuscrits de la Bibliothèque Nationale, tome vingt-troisième. Paris: Imprimerie Nationale,* 1877, pp. vi – x: *El-Malaky, de Malaga, sa patrie .... Fils d'un vétérinaire, il put contracter à la maison paternelle le goût de la botanique. ... Malek el-Kamel régnait en Égypte à l'arrivée d'Ibn el-Beïthâr. Il l'accueillit, le prit à son service et le nomma inspecteur des herboristes du Caire .... Il donne fréquemment le nom des localités où il a découvert des plantes nouvelles .... Dans ses voyages, Ibn el-Beïthâr se mettait en relations avec les savants du pays qui pouvaient lui fournir des renseignements. Leurs noms figurent dans ses récits. ... Le plus important ouvrage d'Ibn el-Beïthâr est celui qui porte en arabe le titre de Djamî el Moufridat, collection des simples .... Le nombre des auteurs cites s'eleve a pres de cent cinquante. ... Les autres ne sont pa seulement d'origiine arabe, mais des Persans, des Syriens, des Chaldéens et des Indiens ....*

96 Leclerc, pp. 106-107: *Prise à petite dose, comme une graine d'orobe, elle calme les douileurs .... Elle est utile contre la toux chronique. A haute dose, elle provoque un sommeil profond, pareil à celui de la léthargie, puis elle tue. ... Diagoras rapporte qu'Érasistrate ... ne voulait pas l'employer contre l'ophthalmie ni contre les affections de l'oreille parce qu'il affaiblit la vue et provoque le coma.*

97 Leclerc, p. xi: *On a singulièrement exagéré le nombre des médicaments nouveaux introduits par Ibn el-Beïthâr. Hottinger s'est avisé de dire ... qu'il y a là plus de deux mille plantes inconnues à Dioscorides.*

98 Leclerc, pp. 426-427.

99 Osbaldeston, T. A. and R.P.A. Wood, trs. *Dioscorides: De Materia Medica.* Johannesburg, SA: Ibidis Press, 2000, pp. 423-427, archive.org; It is the "plant from

Papaver iberos, usually identified as *Papaver somniferum* var *setigerum* L. and common in the Iberian peninsula, is supposedly another newcomer, but Dioscorides covers the *Papaver* species well. *P. setigerum* is closely related to *P. somniferum* and contains small amounts of morphine.[100] Gómez de Ortega (1741 – 1818), botanist and heir to the work of José Quer (1695 – 1764), obtained good opium from poppies grown in the *Real Jardin Botánico* in Madrid as well as from the fields of Andalucia.[101] They have also been found on a French mediterranean island.[102]

---

which harmine was first isolated, as well as a source of harmaline and tetrahydroharmine. Total beta-Carboline content runs almost 4% by weight in the seeds of Syrian Rue. These alkaloids occur in roughly the same proportions as in" *Banisteriopsis caapi*, the basis of ayuhuasca or yage. A maceration of its seeds is still prepared by the old *campesinos* of the Balearic Islands for certain festivals, as I was able to personally verify. The women remain excluded from its use.

100 Small amounts of morphine have been detected in *setigerum*; see Farmilo, C. G. "Detection of Morphine in Papaver setigerum DC," *UNODC Bulletin on Narcotics*, 1953, Issue 1 – 004, pp. 26-31; "The cytological evidence of a close affinity between *P. setigerum* and *P. somniferum* is discussed by Fulton. *P. somniferum* is diploid (n=11) and *P. setigerum* is tetraploid (n=22) with exactly twice the number of chromosomes. No other species of *Papaver* is known to have the number n=11 or a multiple of this number. This information indicates that *P. setigerum* is not the wild ancestral species of the cultivated *P. somniferum*, as was formerly believed since a diploid would not be derived from a tetraploid plant (p. 2/8)."

101 Gómez de Ortega, Casimiro. *Continuacion de la Flora Española, ó Historia de las plantas de España, que escribia Don Joseph Quer*. Vol VI. Madrid: D. Joachîn Ibarra, 1784, bibliotecadigital.jcyl.es, pp. 57-58: *La mejor opinion es la apoyada en la experiencia ... [E]l jugo lechoso de las Adormideras, sacado por incision en nuestra Península, tiene los mismos caractéres, y causa los propios fonómenos que el buen Opio y aun tiene la preeminencia de mayor pureza, y estár libre de partes groseras: esto se consigue con hacer con cuidado la operacion, como describe DIOSCÓRIDES, y como la practiqué en el Real Jardin Botánico en el año de 1762, y logré una onza de purisimo y perfectíssimo Opio, de cuya excelencia no me queda la menor duda. ... Yo tengo Opio exquisito, adquirido por el mismo medio en los campos de Andalucia ....*

102 Candolle, A. P. de. *Flore Française, ou Descriptions succinctes de toutes les plantes qui croissent naturellement en France, tome cinquième, ou sixième volume.* Paris: Chez Desray, 1815, biodiversitylibrary.org, pp. 585-586: *Pavot porte-soie. Papaver setigerum. Cette espèce*

An early mention of the theriaca in a Romance language shows up in the *Libro de Calila é Dimna*, a collection of Indian fables better known under the title *Fabulas de Pilpay ó Bidpay* [The Fables of Bidpay] ordered translated into Castilian at Toledo by Alfonso X the Learned in 1251.[103]

One might say, then, that opium came to Europe from the Middle East, first seeking refuge in Byzantium when any sign of scientific botany disappeared in the West, then was returned to Europe through the work of the HispanoArabs. If one accepts that it had its origins in a triangle whose vertices are Andalucia, Algeria and Cyprus – as De Candolle [1806 – 1893] supposed[104] – it was not reinvented but only resurged where it was born.

---

ressemble au pavot somnifère .... Cette plante a été découverte par M. Requien, dans l'ile du Levant (l'une des iles d'Hyères).

103 Wacks, D. A. "The cultural context of the translation of Calila E Dimna," Framing Iberia. Leiden: Brill, 2007, brill.com; Gayangos, Don Pascual de, ed. *Biblioteca de Autores Espanoles*. Madrid: M. Rivadeneyra, 1860, pp. 49-50: "*ca el home entendudo, maguer que se fie por su fuerza é por su valentia é por su seso, non debe ganar enemigos; así como el home, maguer tenga la triaca et las melecinas, non debe beber la vedegambre á fiucia dollas, ca la bondat es dicha de los que bien facen et non de los que bien dicen*"; Knatchbull, Wyndam, tr. Kalila and Dimna, or The Fables of Bidpai. London: Longman, Hurst, Rees, Orme, and Brown, 1819, p. 231: "for the sensible man, however confident of his own strength and of his high claims, should be as cautious of creating himself enemies by an unreasonable and presumptuous display of his superiority, as a person would hesitate to swallow poison, though he is in possession of its antidote." Here, theriaca is translated as antidote; the original is from the Sanskrit text of Pañcatantra [3rd c. BC]. As regards the *verdegambre* or hellebore, it is so violently toxic – also common in the Mediterranean basin – that in Spain it is denominated *hierba del ballestero* (herb of the archer) due to its efficacy for poisoning arrows.

104 Candolle, Alphonse de. Origin of Cultivated Plants. New York: D. Appleton and Company, 1885, archive.org, pp. 392-393: "Poppy – *Papaver somniferum*, Linnaeus. ... The variety which has been cultivated for centuries escapes readily from cultivation, or becomes naturalized in certain localities of the south of Europe. It cannot be said to exist in a really wild state, but botanists are agreed in regarding it as a modification of the poppy called *Papaver setigerum*, which is wild on the shores of

Besides employing it in theriacas and mixing it with solanaceas and cannabis in other medicinal recipes, Muslim culture used opium recreationally, both in private and in the public *divan.* Long before the spread of Islam, all the territory surrounding the Black Sea, as well as Egypt, Mesopotamia and Iran, were areas where the poppy's black seeds grew for millennia.

With the Arab expansion, opium is disseminated, sourced in the gigantic Persian and Turkish plantations, from the Strait of Gibraltar to Malaysia and China, at times in the form of pills sold with the motto *mash Allah* ('gift of God'). Around the eleventh century those who use the drug in social gatherings or for dreams can be counted in the tens of millions and belong to every social strata. The most common method of ingesting it is to eat it, though the Persians were already accustomed to smoke it in the time of Avicenna. It is also frequent to consume it in grape syrups mixed with hashish.

The traditional Muslim custom was to take little or no opium as a euphoriant until one was nearly fifty years old and then to begin to administer it daily to get the advantages of 'familiarity' mentioned by the Greek and Roman physicians. It is thought of as a drug of senectitude, which permits human beings to grow old without bitterness and to die sweetly; the only undesirable side effect is a tendency toward constipation which can be corrected periodically with some kind of laxative. Eating opium is considered not only a means of restoring psychological equilibrium but also as a means of preserving physical health due to a modification of the metabolism linked to the habit: those who carry on for years or decades consuming great quantities daily of the drug are immune to ailments like the cough or the flu, singularly debilitating for persons of an advanced age. In such cases the truly noxious, as much on the psychological level as on the

---

the Mediterranean, notably in Spain, Algeria, Corsica, Sicily, Greece and the island of Cyprus. It has been met with in Eastern Asia, consequently this is really the original of the cultivated form."

somatic, is the interruption of said use; if this is avoided the opium user remains safe from accidents and a rapid organic impoverishment. The toxicologist Balthazard and other early twentieth century physicians confirmed this symbiosis with the drug that the great Persian and Turkish opium eaters had achieved, to the extreme of maintaining that "the practice is hygienic so long as it is maintained within certain limits."[105]

Perhaps the most frequent commonplace with regards to the traditional predilection of the Muslims for opium may be to suppose that it was a direct consequence of the Koranic prohibition of alcohol.[106] But we have already seen that nowhere in the Koran is found such a prohibition and how the Islamic culture has always admitted (until relatively recently, with few exceptions) the moderate consumption of alcohol, and even the immoderate. Yet it would be repugnant today in the West to compare even on the theoretical level the respective advantages and inconveniences of opium and alcohol, not only from a strictly therapeutic perspective but also as euphoriant drugs in general.

The old Arab criterion is that, ingested in a large quantity over long enough periods of time, both drugs produce a habit whose interruption gives rise to abstinence syndromes and that both are powerful toxins that literally end up embalming their users as if they had been preserved by taxidermists. All the same, the dipsomaniac has a significantly shorter lifespan than the opiomane, transmits congenital

---

105 Aparicio, 1972, p. 159.

106 Burton writes that the English word "alcohol" is derived from the Arabic *Khol* or "powdered antimony for the eyelids. ... The powder is ... applied with a thick blunt needle to the inside of the eyelid, drawing it along the rim .... The latter word, with the article (Al-Kohl) is the origin of our 'alcohol'; though even M. Littré fails to show how 'fine powder' became 'spirits of wine.' I found this powder (wherewith Jezebel 'painted' her eyes) a great preservative from ophthalmia in desert-travelling: the use in India was universal, but now European example is gradually abolishing it" (1885, vol. I, p. 59, fn 1).

defects to his progeny and is more easily involved in conflicts with his obligations to his family, work and society. In places where opium and alcohol can be acquired with equal facility, for an equivalent price, another advantage of the first over the second is that the opiomane doesn't experience clumsiness, verbal jabber and halitosis. Without doubt it was these considerations – ethical and pharmaceutical – that made the leaders of Islam, and the people, prefer the ebriety of the former over the latter. To educe that they fell upon the poppy because their holy book prohibited wine is equivalent to maintaining that Westerners smoke cigars because their laws impede them from smoking crack. Yet drug substitution is often a byproduct of prohibition, as we have seen over the last century during the global crusade against drugs, and as we shall see with Shah Abbas I.

The lack of historical rigor in analyzing the history of opium is often combined with a more or less declared deprecation toward the 'East' with its mythologem of what constitutes a true 'paradise,' a thing not shared by the realistic judgment of many Muslims who considered opium a superior lenitive to alcohol. What distinguishes Arab use from the GrecoRoman is the recommendation of opium for the transition from middle to old age and to overcome the troubles of the latter. This was precisely the principal utility that Plato saw in wine. The true difference observed between GrecoRoman and Arab culture with regards to opium is its use as a euphoriant and not solely as an analgesic and antidote. The theriacas implied of course a daily use of opium but along with this the Muslim admitted the drug as general and permanent solace, seeking to accustom himself to it. This is clear enough from the quantity of the treatments prepared by Avicenna and Rhazes.[107] Having Persia as its focus, this attitude was extended to all the territories that came under the influence of Islam, from the north of Africa and Asia Minor to India, Indochina, the Malay archipelago and China; in the Far East only Japan remained on the margin.

[107] Behr, 1981, p. 47.

Eight hundred years will have to pass before a Muslim ruler – Shah Abbas I [r. 1588 – 1629] would cause an explosion of opiate use. He did so when he tried to restrict access to wine in 1621. Within a year he was forced to repeal his decree in favor of prohibiting the 'poppy boil-up' which had become popular in the absence of access to alcohol.

This tale of drug substitution and the unintended consequences of a decree is told by the Venetian traveler Pietro della Valle [1586 – 1652]. While at Isphahan, the king sent an edict prohibiting all Muslims from drinking or selling wine. Naturally, there were exceptions. Though non-Muslims could continue to drink as they pleased, they were forbidden by capital punishment from either selling or giving wine to Muslims. The king continued to drink, but in secret for fear of causing a scandal, because of doctor's orders. His most important ministers also had permission to drink, so long as the thing was done hidden away in their chambers. At Shiraz the people continued to drink as usual.[108]

He was soon forced to reverse himself. Less than eight months later, the same king published to the sound of trumpets at Isphahan, where he had arrived the day before, that no one under penalty of death, should from now on any longer drink *Cocnar*, which

---

108 Carneau, Etienne, Francois le Comte, trs. <u>*Troisiesme Partie des Fameux Voyages de Pietro della Valle*</u>, Letter 12 from Persia. Paris: Chez Gervais Clouzier, 1653, archive.org, pp. 177-180: *Le vingt huitiéme d'Aoust le Roy envoya un Exprés a Hisphahan, avec des lettres portans deffenses à tous les Mahometans de boire du vin ...; qui se mesme iour & les autres suivans fuerent publieés à son de trompe par tous les carrefours de la ville, permettant neantmoins aux ... Chrestiens d'en boire & d'en faire autant qu'il leur plairoit [but] n'en donnassent point, ni pour de l'argent, ni par present, à aucun Mahometan ... sur peine de la vie .... Le Roy en boit ... mais en cachete ... de peur de causer du scandale à ses sujets; encore est il seul ... d'en boire durant tout le iour un certain nombre de verres, par l'ordre des Medecins. Quelques uns des plus grands & des premiers Ministres de son Estat ... ont eu la permission d'en boire aussi ... secrettement dans leur chambre & sans scandale. Il n'y a que sur les terres d'Imamculi Chan de Scirax, qui est la veritable Perse, où l'on ait la liberté entiere d'en boire autant qu'il leur plaira ....*

was a certain liquor extracted from the bark of the heads of poppies which was in great use among the Persians, and particularly the soldiers, since their wine had been prohibited. *Cocnar* was said to weaken the body and stun its users. It was prohibited with so much rigor that the carafes of this liquor were broken in all the boutiques of the market which were selling it and the death penalty ordered alike for those who drank it, as well as for those who fabricated it or who exposed it for sale. But the king gave them a general permission to drink wine, as before, in place of *Cocnar*. ... In this way Bacchus rules in Persia more powerfully than ever, as the king, with all his power and all the diligence he brought to bear, could little chase it from his kingdom.[109]

---

109 Carneau, et al, trs. Letter 14 from Persia, pp. 257-258: *Le vingt quatriéme d'Avril, le Roy fit publier à son de trompe dan Isphahan, où il estoit arrivé le iour auparavant que nul, sur peine de la vie, ne beust plus dorénavant du Cocnar, qui est une certaine liqueur extráite de l'écorce des pommes de Pavots, qu'ils appellent Chas cehase, qui estoit grandement en usage parmy les Perses, & particulierement entre les soldats, depuis que le vin leur avoit est é defendu; parce que ce breuvage ... foit extremement pernicieux à la santé, & qu'entre les autres mauvais effets qu'il produit, il affoiblit notablement le corps, & rend la personne comme estourdie. Le Roy ... defendit l'usage ... avec tant de rigueur que tous les vase de cette liqueur furent brisez dans les boutiques des marchands qui la vendoient; & la peine de mort ordonnée tant à ceux qui en boiroient, comme aux autres qui en feroient la composition, ou qui l'exposeroient en ventre. Mail le Roy ... leur donna une permission generale de boire du vin, comme auparavant, au lieu du Cocnar .... Ainsi la deffense qui sembloit insupportable à ses peuples, fut levée aprés quelques mois, & la licence si ardemment souhaitée de boire du vin, comme auparavant, leur fut remise. ... Par ce moyen Bacchus regnera dans la Perse plus puissamment que iamais, sans que le Roy, avec tout son pouvoir, & toute la diligence qu'il y a apportée, l'ait peu chasser de son Thrône;* see also, Schipano, Mario, ed. Viaggi di Pietro della Valle, Il Pellegrino, Descritti da lui medesimo in Letterre familiari, *La Persia, parte seconda.* Venice: Presso Paolo Baglioni, 1667, archive.org, pp. 193-196, 281-282; Shahnavaz, S. "AFYŪN," Encyclopaedia Iranica, I/6, iranicaonline.org, pp. 594-598.

C. Cannabis

Cannabis does not appear to be mentioned in Sanskrit until the tenth century. Yet the products derived from cannabis (grifa, kif, hashish) were known in the Far East from some of the earliest written records. Without any doubt, the plant was an important point of contact between the Arabs and the original populations of those territories they conquered.

Figure 87. The Old Man of the Mountain (miniature from the Travels of Marco Polo, 1400s).

1. The Diversity of Arab Use. In the thirteenth century a contemporary of Omar Khayyam, Hassan Ibn Al-Sabbah [c. 1050 – 1124, Sinān, the so-called Old Man of the Mountain] founded the order of the Hashishins, affiliated with the Ismailites. The three stories that have come down about Al-Sabbah agree that he intoxicated young men, either with opium, wine or hashish.

Marco Polo says he first created an earthly paradise:

He thought moreover of an unheard-of wickedness, that he should make men into bold murderers or swordsmen, who are commonly called assassins, by whose courage he might kill whoever he wished and be feared by all. He dwelled in a *most noble* valley *shut in* between two *very high* mountains *where* he had made them make the largest garden & the most beautiful that ever was seen *in this world.* There are *abundance and delight* of all the good *plants, flowers, and* fruits of the world, *and trees which he had been able to find.* ... And besides he had made them make *in that garden many beautiful fountains* ... through some of which *it was seen* ran wine & through some milk & through some honey & through some *the clearest* water. There were *set to dwell* ladies & damsels the most beautiful in the world, who *all* knew *very well* how to play on all instruments & sing *tunefully* & *sweetly* dance better than other women *of this world* .... *Their duty was to furnish the young men who were put there with all delights & pleasures.* ... *No sad thing was spoken of there, nor was it lawful to have time for anything but play, love & pleasure.* ... And the Old Man made his men understand that *in* that garden was Paradise.[110]

Marco Polo then describes how the Old Man would use opium to trick the young men into believing in his paradise:

And the Old Man kept with him at his court all the young men *of the inhabitants of those mountains* of the ocuntry from twelve years to twenty .... *Sometimes* the Old Man, *when he wished to kill any lord who made war or was his enemy*, made them put some of these youths into that Paradise .... For he had *opium* to drink given them by which they fell asleep *and as if half dead* immediately *as soon as they had drunk it, and they slept quite three days and three nights.* Then he had them taken *in this sleep* and put into that garden *of his, into different rooms of the said palaces*, and *there* made them wake, *and they found themselves there.* ... And when the youths were waked up and they find themselves in there ... they believe that they are *most* truly in Paradise.[111]

Then the Old Man would use opium again to separate them from this paradise:

---

[110] Moule, A. C. & Paul Pelliot, trs. Marco Polo: The Description of the World, vol. I. London: George Routledge & Sons Ltd., 1938, archive.org, p. 129, italics original.

[111] Moule & Pelliot, trs., p. 130.

And *after four or five days* when the Old Man wishes any of them *his assassins* to send to any place and to have any man killed, *then* he has the drink of *opium* given *again* to as many as pleases him *of these youths to make them sleep*, and when they are asleep he has them taken into his palace *which was outside the garden.* And when these youths are awaked and they find themselves *out of their garden* in that castle in the palace, they make great marvel at it and are not *very* glad of it, *that they find themselves outside of the Paradise*, for from the Paradise from which they came they ould never of their own will be parted. ... [A]nd *many* had a wish to die that they might be able to go there, and much desired that day when they should go there.[112]

Finally, the Old Man promised them they should return to that paradise if they would become his assassins:

And the Old Man answered them, Son, this is by the commandment of our prophet Mahomet, that whoever defends his servant he will grant to him Paradise; and if thou art obedient to me thou shalt have this favour. Through this means he had so inspirited all his people to die ... because none feared death if only he could do the commandment and will of the said Old Man, and they exposed themselves like madmen to every manifest danger, wishing to die together with the king's enemy and despising the present life. And for this reason he was feared in all those countries as a tyrant. ... And when the Old Man wished to have any lord or any other man killed he took some of these his assassins and sends them where he wished, and told them that he wished to send them *carried by his angels* to Paradise, and that they go to kill such a man, and if they should die that they will go immediately to Paradise. Those to whom this was commanded by the Old Man did it very willingly more than anything that they could do; and they went and did all that the Old Man commanded them *for the great desire that they had that they might come back to Paradise.*[113]

This would all just be another traveler's tale except that a very similar story shows up in a Chinese travelogue, the *Xishiji.* Written by Lui-yu in 1263, it recounts the stories of Chang-de, a tax officer who embarked on a journey to northwestern Iran.[114] In Cheng-de's

---

112 Moule & Pelliot, trs., p. 131.

113 Moule & Pelliot, trs., pp. 131-132.

114 Chen, Li-wei, "The Mountain without the Old Man: Xishiji on Ismailies," in the *Proceedings of the 2nd International Ismaili Studies Conference 'Mapping a Pluralist Space in*

account, the young men are lured with material goods, intoxicated with wine, placed in a chamber of delights, then returned to reality:

> *Its kingdom's soldiers were all assassins. It used to be that as [they] spotted any strong man, they lured him with material goods. They ordered him to kill his father and brother(s) and recruited him. They intoxicated him, excorted him to a (chamber) basement and entertained him with music and beauty. They let him indulge in sensual pleasure. Several days afterwards, they placed him back to where he came from. At the time he woke up, they asked them what he saw. They taught him that if he could die as an assassin, he would live in joy and comfort like that. As a result, they taught him classic texts and mantras for him to recite daily. Therefore his mind was blinded (convinced or seduced?) and he was willing to die without regret. ... They ordered to send assassins to hide in those kingdoms which did not surrender. They stabbed their lords, and women as well, and they died.*[115]

The comparative value of this separate text shines brightest in the choice of the vehicle of ebriety: "In *Xishiji*, the recruitment team drugged those strong men with wine rather than opium. It is likely that binge drinking of wine had a more negative connotation than consuming opium in 13th century China. However, wrongdoers were more likely to be associated with overdosing hashish in the Islamic world."[116]

The third version of the story comes by way of Fitzgerald's translation of The Rubaiyat of Omar Khayyam. In this one, Hassan al Sabbah uses hashish to madden his assassins. Discontented with his low government post, he

> plunged into the maze of intrigue of an Oriental Court, and failing in a base attempt to supplant his benefactor, he was disgraced and fell. After many mishaps and wanderings, Hasan became the head of the Persian sect of the Ismaílians – a party of fanatics who had long murmured in obscurity, but rose to an evil eminence under the

---

Ismaili Studies," held March 9-10, 2017, at Carleton University, Ottawa, Canada, edited by Karim H. Karim, pp. 123-125.

[115] Chen, Li-wei, p. 127.

[116] Chen, Li-wei, p. 129.

guidance of his strong and evil will. In A. D. 1090, he seized the castle of Alamút, in the province of Rúdbar, which lies in the mountainous tract south of the Caspian Sea; and it was from this mountain home he obtained that evil celebrity among the Crusaders as the Old Man of the Mountains, and spread terror through the Mohammedan world; and it is yet disputed whether the word *assassin*, which they have left in the language of Modern Europe as their dark memorial, is derived from the *hashish*, or opiate of hemp-leaves (the Indian *bhang*), with which they maddened themselves to the sullen pitch of Oriental desperation ....[117]

Once again, the reason behind the choice of drug is telling:

The Nezārīs of the Alamūt period were not the inventors of the policy of assassinating religio-political adversaries in Muslim society [but they] did assign an important political role to this method of struggle. ... It was under such circumstances that the Crusaders and their occidental chroniclers, surprised by the seemingly irrational behavior of the *fedā' īs*, began to fabricate a number of legends about these devotees of the Nezārī Isma 'ilis who had become famous in Europe as the "Assassins," the followers of a mysterious "Old Man of the Mountain." [T]he seemingly blind obedience of the *fedā' īs* to their leader was attributed, by their occidental observers, to the influence of an intoxicating drug like hashish ... which provided a rational explanation for a behavior that otherwise seemed irrational to Westerners. ... It may be noted, however, that the Muslims did refer to the Nezārī Isma'ilis with abusive terms such as *hašīšiya*, *hašīšīn*, etc., without any derivative explanation ... and these terms, meaning low-class rabble, were picked up by the Crusaders who transformed them into the variants of the term "Assassin" in European languages.[118]

In each story the choice of drug maximizes the social opprobrium for its intended audience.

Deeply influenced by the Sufis, Hassan's kingdom lasted until it was exterminated by the Mongols. A model for the European military orders like the Knights Templar and the Teutonic Knights, the Hashishins (whose fame for cruelty, as Fitzgerald suggests, could be

---

[117] FitzGerald, 1948, p. 4.

[118] FEDĀ'Ī, Encyclopaedia Iranica, iranicaonline.org., pp. 2/4, 3/4.

the origin of the word 'assassin') were said to have received an abundant provision of cannabis before going into battle and were distinguished for their bravery during the Crusades. Naturally, this fame comes from the same Crusaders, who as the 'good' invaders demonstrated a total blindness to the atrocities they themselves committed.

Saladin [Salah al-Din al Ayubbi, 1137 – 1193] tried to destroy the Assassins root and branch and capture their leader, Sinān, but ended by making an uneasy truce with them instead:

Saladin, believing that he had the arch-enemy in his power, sent a body of troops to surround him; but hostile soldiers and peaceful messengers were alike held back by a mysterious force which numbed their limbs. ... The awed reports of his baffled and perplexed envoys worked upon Saladin's fears. He remembered the two former attempts upon his life, and began to doubt whether anything human could save him from the supernatural agencies of this devil or saint. ... He had chalk and cinders strewed around his tent, to detect secret footsteps; his guards were supplied with linklights, and the night watches were frequently relieved. But unearthly terrors surrounded him, and his sleep was troubled. ... Presently Saladin awoke from his uneasy dreams to see a figure gliding out at the tent door. Looking round he noticed that the lamps had been displaced, and beside his bed lay some hot scones of the shape peculiar to the Assassins, with a leaf of paper on the top, pinned by a poisoned dagger. There were verses on the paper: "By the Majesty of the Kingdom! what you possess will escape you, in spite of all, but victory remains to us: We acquaint you that *we hold you*, and that we reserve you till your reckoning be paid." Saladin gave a great and terrible cry .... The dread Master had been actually at his pillow: it was nothing short of a miracle. ... Then Saladin said: "I have *seen* him – and that is very different from hearing of him. Go to this man and ask him for a safe-conduct, and pray him not to punish me for my past errors." ... Saladin therefore departed, in such haste that he even left his artillery behind him; and at the Bridge of Ibn-Munkidh he received a safe-conduct from the Master of the Assassins. ... As a political measure, moreover, the binding of the Master by ties of mutual toleration was a master-stroke. It cut away from the still disaffected Shiites in Egypt their hope of Sinan's sinister support, and deprived the Crusaders of a secret weapon.[119]

---

[119] Lane-Poole, Stanley. Saladin and the fall of the Kingdom of Jerusalem, ch. X,

The Arab pharmacopeia recommended cannabis for many different ailments, and its use as a general euphoriant was sometimes combined with opium and at other times with wine. In the "Tale of the Ensorcelled Prince," narrated within the famous "Tale of the Fisherman and the Jinni" in the Thousand Nights and a Night, a philandering wife uses cannabis to drug her husband to sleep so that she can go to her lover in the night. While pretending to be napping, one afternoon he overhears a slave-girl conversing with another who accidentally admits the truth:

"Nay, more, doth she not drug every night the cup she giveth him to drink before sleep-time, and put Bhang into it? So he sleepeth and wotteth not whither she goeth, nor what she doeth; but we know that, after giving him the drugged wine, she donneth her richest raiment and perfumeth herself and then she fareth out from him to be away till break of day; then she cometh to him, and burneth a pastile under his nose and he awaketh from his death-like sleep." When I heard the slave-girls' words, the light became black before my sight and I thought night would never fall. Presently the daughter of my uncle came from the baths; and they set the table for us and we sat and ate together a fair half-hour quaffing our wine as was ever our wont. Then she called for the particular wine I used to drink before sleeping and reached me the cup; but, seeming to drink it according to my wont, I poured the contents into my bosom; and, lying down, let her hear that I was asleep. Then, behold, she cried, "Sleep out the night, and never wake again: by Allah, I loathe thee, and I loathe thy whole body, and my soul turneth in disgust from cohabiting with thee; and I see not the moment when Allah shall snatch away thy life!"[120]

In other quatrains, Omar Khayyam sings the praises of hashish as an intoxicant, especially when mixed with wine:

Truces and Treaties (1176 – 1181). NY: G. D. Putnam's Sons, 1906, archive.org, pp. 148-151.

[120] Burton, 1885, vol. 1, pp. 70-71. Burton adds a footnote: "The Arab 'Banj' and Hindú 'Bhang' ... meaning a preparation of hemp (*Cannabis sativa* seu *Indica*) .... Amongst Moslems, the Persians adopted the drink as an ecstatic ..." (p. 70, fn. 2).

Are you depresssed? Then take of *bang* a grain,
And next a pint of rose-hued grape-juice drain.
"Sufi you are? Nor eat of this or that?"
Go! Feast on stones, since stones your fare remain!

Though rich, the toper comes to povery,
And stirs the world by his debauchery.
That emerald in my ruby bowl I'll pour
That I may wholly blind Care's serpent eye.

Hashish is better for all men's heart pains,
They say, than cup and wine to lute's soft strains;
By Law one wine drop clearly better than
A hundred bang users' blood thus remains![121]

The use of some variety of cannabis with wine, already mentioned by Democritus and Galen, suggests that in that era there was a recipe, today lost, for effectively combining both drugs. The mixtures we know of – without wine, of course – are the *dawamesk* mentioned by Baudelaire and Gautier, an opioid compound, and the *majoun* of North Africa, potentiated with belladonna or daturas and sometimes with opium as well. Another form of intoxication is that already mentioned by Herodotus, burning cannabis in well-closed places and simply breathing in the smoke.

Although the medicinal use of cannabis remained unaltered at least from the first millennium before the Christian era – multiplied

---

[121] Thompson, Eben Francis, tr. The Quatrains of Omar Khayyam of Nishapur. London: Privately Printed, 1906, archive.org, quatrains numbered 294, 627, 842 on pages 99, 210, 281; Thompson adds a footnote (p. 210): "Emerald, 'zumurrud,' which Nicolas explains is hashish ... but emerald may just as well mean wine .... The emerald is believed by the Orientals to possess the power of blinding serpents"; see also, Rittenhouse, Jessie B., ed. The Rubaiyat of Omar Khayyam, comprising the metrical translations by Edward Fitzgerald & E. H. Whinfield and the prose version of Justin Huntly McCarthy. Boston: Little Brown, and Company, 1900, archive.org, quatrains numbered CCC, CCCXI, CCCXIV, pages 121, 123, 138.

several times over by combining the Persian pharmacopeia with the Indian, Egyptian and Chinese – there are reasons to suppose that it was not for the Arabs only a drug of the comfortable classes (able to afford physician-prescribed medicine) but rather one of groups distinguished by religious faith or social condition. There seems to have been a drug favored by small *campesinos*, day laborers and slaves, called hashish *al-haráfísh*, literally "rascals' grass."[122] On the other side, there is the hashish *al-fokora* ("herb of the *fakirs*") and Makrizy – a historian of the fifteenth century – mentions a liquid solution employed by these aesthetes to "liberate the spirit."[123] He cites in support of this position a poem by a sheik who proposes: "Leave wine/ take this cup that exhales the perfume of amber/ and shines with the dazzling green of the emerald."[124] From the twelfth century various preparations of cannabis (and opium) are important points of departure for understanding the terminology of certain mystics and for institutions like the ecstatic dance of jubilation or the ecstacy of erotic inhibition.[125]

Nevertheless, except within the mystic orders linked to the Sufis, cannabis has no religious connotation in the Arab world, the opposite of that which occurred in Buddhism and Hinduism. Islam is too perfect a montheistic faith to admit institutions of communion, and no drug can serve as a mystic vehicle in its orthodoxy. Though drugs may be called the gifts of Allah, or poisoned sweets handed out by the djinns, they will never officially be either entheogens or

---

[122] In his translation of the Thousand Nights and a Night, Burton suggests that cannabis is the same herb described by Rabelais in chapters 49, 50 and 51 of *Pantagruel* as well as that mentioned in the Decameron: "Hashish al haráfísh = rascals' grass, *i.e.* the herb Pantagruelion. ... [V]arious preparations of the drug are sold at an especial bazar in Cairo. See the 'powder of marvellous virtue' in Boccaccio, iii., 8; and iv., 10" (1885, vol. 1, p. 70, fn. 2).

[123] Leonicio, 1971, p. 74.

[124] Leonicio, 1971, p. 74.

[125] Massignon, 1922, p. 86 *ff*; in Eliade, p. 316, n. 1.

enechthrogens. Hence the connections between cannabis and the *canaille* and the elaborator of philters in folk medicine, or with saints and *fakirs*, does not infer any modification in the neutral status of this drug within the totality of available psychoactive drugs, just as it does not change the nature of the *aguardiente* of Galicia that it is consumed by poor fisherman, landowners and parish priests. The Islamic political-religious authority says nothing in favor or against it, as occurs with opium. The only known exception to this rule takes place in 1378 when an emir of Joneima decreed that the eaters of hashish were to be punished with the extraction of their teeth; but this law, of very local impact, seems to have been repealed shortly afterwards.[126]

2. The Fundamentalist Reaction. Within the ranks of the jurisconsults – the so-called *alfaqies* – one can observe attempts to achieve an illegalization of hashish, interesting because it helps make explicit the categories in play. In chronological order the first of these texts appears at the end of the thirteenth century; Ibn Ganim signed it, his express aim to defend the proposition that "whosoever drinks wine is a sinner and who eats hashish an infidel."[127] The difference in treatment accorded the two drugs observes the distinction that no one in the Islamic faith used wine as a mystic vehicle but there is no shortage of those who considered hashish a "dwelling place near to God and summation of the divine presence."[128] The thesis of Ibn

---

[126] Lewin, Louis. Phantastica Narcotic and Stimulating Drugs Their Use and Abuse. New York: E. P. Dutton & Co., Inc., 1964, p. 107: "It is recorded that in the year 1378 the Emir Soudoun Sheikhouni tried to end the abuse of Indian hemp consumption among the poorer classes by having all plants of this description in Joneima destroyed and imprisoning all the hemp-eaters. He ordered, moreover, that all those who were convicted of eating the plant should have their teeth pulled out, and many were subjected to this punishment. But by 1393 the use of this substance in Arabian territory had increased."

[127] Ibn Ganim, *Maylis fi damm al-hasisa*, pp. 40-41, in Lozano Camara, 1990.

[128] Ibn Ganim, *Maylis fi damm al-hasisa*, p. 40, in Lozano Camara, 1990.

Ganim appears intolerable since it not only disfigures the 'intoxicating' quality of cannabis but also represents the evil of the drug as being concentrated in that the devotee is 'distracted from prayer.'

The next treatise along these lines, written at the close of the fourteenth century,[129] presents hashish as something introduced into the Arab world by "the Tartars,"[130] and imputes to it 120 specific harms, among which are included "being complacent with adultery, sudden death, leprosy and passive sodomy."[131] His argument is that it is the worst of drugs, because along with its many specific harms one can add "a first moment of ecstacy, captivation and delightful vigor."[132] The pleasure of ebriety is always a guilty one since it comes at the expense of 'reason,' and acts of this kind are so reproachable that "intoxication is [even] prohibited for animals."[133] The only excuse a person may allege for using psychoactive drugs is some specific therapeutic purpose, and the more doubtful the pleasure induced by a substance, the less suspect will it be for the good believer; thus, for example, *beleno* is more dignified, in principle, than wine or hashish.[134]

Within this restrictive tendency it is worth mentioning the *alfaqui* Ibn al-Yazzar, who around the year 1580 wrote in Cairo a treatise proposing to extend to a certain theriaca or *electuario* (the so-called *bars*) the attitude of al-Zarkasi toward wine and hashish. Though it does not offer the exact composition of this theriaca,[135] the text of al-

---

129 Al-Zarkasi, *Zahr al-aris*, in Lozano Camara, 1990, pp. 117-146.

130 Rosenthal, 1971, p. 54 *ff.*

131 Al-Zarkasi, pp. 122-123.

132 Al-Zarkasi, pp. 129-130.

133 Al-Zarkasi, p. 144.

134 Al-Zarkasi, p. 138.

135 While the exact composition of *bars* is disputed, "there can be no doubt that [it] was a compound drug" (Rosenthal, Franz. The Herb: Hashish versus Medieval Muslim Society. Leiden, NL: E. J. Brill, 1971 (GB), p. 31). Ingredients may have included hashish, laudanum, opium syrup, hemp, pepper, saffron or *Datura stromonium* (pp. 32-33).

Yazzar indicates that at the end of the sixteenth century the Arabs were using it recreationally. This happens at the exact moment coffee is being persecuted in Egypt, Syria and Turkey, and al-Yazzar mentions that the cheapness of *bars* can be contrasted with the "disproportionately high cost of coffee." The picture he paints verges on the pathetic:

> Now, when *bars* leads to pillage and the dishonor of the harem, and makes all the eloquent men of good intentions mute, made assiduous patrons of the drugstores, we write this elegant composition where we invite you to cry for a people, become a desolate desert.[136]

Therefore, in his opinion, "the healthy ought not to take the triaca more than once a week,"[137] since otherwise a guilty pleasure would take precedence over an innocent therapy. For the rest, the treatise attacks the opium present in *bars* – alleging that it "converts the user into a shadow" – but no more than its other ingredients; saffron (*azafran*) for example, has "a property of making one happy that, in large doses, annuls mental sensibility" and *nardo* (tuberose or spikenard) "produces euphoria, for which reason its illegality admits no discussion."[138]

It seems that the counsels of al-Yazzar did not become general Islamic law, nor those of al-Zarkasi, though they were followed here and there by different regents. Their principal value, from a historical point of view, is to mark a point of inflection in the evolving Arab concept of ebriety. In the beginning, to get drunk is guilty because it instigates insensate conduct leading to lying; as sententiously stated the neoclassic poet Ibn Khafajah, around 1090, this does not suppose a

---

[136] Ibn al-Yazzar, *Qam al-wassin fi damm al barrasin*, in Lozano Camara, 1990, p. 182; neither the diatribes against nor the various prohibitions of the substance seem to have modified the habits of their users (Rafeq (2001), pp. 130-131).

[137] Ibn al-Yazzar, *Qam al-wassin fi damm al barrasin*, in Lozano Camara, 1990, p. 160.

[138] Font Quer, 1982, p. xli.

condemnation of ebriety, because to be sober belongs to the animals. But later – not before the thirteenth century arrives – any form of ebriety is guilty since to be intoxicated is not a sign of being civilized but a prohibited pleasure, opposed to healthy reason. The later arguments of the European Inquisition on the subject of drugs will notate this line of reasoning, always exonerating alcoholic drinks.

Figure 88. A Sufi in the extasy of meditation.

D. Coffee

The origins of the plant coffee are lost in the mists that cling to the mountains of Ethiopia where the misnamed shrub *Coffea arabica* (L.) most likely originated. For the pastoral Oromo, the fruit of the wild plant is a gift from *Waqa* and a great medicine.[139] The wandering Gallae were said to crush, roast and eat the berries with grease on their travels.[140]

The beverage coffee, however, is most likely the fortuitous product of the Arab transmission of the art of distillation, the Sufi requirement for all-night prayers, and a shortage of the Yemeni stimulant *qât* (*Catha edulis*). The amusing tale of Kaldi the goat-boy is not verifiable. Kaldi noticed that his goats, after eating the berries of a particular bush, began to dance about with joy. He then informed two Christian monks by the name of Sciadli and Aidrus. These were then responsible for roasting and grinding the beans to brew the first black cup with its magnificent aroma and bitter taste.

Yet this story arrives no earlier than the seventeenth century out of the feverish imagination of a Christian Maronite monk, A. Faustus Naironi. He was clearly determined to appropriate the

---

139 The Oromo believe the plant to have sprung from the tears of their sky god: Schaefer, Charles G. H. "Coffee Unobserved: Consumption and Commoditization of Coffee in Ethiopia before the 18th century," in Le commerce du café, p. 24, quoting L. Bartels. Myths and Rites of the Western Oromo of Ethiopia: An Attempt to Understand. Berlin: Dietrich Reimer Verlag, 1983, p. 306; the Oromo word for the fruit is *bun* or *bunito*, a linquistic coincidence with the *bunchum* of Rhazes (850 – 922) and the *bunn* of Avicenna (980 – 1037), suggesting the fruit at least was known at least as early as the tenth century (Ukers, William H. All About Coffee, second edition. New York: The Tea and Coffee Trade Journal Company, 1935, pp. 7-8; Schaefer (1983), p. 24).

140 Walsh, Joseph A. Coffee: its History, Classification and Description. Philadelphia, PA: Henry T. Coates and Co., 1894, p. 2, citing Bruce's 1678 Travels to Discover the Source of the Nile.

invention of such a popular drink to canny European Christians.[141] In contrast, the more reliable Arab traditions trace the origin of the drink to the Sufis of Yemen.[142]

In one the "sheik, imam, scholar, and mufti Jamâl ad-din abî 'Abd allah Muhammad b. Sa'îd known by the name of adh-Dhubhânî (d. ca. 1470), from Dhubhân, a town well-known in the Yemen" left the port of Aden for a country in which "the inhabitants used coffee."[143] When he returned,

> he fell ill and remembered coffee. He took it and found it useful in his recovery. He discovered among the properties of coffee that it drove away sleep and laziness, transmitting to the body lightness and vivacity. When he began following the Sufi rule, he found, with the other Sufis, in the drinking of coffee an aide in realizing their devotion (the practice of their cult) .... At Aden, the people, the *fuqahâ* [the learned]

---

[141] Ukers (1935), pp. 10-11; Bacqué-Grammont, Jean-Louis, "*Autour des premières mentions du café dans les sources ottomanes*," in Le commerce du café avant l'ère des plantations coloniales, ed. Michel Tuchscherer. Cairo: Institut Français d'archéologie orientale, 2001, p. 19, quoting the story repeated by A. F. Naironi in *De saluberrima potione cahue seu cafe muncupata discursus*, Rome, 1671 and Jean de La Roque in *Voyage dans l'Arabie Heureuse par l'Océan oriental et le détroit de la mer Rouge*, Amsterdam, 1716, p. 251-294; Arendonk, C. van. "Kahwa," in The Encyclopaedia of Islam, ed. E. van Donzel, et al, vol. IV, Iran-Kha. Leiden: E. J. Brill, 1978, p. 450; Jacob, H. E. Coffee: The Epic of a Commodity, tr. Eden and Cedar Paul. Short Hills, NJ: Burford Books, 1998, p. 11.

[142] Hattox, Ralph S. Coffee and Coffeehouses: The Origins of a Social Beverage in the Medieval Near East. Seattle, WA: University of Washington Press, 1985, p. 14; the Arabic word for coffee the drink is *Qahwa*: "*Qahwa* was a word in common use before coffee itself was known: it has a long pedigree as one of the epithets of wine. The Arabic root *q-h-w/y* denotes the idea of making something repugnant, or lessening one's desire for something" in the sense that wine is said to take away one's desire for food just as coffee takes away one's desire for sleep (Hattox, 1985, pp. 18-19; De Sacy, 1826, p. 414).

[143] Hattox (1985), pp. 14-15; De Sacy, Silvestre. *Chrestomathie Arabe*, vol. I. Paris: A L'Imprimerie Royale, 1826, pp. 416-419; Khiari, Farid. *Licite, illicite? Qui dit le droit en islam?* Aix-en-Provence, FR: Edisud, 2005, pp. 37-39, tr. gwr.

as well as the commoners, followed the Sufis in the consumption of coffee in order to find help in their quest for knowledge, in their crafts and in their labor.[144]

In another story "'Alî b. 'Umar ash-Shadhulî [1354 – 1425 AD], ... one of the sheiks and masters of the Shâdhulite order and their orator in the divine sciences" popularized the drink after "*qât* disappeared from Aden."[145] He suggested that instead his followers should "try ground coffee (which he himself consumed). They did this. They found that it had the same effect (as *qât*), and moreover was less expensive and less trouble when stocking up food provisions for the year."[146]

In a third it was Abū Bakr ibn 'Abd Allāh, known as al-'Aydarūs, who survived his many journeys by feasting on coffee berries:

> He found that it made his brain nimble, and that it promoted wakefulness and stimulation for (the performance of) religious duties. So (he began) taking it for nourishment and food and drink, and he directed his followers to do so too, until (the practice) became widespread in the Yemen.[147]

Though the drink had been well known and in common use for at least a century, at Mecca in 1511 coffee was prohibited for the first time. Emir Khâyir Bek al-Mi'mâr was appointed by the Sultan to look after his personal property at Mecca, also holding the post of *mohtesib*,

---

144 Hattox (1985), pp. 14-15; De Sacy (1826), pp. 416-419; Khiari (2005), pp. 37-39, tr. gwr.

145 De Sacy (1826), p. 419: "*(L)a substance nommée cafta vint à manquer à Aden* (The substance named *cafta* came to be lacking at Aden);" Hattox (1985), p. 18: "there was no *kafta* ...."

146 Hattox (1985), p. 18; De Sacy (1826), pp. 419-420; Khiari (2005), pp. 39-40, tr. gwr.

147 Hattox (1985), p. 21, translating from and citing the *al-Kawākib al-sā'ira bi-a 'yān al-mi'a al-'āshira*, ed. Jibrā'il Jabbūr, 3 vols. (Beirut: American University of Beirut, 1945-58), 1:114.

or inspector of markets.[148] On the grounds of the Holy Mosque he discovered a small group drinking coffee together after Friday evening prayers. On his authority and duty as *mohtesib* to command good and forbid evil, he ordered them to disperse.[149]

The next morning he invited theologians, jurists, physicians, important men of the city and other witnesses to an assembly where he "literally put coffee on trial."[150] First, coffee was being drunk in places where men and women mingled, music and chess was played for money, and coffee cups circulated as if they were wine cups; the assembly quickly condemned these kinds of gatherings.[151] Second, he wanted coffee itself prohibited. But this the assembly could not agree on, due to the doctrine of original permissibility (*al-ibāha al-aslīya*).[152]

Anticipating their reluctance, the *mohtesib* then called two doctors who condemned it as harmful to one's health and capable of leading to conduct unbecoming to a good Muslim. Finally, a couple of witnesses testified that coffee had altered their senses.[153] All this was submitted to the Sultan for his approval:

---

148 Hattox (1985), pp. 33-34: "the inspector of markets ... not only looked after weights and measures and trade practices in general, but also was something of an arbiter of morals, whose duties included 'forbidding reprehensible things.' The office had come to combine something of the functions of the Bureau of Consumer Affairs and the vice squad."

149 Khiari (2005), pp. 47-48; De Sacy (1826), pp. 431-432; Hattox (1985), pp. 32-33.

150 Standage, Tom. *A History of the* World *in* 6 Glasses. New York: Walker and Company, 2005, p. 138.

151 Khiari (2005), pp. 48, 53; Hattox (1985), p. 34; De Sacy (1826), p. 432.

152 "[U]nless something is expressly prohibited by the Qur'ān or *sunna*, it is permitted" (Hattox, 1985, pp. 61-62). "This is usually based on Qur'ān 2:29: 'It is He who created for you all that is on the earth' (*Khalaqa lakum mā fī al-ard jamī 'an*)" (1985, p. 153). Compare Gen. 1: 29: "Behold, I have given you every herb bearing seed" (www.blue letterbible.org, KJV).

153 Khiari (2005), pp. 48-49; Hattox (1985), pp. 34-35; De Sacy (1826), pp. 432-434.

What is your opinion ... of the drink named coffee which has propagated in the noble Mecca ... to the point where it is drunk even within the sacred mosque ...? Some ... are certain that consuming a great deal leads to intoxication, and some doctors ... have said it is harmful to one's health. ... Should the one in authority ... halt this reprehensible thing and forbid its consumption ...? What is the law in this matter? Give us a fatwa – may God reward you – and show us clearly the answer, may God help you, amen![154]

Without waiting for the Sultan's reply, Khâyir Bek al-Mi'mâr immediately

published a law forbidding the drink and the sale of coffee. He redoubled his zeal in its interdiction, even going so far as to chastise – which was unforeseen by the law – a group of sellers of coffee and to bring pressure on their businesses. He removed the coffee he found in their shops and he burned it in the middle of the marketplace. ... If it was brought to [his attention] that someone was continuing to drink coffee, he beat him – which was not called for in the law – and exhibited him in the markets.[155]

But the Sultan's reply only condemned the bad conduct but permitted coffee itself.[156] The *mohtesib* was ordered to Cairo but never arrived.

In spite of this, coffee would be prohibited many times in the Islamic world over the next two centuries. In Mecca in 1526 a newly appointed judge closed the coffee shops; a year later he died and they reopened.[157] In 1544, upon receiving a decree from Istanbul, the coffee shops in Mecca were again closed – for one day.[158]

---

[154] Khiari (2005), pp. 53-54.

[155] Khiari (2005), p. 42.

[156] Khiari (2005), p. 54.

[157] Khiari (2005), p. 43; De Sacy (1826), p. 425; Hattox (1985), pp. 37-38.

[158] Khiari (2005), p. 45; De Sacy (1826), p. 428; Hattox (1985), p. 38; Galland, Antoine. De l'origine et du progres du cafe. Caen: Chez Jean Cavelier, 1699, p. 43.

In 1512, the religious authorities in Cairo pronounced a fatwa against coffee, though the habit continued.[159] Two decades later in the same city, a mob whipped up to a frenzy by a fundamentalist preacher attacked the coffee shops and beat those drinking coffee there.[160] A local judge then invited all who wished to partake of the substance while he carefully examined their behavior in his presence; finding no alteration, he ruled the new drug legal.[161] In 1539 the commander of the night watch attacked the coffee shops in Cairo, imprisoning the coffee drinkers he found there, each of whom received seventeen blows of the cane; within a few days the shops had reopened.[162] A decade later another judge again closed the shops selling coffee at Cairo, which lasted until he tried it for an illness that was cured by the black drink.[163]

At Damascus, Syria, in 1543 the chief judge declared the coffee shops dens of vice, which were then raided with the drinkers receiving a beating.[164] New laws were enacted in 1553 and 1563 but to no effect.[165] In 1570 a contemporary observed that it was the custom "to offer a cup of bitter coffee to visitors who arrive at the house of a deceased to present their condolences."[166] At Aleppo in 1573, the

159 Pascual, Jean-Paul. "*Café et Cafés à Damas: Contribution à la Chronologie de Leur Diffusion au XVIème Siècle*," *Berytus Archaeological Studies*, vol. XLII (1995-1996), p. 143, quoting Ibn Ayyub who cites Ibn Tūlūn.

160 Khiari (2005), p. 44.

161 Khiari (2005), p. 44.

162 Khiari (2005), p. 45; Hattox (1985), p. 40.

163 Khiari (2005), p. 83.

164 Pascual (1995-1996), p. 146, quoting Ibn Ayyūb, citing Ibn Tūlūn.

165 Rafeq, Abdul-Karim. "The Socioeconomic and Political Implications of the Intro-duction of Coffee into Syria (16th-18th centuries)," Le Commerce du Café, ed. Michael Tuchscherer. Cairo: Institut Français d'Archéologie Orientale, 2001, p. 129 et seq.

166 Pascual (1995-1996), p. 149.

German physician, botanist and traveler Leonhard Rauwolf (d. 1596) found the ban openly disregarded:

Among the rest they have a very good drink, by them called *Chaube* (Coffee) that is almost as black as ink, and very good in illness, chiefly that of the stomach; of this they drink in the morning early in open places before every body, without any fear or regard out of *China* cups, as hot as they can, they put it often to their lips but drink but little at a time, and let it go round ....[167]

In spite of *fatwas* against them, the elites embraced the new coffee houses (*kahwekhāne*) that opened in Istanbul in the middle of the sixteenth century:

[They] soon attracted gentlemen of leisure, wits and literary men seeking distraction and amusement, who spent the time over their coffee reading or playing chess or backgammon, while poets submitted their latest poems for the verdict of their acquaintances. This new institution was jokingly called also *mekteb-i ʿirfān* (school of knowledge). The coffeehouse met with such approval that it soon attracted civil servants, *kādīs* and professors also ....[168]

Even so the religious and political opposition to the new drink at one point caused ships loaded with coffee for Istanbul to be burned:

It (coffee) was strictly forbidden and *fatwas* were issued banning it. They declared that *not only was it a burnt substance*, but the way in which it was drunk – the cup being passed round the gathering [as if it were wine] – resembled debauchery. It is related

---

167 Ray, John, ed. A Collection of Curious Travels and Voyages in Two Tomes: The First Containing Dr. Leonhart Rauwolff's Itinerary into the Eastern Countries ...., tr. Nicholas Staphorst, 2nd ed., vol. II. London: Printed for J. Wathoe, et al., 1738, part 1, chapter 7, p. 68, www.archive.org

168 Arendonk, C. van. "Kahwa," in The Encyclopaedia of Islam, ed. E. van Donzel, et al, vol. IV, Iran-Kha. Leiden: E. J. Brill, 1978, p. 451; compare the "penny universities" in London a century later (Birnbaum, E. "Vice Triumphant," *The Durham University Journal*, December 1956, New Series, Vol. XVIII, No. 1 (Vol. XLIX, No. 1), p. 22, n. 7).

that Ebü 's-Su'ûd Efendi [(1491 – 1575), the Shaikh al-Islam or supreme religious authority of the Ottoman Empire] caused ships that brought it to be reloaded and their coffee cargoes to be sunk in the sea.[169]

Yet travelers to Constantinople reported the drink for sale:

This suppression continues still today and the coffee that is sold publicly in Constantinople, is carried in the markets, and upon the busiest streets, and in large *Cafetieres* with fire beneath them, and it is distributed in cups to all those who wish it. There is no shame in taking it in public .... Just because there are no longer coffee shops in Constantinople doesn't mean there is less coffee ....[170]

Throughout the sixteenth and seventeenth centuries the bans on coffee were renewed officially but were not strictly obeyed:

Edicts issued in the reigns of Murad III (982/1574 – 1003/1595) and Ahmad I (1012/1613 – 1016/1617) were not strictly enforced and still less obeyed. ... Murad IV (1032/1613 – 1049/1640) issued a strict prohibition of coffee (and tobacco). He had all the coffee-houses torn down and many forfeited their lives for the sake of coffee. Under Mehemmed IV (1058/1648 – 1099/1687), while the sale of coffee in the streets was allowed, the prohibition of coffee-houses was at first renewed by the Grand Vizier Köprülü ....[171]

As the prohibitions became more and more unworkable, the punishments became more and more elaborate. Murad Khan IV [r. 1623 – 1640], who would try vainly to make Turkey great again, would stalk the streets, decapitating coffee drinkers in mid-sip: "Many forfeited their lives for the sake of coffee."[172] Under Grand Vizier Köprülü Mehmed Pasha [r. 1656 – 1661], "[f]or a first violation of the

---

169 Birnbaum (1956), p. 23, n. 19, quoting Hajji Khalifa's *Mîzân ul-Hakk*, p. 53.

170 Galland (1699), p. 61-62.

171 Arendonk (1978), pp. 451-452; Ukers (1935), pp. 16-17.

172 Houtsma, M. Th., et al., eds. "Kahwa," E. J. Brill's First Encyclopaedia of Islam, 1913 – 1936, vol. 4, ITK – KWATTA. Leiden: E. J. Brill, 1993, p. 633 (GB).

order, cudgeling was the punishment; for a second offense, the victim was sewn in a leather bag and thrown into the Bosphorus."[173]

Toward the end of the seventeenth century, the expense of the wars, especially after the disastrous Battle of Vienna (1683), forced the Ottoman Empire to rescind the bans: "By the end of the 17th century coffee was imported from the Yemen in large quantities; from 1688 the government levied a considerable customs duty, which produced badly needed revenue for the Treasury."[174] From forbidden drug it became a source of Arab pride, combining well with opium and relegating wine to a lesser plane, after having won its battle against an initial intolerance.

Figure 89. Koprulu Mehmed Pasha.

[173] Ukers (1935), pp. 16-17.

[174] Birnbaum (1956), p. 24.

E. Tobacco

Though unable to enforce a ban on coffeehouses, Sultan Ahmed I [1603-1617] also tried to prohibit a different drug sweeping through the Empire:

Some time in the latter half of the ninth century of the *Hijira*, after some Spanish ships had discovered the New World, the Portuguese and English ... came to an island close to the mainland, called in the *Atlas 'Gīneyā'*. A ship's doctor, who had been smitten with a lymphatic disorder ... decided to try and cure it with hot and dry things, in accordance with the laws of treatment by opposites. ... It [tobacco] did him good ... The ship's company saw this and, regarding it as a beneficial medicine, followed the doctor's example .... One saw another and they all began to smoke. When the ship arrived in England, the habit spread ....[175]

In 1609, the sultan forbade

the growing and consumption of tobacco which English traders had recently brought into his domains, citing as his reason that people were not going about their business but spending night and day smoking in the coffee-houses. Tobacco was so popular that the ban was ineffective and had to be repeated in 1614, by which time it was so profitable a crop that it competed for land with the traditional occupation of apiculture, and the price of honey rose accordingly. ... Sultan Osman [1618-1622] had repeated the ban – reinforced with a juridical opinion ....[176]

Yet a traveler in the early 1600s noticed that the Turks would smoke even under threat of mutilation:

[T]hey also delight in Tobacco: which they take through reedes that have joyned unto them great heads of wood to contain it ... and were it not sometimes lookt into (for *Morat Bassa* not long since commanded a pipe to be thrust through the nose of a *Turke*, and to be led in derision through the Citie.) no question but it would prove a

---

[175] Chelebi, pp. 50-51.

[176] Finkel, Osman's Dream, pp. 212-213.

principall commodity. Neverthelesse they will take it in corners; and are so therein, that that which in England is not saleable, doth passe here amongst them for most excellent.[177]

Clerics condemned the abominable habit. Various pamplets were circulated against it. Fatwas were decreed. But, wrote the historian Katib Chelebi, the authorities could not abolish the new custom. From

about the year 1010/1601, to the present day, various preachers have spoken against it individually, and many of the Ulema have written tracts concerning it, some claiming that it is a thing forbidden, some that it is disapproved. Its addicts have replied to the effect that it is permissible. After some time had elapsed, the eminent surgeon Ibrāhīm Efendi devoted much care and attention to the matter ... giving warning talks ... and sticking copies of fetwas onto walls. He troubled himself to no purpose. The more he spoke, the more people persisted in smoking. Seeing that it was fruitless, he abandoned his efforts. ... It has become a thing common to East and West, and no one has succeeded in suppressing it.[178]

Murad Khan IV [r. 1623 – 1640] also tried suppression. He

had come to the throne when barely 12 years old, in a period of anarchy, and had been obliged to take ruthless measures against the mutinous Janissaries. He closed the coffee-houses and forbade smoking on pain of death, on 16 September 1633, a fortnight after the great fire which destroyed one-fifth of Istanbul. The coffee-houses were breeding-grounds of disaffection. The reason for the Sultan's objection to smoking is less obvious: some say he was persuaded to outlaw tobacco by Qādīzāde Mehmed Efendi [d. 1635] ... who regarded it as a sinful innovation.[179]

The pretext for banning smoking was the same as for the closing of the coffee shops: the danger of a new fire. But the

---

177 Sandys (1621), p. 66.

178 Chelebi, pp. 50-51.

179 Chelebi, Katib, p. 59, ft. 2.

underlying reason was also the same: to prevent public disorder. Any gathering of the people was suspect:

> *La fermeture des cafés fut immédiatement suivie d'une seconde ordonnance qui proscrivait l'usage du tabac sous peine de mort. Le prétexte était le danger d'un nouvel incendie; mais au fond c'était ... destinée à prévenir les rassemblemens des désoeuvrés, et à supprimer tous le lieux de réunion où l'on pouvait s'entretenir des affaires publiques. Le despote craignait, non sans raison, qu'on milieu de tasses et des pipes, l'esprit de trouble et de résistance ne prît un développement qu'il deviendrait difficile d'arrêter.*[180]

These restrictions brought forth a malign epigram from an anonymous critic: "You hunt the black eunuchs which cause us sleepless nights, say the people; having forbidden the black (coffee), and having condemned the innocent smoking of tobacco, you dissipate the bloody smell which rises from oppressed hearts [tr. gwr]."[181]

But words did not deter him and each night he made the rounds in person. Whoever was found with a pipe or a cup of coffee paid with their head. Each morning the bodies of victims, abandonned in the streets, gave witness to the pitiless justice of the night.[182]

---

[180] Hammer, J. (1837), vol. 9, book 47, p. 209: "The closure of the cafés was immediately followed by a second ordinance which proscribed the use of tobacco under penalty of death. The pretext was the danger of a new fire; but at base this was ... destined to prevent disorderly assembly, and to suppress all the gathering places qhere one could discuss public affairs. The despot feared, not without reason, that in a place of cups and pipes, the spirit of trouble and resistance might develop that would be difficult to halt (tr. gwr)."

[181] Hammer (1837), p. 209: *Chassez les eunuques noirs que nous font des nuits sans sommeil, disait la voix populaire; avant de proscrire le nègre (le cafè), et avant de condamner l'innocente fumée de tabac, dissipez la vapeur sanglante qui s'élève des coeurs opprimés.*

[182] Hammer, p. 209-210: *Chaque nuit le Sultan faisait la ronde en personne; quiconque était trouvé sans lumière dans les rues, quiconque était rencontré avec une pipe ou une tasse de café, était livré au bourreau. Chaque matin les cadavres des victimes, abandonnés au milieu des rues, venaient témoigner de l'impitoyable justice de la nuit. ... Chaque jòur quelques amateurs imprudens des denrées prohibées payaient de leur tête leur fatale passion.*

The sultan may have been the origin of the tradition of allowing a condemned man a last smoke as his soldiers smoked even while awaiting execution:

People being undeterred, the imperial anger necessitated the chastisement of those who, by smoking, committed the sin of disobedience to the imperial command. Gradually His Majesty's severity in suppression increased, and so did people's desire to smoke, in accordance with the saying, 'Men desire what is forbidden,' and many thousands of men were sent to the abode of nothingness.

When the Sultan was going on the expedition against Baghdad, at one halting-place fifteen or twenty leading men of the Army were arrested on a charge of smoking, and were put to death with the severest torture in the imperial presence. Some of the soldiers carried short pipes in their sleeves, some in their pockets, and they found an opportunity to smoke even during the executions. At Istanbul, no end of soldiers used to go into the barracks and smoke in the privies. Even during this rigorous prohibition, the number of smokers exceeded that of the non-smokers.[183]

The traveler Tavernier was extorted out of his tobacco by

two Troops of Tartars well mounted. When they saw us, they made a Lane for us to pass through them, with a design most certainly to have fall'n upon us .... Thereupon we alighted and Barricad'd up our selves with our Chariots. ... The Commander answer'd, that he had divided his men in that manner only to do us Honour, but since we desir'd they should be gone, they requested us but to lend them a little Tobacco. A boon which we readily granted them, and so we pass'd on.[184]

After the death of Murad Khan IV, according to Katib Chelebi,

the practice was sometimes forbidden and sometimes allowed, until the Sheykh al-Islam, the late Bahā'ī Efendi, gave a fetwa ruling that it was permissible, and the practice won renewed popularity among the people of the world. Occasional reprimands from the Throne to smokers have generally been disregarded, and smoking is at present practised all over the habitable globe. ... The purpose of all

---

183 Chelebi, K., pp. 50-52.

184 Tavernier, "The Design of the Author," 1678, fifth and sixth unnumbered page.

this is to demonstrate the facts: there is no question of interference with those who have the addiction. To try to put them off is not a practical possibility, and is generally agreed to be in the category of preaching to the winds. ... Yet the following course is preferable: not to declare things forbidden, but always to have recourse to any legal principle that justifies declaring them permitted, thus preserving the people from being laden with sins and persisting in what has been prohibited. ... The great doctors of the law have in former times pronounced it disapproved, while certain provincial muftis have declared it forbidden. More recently the late Bahā'ī Efendi pronounced it lawful, not out of regard for his own addiction but because he considered what was best suited to the condition of the people and because he held fast to the principle that permissibility is the norm. ... It is that the people will persist in using the forbidden thing, with baneful results. Further, declaring it to be lawful is in the general interest, as being an act of compassion towards the addict and protecting the public from sin.[185]

Having lived through Murad IV's repression of tobacco and having witnessed the counterproductive results, Katib Chelebi proposed what the Ottoman Empire eventually did, which was to licence, tax and regulate the substance:

Hereafter the most necessary and useful thing for the rulers of the Muslims to do is this: they should farm out exclusive concessions to deal in tobacco-leaf in every part of the Guarded Domains, appointing custodians. Tobacco will bear a fixed contribution to the Treasury of 20 piastres per *okka*. It should be sold in one appointed place in every city and should not be allowed in the markets at large. This will yield 100 million aspers a year.

During the rigorous prohibition enforced under the late Ghazi Sultan Murad, many people, not daring to smoke tobacco in pipes, used to repel the craving by crushing the leaf and snuffing it up their noses, but subsequently they have abandoned this foolishness, for smoking without fear has become possible. ...

The fool may interfere, saying:
'Scatter the stupidity of smoking with the wind of fortitude
For it has obstructed with its heat the sun of the mind.'
The addict replies:

[185] Chelebi, K., pp. 55-56.

> 'The joy and savour of tobacco are not found in honey and sugar', and goes on smoking, quite undismayed. The best course is not to interfere with anyone in this respect, and that is all there is to it.[186]

Naturally, he was ignored.

Figure 90. Katib Chelebi.

186 Chelebi, K., p. 58.

The attack on tobacco was part of a larger condemnation of innovation itself:

> Tobacco, taverns and coffee-houses were inextricably linked and, economic considerations aside, Murad's ban on tobacco of a few months earlier can be seen as an attack on the unregulated life of the coffee-houses and taverns as much as on the noxious weed itself – now he took more direct action. ... [T]he climate of austere morality ... continued throughout the 17th century – named the Kadizadeli movement after Kadizade Mehmed ... [who] promoted a puritanical strain in religious thinking [and a] quest for an uncorrupted Islam shorn of the innovations which had accrued since the time of the Prophet.[187]

Another historian who lived through this period, Evliya Chelebi, was careful to admit that he did not speak from any personal knowledge of these prohibited drugs:

> Since I was born, I never tasted in my life, of fermented beverages, or prohibited things, neither tobacco, nor coffee, nor tea, nor [he appends a very long list of items he has never touched]. ... I have spoken only for their pleasure's sake, of all this prohibited fermented beverages and electuaries. It is through my friends that I learnt the use of these opiates and fermented liquors .... God knows, that I partook not of a drop by the invitation of those drunkards, but mingling amongst them I became perfectly aware of their conditon.[188]

After the death of Murad Khan IV, his son Ibrahim [r. 1640 – 1648] was followed by his grandson Mohammed IV [r. 1648 – 1687] who had as little interest as Ibrahim in matters of government. Kösem, the sultana valide, took over the running of the empire until 1651 when Turhan, the mother of Mohammed IV, had Kösem, his grandmother, strangled.

In the confusion of this era, the people enjoyed their wine, buza, tobacco and coffee due to lax enforcement of the edicts against

---

[187] Lane-Poole, p. 214.

[188] Efendi, Evliya, pp. 246, 54.

them. Since the prohibition on smoking tobacco had not been repealed, lovers of the leaf eluded the existing penalties by taking tobacco in the form of snuff, first imported into the Ottoman empire in 1642.[189]

"Production of tobacco [was finally] legalized in 1646,"[190] but this would not end the fight. In 1650, the *sipahis* revolted against a no-smoking order by one of their leaders. The commander ordered the closure of the tobacconists and burned the pipes he found there. But the *sipahis* replied, "Let us smoke peacefully if you don't want smoke from the flames of revolt."[191]

Grand-vizier Mohammed Köprülü Mehmed Pasha, [g.v. 1656 – 1661] attempted to restore order. Though production of tobacco may have been officially allowed, there were many who refused to accept any of the new innnovations. One of his first tasks was to suppress the disorder caused by the Kadizadelis, a rigidly orthodox Islamic sect: "Their puritanical message had once more fallen on receptive ears during the bitter factionalism of Mehmed IV's early years."[192]

Eight days after his elevation to the position of Grand Vizier, the partisan fanatics of the deceased Kadizadeli, hoping for power under the administration of the new grand vizier so as to continue their persecutions against the Sufis and the dancing Dervishes, assembled in the mosque of Mohammed II. They resolved to destroy all the

---

189 Hammer, vol. 10, book 49, pp. 16-17: *Comme on n'avait pas rapporté la loi par laquelle Mourad avait interdit l'usage du tabac à fumer, sous les peines le plus sévères, au nombre desquelles se trouvait la peine de mort en cas de récidive, les amateurs des jouissances irritantes que procure le tabac éludèrent la pénalité existante en prenant du tabac à priser, afin, dit l'auteur du Choix des histoires, de se donner le plaisir de l'éternuement; les annales ottomanes signalent dans le cours de cette annee 1642 (1052) l'introduction du tabac à priser dans l'empire.*

190 Finkel, p. 309.

191 Hammer, vol. 10, book 52, p. 345: *L'aga avait ordonné de fermer las tabagies et de briser les pipes qui s'y trouvaient; mais les sipahis avaient battu ses gens et avaient dit: «Laissez-nous fumer tranquillement, si vous ne voulez pas que de cette fumée s'élance la flamme de la révolte.»*

192 Palmer, p. 254.

cloisters of these orders, to force the members to confess to the one true faith, to kill all those who refused, to allow only one minaret for each mosque, suppressing all the others as a useless luxury, to condemn as guilty heresies the use of gold and silver vessels, of habits of silk, tobacco, coffee, opium, singing hymns, or dancing to the sound of a drum or flute. In a word, they vowed damnation to all those who did not partake of the doctrines of Kadizadeli and to inflict upon those who persisted in their heresy all the temporal punishments which were within their power.[193]

Upon news of these civil disorders, the grand-vizier sent a message to the preachers, fomenters of all these troubles, to exhort them to return to order. When they ignored him, he sent the sultan a report on the need to chastise the rebels. The sentences of death signed by Mohammed [IV] against the authors of these disturbances were commuted by Köprülü to banishment.[194]

His successor Köprülüzade Fazil Ahmed Pasha [g.v. 1661 – 1676] disciplined the army and captured the island of Crete. His

---

193 Hammer, vol. 11, book 53, pp. 5-6: *Huit jours après l'élévation de Koeprilü au grand-vizirat ... partisans fanatiques de Kazizadeé, espérant pouvoir, sous l'administration d'un vieillard, continuer leurs persécutions contre les soffis et les derwischs dansans, se rassemblèrent dans la mosquée de Mohammed II; ils résolurent de détruire tous les cloîtres de ces ordres, d'en forcer les membres à la confession de la vraie foi, de tuer tous ceux qui s'y refuseraient, de ne laisser subsister qu'un minaret dans chaque mosquée, en supprimant tous les autres comme un luxe inutile; de condamner comme de coupables hérésies l'usage des vaisselles d'or et d'argent, des habits de soie, du tabac, du café et de l'opium, le chant des hymnes, les danses au son du tambour et de la flûte; en un mot, de vouer à la damnation tous ceux qui ne partageraient pas les doctrines de Kazizadé, et d'infliger à ceux qui persisteraient dans leur hérésie toutes les punitions temporelles qui seraient en leur pouvoir.*

194 Hammer, vol. 11, book 53, p. 6: *A la nouvelle de ces désordres, le grand-vizir envoya un message aux scheïkhs prédicateurs, fauteurs de tous ces troubles, pour les exhorter à rentrer dans l'ordre; mais cette démarche étant restée san résultat, il adressa au Sultan un rapport dans lequel il lui représenta la nécessité d'anéantir les rebelles. Les sentences de mort signées par Mohammed contre les auteurs des troubles, furent commuées par Koeprilü en ordres de bannissement*; Palmer, p. 254.

spiritual adviser and that of Mohammed IV was Vani Efendi, an old hunchback who preached against dancing, singing, the cafes, taverns, opium dens, tobacco sellers and buza shops: "As in the days when Kadizade Mehmed had had the ear of Sultan Murad IV, coffee-houses were pulled down and smoking was again banned."[195] Yet, in spite of the previous decisions of the muftis and sheikhs, in spite of the ordinances of the sultans and the grand-viziers, the use of coffee and tobacco [were] found as often on the banks of the Bosphorus as on the banks of the Seine.[196] Outside Adrianople, for example, Dr. John Covel found a glade with many "sitting upon carpet with tobacco, coffee ...."[197]

In the end it was the simple lack of money that ended the official prohibition of tobacco. After the disastrous defeat at the Battle of Vienna (1683), the empire's "resources were stretched to the limit .... The struggle to finance and man the war effort overrode all other considerations druing the final years of the seventeenth century."[198] "[B]y the 1690s [tobacco] was grown across the empire where climatic conditions permitted; ... both production and export of tobacco were taxed."[199]

---

195 Finkel, p. 278.

196 Hammer, vol. 11, book 55, p. 286: *[L]e grand-vizier Mohammed Koeprilü avait de nouveau interdit l'usage à Constantinople peu d'années auparavant, défense que son fils Ahmed ne put maintenir, malgré les sévères prédications de Wani qui proscrivait cette jouissance matérielle (pour les autres bien entendu), et en dépit des considérations politiques, qui tendaient à faire envisager les cafés comme les rendez-vous des détracteurs et des ennemis du gouvernement. Ainsi, malgré les décisions antérieures des mouftis et des scheïkhs, malgré les ordonnances des sultans et des grands-vizirs, l'usage du café et celui du tabac se sont acclimatés aussi bien sur les rives du Bosphore que sur celles de la Seine.*

197 Covel, Dr. John. "Extracts from the Diaries of Dr. John Covel (1670 – 1679)," in Early Voyages and Travels in the Levant, ed. J. Theodore Bent. NY: Burt Franklin, p. 173, babel.hathitrust.org.

198 Finkel, p. 325.

199 Finkel, pp. 308-309.

10
Christianity and Ebriety (II)

The assault itself is due to the malice of the demons, who through envy endeavor to hinder man's progress; and through pride usurp a semblance of Divine power.[1]
-- *Thomas De Aquinas*

A. From the High Middle Ages to the Lower
B. The Opening of the Internal Crusade
   1. Drugs and Apostasy
   2. Eroticism as Pharmacological Aim
C. Lotions and Potions
   1. Composition
   2. Verification
D. Practice and Aspiration of Medicine
E. The Aguardientes and Alcohol

---

[1] The "Summa Theologica" of St. Thomas Aquinas, literally translated by The Dominican Fathers. London: Burns Oates & Washbourne, Ltd., 1922 (GB), part I, QQ. CIII – CXIX, Q. 114, Art. 1: "Whether men are assailed by demons," p. 141.

Figure 91. Lucifer and Saint Michael weighing souls (romantic painting from the Ribes valley).

Figure 92. Lucifer in a detail from The Judgment of Souls, the Legend of Saint Michael by Arguis.

During the High Middle Ages those accused of witchcraft are still particular individuals. They are persons of flesh and bone, for whom it is recognized – even in principle – the right that any accusation against them of dabbling in magical arts or possessing malevolent herbs should be proved. Lacking these prerequisites, their accusers were obligated to pay a fine. A denunciation could not be made anonymously nor could it be remunerated; neither are there papal bulls that reward with spiritual and chrematistic advantage those who professionally hunt witches. It could even be said that the law (notwithstanding its general barbary) abhored defenselessness as a principle.

All this changed from the twelfth century onwards. It is around this time that individual witches and sorcerers are converted into mere members of a universal and eternal sect that in itself constitutes an epidemic. The same state of emergency reappears that provoked the Senateconsult on the Bacchanals. With it also bursts onto the scene the habitual system for resolving these kinds of plagues: anonymous and compensated denunciations, stereotypical accusations and secrecy and torture in the proceedings.

After centuries of references to a witch in the singular, the first mention of conventions and secret meetings of a Satanic sect shows up in the *Canon Episcopi*, a text that began to be disseminated widely around the year 1000. The proclamation presents itself – falsely – as something that had been declared some seven centuries earlier in the Council of Ancyra in AD 314.[2] The acts denounced thus acquired the

---

[2] Baroja, 1971, p. 60; *Al concilio celebrado en Ancyra el año 314 se atribuyó así un canon .... Como va dicho, la autenticidad de este texto es muy poco probable* ("From the council celebrated in Ancyra in the year 314 is attributed this canon .... As has already been said, the authenticity of this text is very unlikely" [tr. gwr]); Baroja, 1966, p. 88; see also Migne, J.-P., ed. *Burchardi Womaciensis Ecclesiae Episcopi, Decretorum Liber Decimus, De Incantatoribus et Auguribus, in Patrologiae Cursus Completus*, vol. 140. Paris: Apud Garnier Fratres, 1880 (GB), p. 831.

added historical patina of being things that had always occurred, and had also always been condemned. Yet the wording can only be reliably dated to the ninth and tenth centuries, though it is widely known from the eleventh onwards: "It was cited as an authority and its text was discussed throughout western Europe. It was even used as the basis for a general theory of the cult of witchcraft ...."[3] Says one of its paragraphs:

> It should also be added that certain criminal women, disciples of Satan, seduced by the illusions and devices of the Devil, believe and confess that they ride through the air on certain beasts at night in company with Diana the pagan goddess (or Herodias), and a host of other women, obeying the goddess' orders as if she was their absolute mistress.[4]

---

[3] Baroja, 1971, p. 61; *... y comentado y aplicado en toda la Europa occidental. Ha dado base incluso a una teoría general sobre el «culto brujeril», como veremos* (Baroja, 1966, p. 88).

[4] Baroja, Julio Caro. The World of the Witches, tr. O. N. V. Glendinning. Chicago, IL: University of Chicago Press, 1971, p. 60; *Illud etiam non omittendum, quod quaedam sceleratae mulieres, retro post Satanam converseae, daemonium illusionibus et phantasmatibus seductae, credunt se ac profitentur nocturnis horis cum Diana paganorum dea (vel cum Herodiade) et innumera multitudine mulierum equitare super quasdam bestias et multa terrarum spatia in tempestate noctis silentio pertransire, ejusque jussionibus velut dominae obedire, et certis noctibus ad ejus servitium evocari* (Baroja, 1971, p. 268, n. 7); Murray, 1962, p. 3.

A. From the High Middle Ages to the Lower

Around the year 1000 various factors cause backwards Europe to experience a general recovery. The reestablishment of some commercial routes, the ploughing up of land invaded by forest into large cultivated fields, the drainage of the swamps and the running of cattle on lands along the seacoast, the founding of new cities and towns at the foot of the castles and monasteries, and the control of the northern shores of the Mediterranean (previously dominated by Vikings, Byzantines and Saracens) produces a rise in excess agricultural commodities which allows a flowering of fairs and markets of ever growing size.

To this economic recovery one can add a certain political, military and cultural restoration, as the conflict between the Papacy and the Holy Empire results in pyrrhic victories and real defeats for both, permitting a pluralism unknown until then for European society. Together with the resurrection of the infantry thanks to the Swiss pike, which marks the beginning of the end of the feudal heavy cavalry, a seachange of rejection before the privileges of the clergy provokes various popular religious movements, chiefly in the south of France and the north of Italy.[5] Some cities even manage to enact democratic

---

[5] Under ecclesiastical authority, the high nobility tried to liquidate the Milanese Patarenes, the Petrobrusians and Henritians, the 'Poor of Lyon,' the Waldenses, the Neomanicheans, the Catharians and other heretics. The **Patarenes** "used to assemble in the Pataria, or ragmen's quarter of the city (*pates* being a provinciaal word for a rag). [They were a] medieval group of lay craftsmen, tradesmen, and peasants organized in Milan about 1058 to oppose clerical concubinage and marriage; the group later widened its attack to oppose generally the papacy's moral corruption and temporal powers" ('Patarenes,' The Encyclopaedia Britannica, 11th edition, vol. xx. Cambridge, UK: At the University Press, 1911 (archive.org), p. 902); see also britannica.com; "Five years after the death of *Arnold* of *Bress*, according to Historians, *Peter Waldo*, a Citizen of *Lions*, appeared [in 1160]; I find, that in the Year 1167, there was caused to be burnt at *Vezelay* in *Burgundy*, near unto *Lyons*, of which place *Waldo*

constitutions more or less analogous to the Greek *polis*, under the protection of an incipient but very active (compared to the other classes) bourgeoisie. To this renewal one can add the discovery of the classical world, made possible by the schools of translators founded by Alphonso X and Frederick Barbarossa (1123 – 1190)[6] in Toledo and Sicily respectively, united to the flowering of an HispanoArab and Hebrew culture that achieves its principal impact on the same clergy,

---

was, some of his followers, under the name of *Donarii*, or *Poplicani*; which is one of the names given unto the ***Waldensis*** .... *Some of the chiefest citizens of Lyons being one day together, it happened that one of them died suddenly ... which struck such a terror into one of the Company, that immediately he distributed great treasures unto the Poor, so that very great multitudes followed him, whom he taught to profess voluntary poverty, and to imitate Jesus Christ and his Apostles: And having some competent knowledge of Letters, he taught them the New Testament in the Vulgar Tongue.* ... Of this *Waldo* they were called *Waldensis*; and of the City of *Lyons*, of which he was, Leonists, or the **Poor of Lyons**, as before they had been called ***Petrobrusians***, from *Peter de Bruis*; and ***Henritians*** of *Henry* .... And as for the ***Catharians*** and ***Manicheans*** in particular, we cannot doubt that Italy, France and Germany was infected with them .... Wherefore, about the Year 1017, some of them were put to death at Orleans ..." (L'arroque, M. The History of the Eucharist, tr. Jos. Walker. London: George Downes, 1684 (GB), pp. 474, 475, 481). Perhaps the prototype of these reformers would be a disciple of Peter Abelard (1079 – 1142, famed lover of Heloise), Arnold de Brescia, executed by papal decree in 1155 after stirring up revolt in the citizens of Rome, stuggling "for ten years to found amongst the disorderly and disunited masses a republic on ancient Roman lines" (Patrick, D. and F. H. Groome, eds. Chamber's Biographical Dictionary: The Great of All Times and Nations. Philadephia, PA: J. B. Lippincott Company, 1898 (archive.org), pp. 7, 43), and causing the Pope to have to flee the city. Brescia argued that those dedicated to the cultivation of the spirit should not accumulate earthly goods.

[6] Frederick I, whose "chief traits were a resolute will that at times degenerated into a gross cruelty, administrative skill, martial ardour, a love of danger, and a magnanimous ambition" (Patrick, D. et al., eds., pp. 381-382); "Gerard de Cremona (1114 – 87), a physician of Toledo, made translations, it is said by command of Barbarossa, from Avicenna and others" (The Encyclopaedia Britannica, vol. XV. Chicago: R. S. Peale & Co., 1890 (GB), p. 807).

the only estate with the ability to assimilate and understand the nature of this threat.

There is, then, a larger interchange of goods and ideas, and the memory of an ancient humanity becomes a medieval commonplace. At the same time, administrative organization becomes more efficient, there are viable strategies for better control of customs and opinions, and the fissures in the previously monolithic social edifice stimulate the consumption of a Christian catechism with a new religious evolution especially dangerous because of its spirituality. The campaign against superstition is relaunched with new vigor, with consequences certainly similar to those observed during the High Middle Ages, as it is not possible to combat one magic except in the name of another, based only on the power of intimidation.

In this era, traditional plant remedies are classified as superstition. An appeal to the Catholic Saints is said to be the only approved, safe and effective medicine for every kind of infirmity. For example, a text entitled *Reprobation of Superstitions and Witchcraft* proposes remedies like the following for hydrophobia:

"In this kind of rabies, Santa Catalina and Santa Quiteria have special grace, and by commending themselves to these saints with masses, offerings, generous gifts and devout prayers many people have been healed."[7]

The *Malleus Maleficarum* (1486) is even more explicit about the power of witches to harm and the remedies permitted to cure:

It has already been stated that witches can afflict men with every kind of physical infirmity; therefore it can be taken as a general rule that the various verbal or practical

[7] *En este mal de la rabia, comúnmente se dice que tienen especíal gracia Santa Catalina y Santa Quiteria, y encomendándose a ellas con mísas, ofrendas, limosnas y oracíones devotas, muchas personas han sanado de la rabia* (Ciruelo, Pedro. *Reprobacion de las Supersticiones y Hechizerias*. Medina del Campo, España: Casa de Guillermo de millis, 1551, folio 39, verso, bibliotecadigital.jcyl.es).

remedies which can be applied in the case of those infirmities which we have just been discussing are equally applicable to all other infirmities, such as epilepsy or leprosy, for example. ... And as lawful remedies are reckoned among the verbal remedies and have been most often considered by us, they may be taken as a general type of such remedies.[8]

This makes sense when one considers that eggs were the presumed cause of leprosy and epilepsy: "For we have often found that certain people have been visited with leprosy or the falling sickness by means of eggs which have been buried with dead bodies, especially the dead bodies of witches, together with other ceremonies of which we cannot speak, particularly when these eggs have been given to a person either in food or drink."[9]

Never before did so many preachers possessed with hatred of the flesh flourish, spouting their messages in between sobs and gutteral moans. The best example is the extremely famous Dionysius Cartujano [Denys the Carthusian, 1402 – 1471] who slept standing on his feet, prayed constantly, preferred rotten food to fresh, and shouted in horror if an unaccompanied woman should approach him. In spite of the fact that he was a deafmute, his sermons aroused to the point of paroxysm crowds avid for sanctity.[10]

---

[8] Summers, Montague, tr. The Malleus Maleficarum of Heinrich Kramer and James Sprenger. London: John Rodker, 1928, Part II, Question II, Chapter VI: Prescribed Remedies; to wit, the Lawful Exorcisms of the Church, for all Sorts of Infirmities and Ills due to Witchcraft; and the Method of Exorcising those who are Bewitched (archive.org); Huxley, 1972, p. 126.

[9] Summers, tr., Part II, Question I, Chapter XI.

[10] "In his cell Denys gave himself up heart and soul to the duties of Carthusian life ... letting his zeal carry him even far beyond what the rule demanded. ... It is true that the took not more than three hours' sleep a night .... [P]osterity has surnamed him "Doctor ecstaticus." During his ecstasies many things were revealed to him which he made known only when it could profit others, and the same may be said of what he learnt from souls in purgatory, who appeared to him very frequently, seeking relief through his powerful intercession" (Gurdon, Edmond. 'Denys the Carthusian,' The

Devotion took on very peculiar characteristics in the thirteenth century:

The people of the mountains of Umbria wished, around the year 1500, to kill the hermit San Romualdo so as not to lose his bones. The monks of Fossanova, where Thomas De Aquinas had died in the year 1274, fearing that these holy relics might disappear, literally embalmed the body of the holy master, detaching the head and cooking and preparing it. During the time it took to bury the body of Santa Isabel of Turingia, a mob of devotees cut or tore off not only pieces of the cloth in which her face was enwrapped, but also the hair and fingernails and even bits of her ears and the nipples of her breasts. On the occasion of a solemn festival, Carlos VI of France destributed the ribs of his ancestor San Louis, among Pierre D'Ailly and his cousins Berry and Borgona, and gave a leg to the prelates to share among them, as they do after a meal [tr. gwr].[11]

The same Thomas De Aquinas, who is represented as the introducer of Aristotelian realism, discarded the thesis of Augustine on the imaginative dream of witches. In his commentary on the Book of Job, Aquinas accuses the witches of being able to alter physically and not only fantastically the course of events. Witchcraft causes an infinity of practical sabotage: "Consider that since all this

---

Catholic Encyclopedia, vol. 4, ed. C. G. Herbermann. New York: Robert Appleton Company, 1908 (newadvent.org), pp. 1933-1936).

[11] *El pueblo de las montañas de Umbría quería, por el año 1500, matar al ermitaño San Romualdo, para no perder sus huesos. Los monjes de Fossanova, donde habia muerto Santo Tomás de Aquino el año 1274, ante el temor de que pudiesen desaparecer las santas reliquias, habían confitado literalmente el cadáver del santo maestro, le habían quitado la cabeza y lo habían cocido y preparado. Durante el tiempo que se tardó en enterrar el cadáver de Santa Isabel de Turingia, un tropel de devotos cortatba o arrancaba no sólo trozos de los paños con que estaba envuelto su rostro, sino también los pelos y las uñas e incluso trozos de las orejas y los pezones de los senos. Con ocasión de una fiesta solemne, distribuye Carlos VI [de Francia] costillas de su antepasado San Luis, entre Pierre d'Ailly y sus primos Berry y Borgoña, y da una pierna a los prelados para que se la repartan, como así lo hacen después de la comida* (Huizinga, Johan. *El otoño de la Edad Media*, fourth edition, tr. José Gaos. Madrid: Alianza Editorial S. A., 1982 (alatinacolonia2013.files.wordpress.com), p. 237).

aforementioned adversity comes from Satan, it is necessary to confess that with God's permission demons can bring about turbulence in the air, can stir up the winds and can make fire fall from heaven."[12]

But the permisison of God does not presuppose the authorization of men. The science of Satanism or demonology is a well-developed disclipine now, describing a pyramidal organization. At its apex is Lucifer, the favorite traitor angel of the Father dethroned for his arrogance; the level below finds the seditious angels that were on his side, divided into masculine demons (*incubus*) and feminine (*succubus*); at the base the possessed or reprobates are tortured, presided over by a guild of sorcerers or apostates. The principal interest of this mythological entourage is the light it sheds upon both religious extremes: its images are based as much on interpretations of the Book of Revelation as on the pagan heritage, a creation made up of equal parts persecutors and persecuted. Thanks to the influence of the demonologists, this mythical concoction ends up becoming its own inverted monotheism.

For its part, the promising economic and political perspective at the initiation of the first Christian millennium only very late fell into serious crisis. The Great Hunger of 1315 – 1317 closed a catastrophic era, preceded by a banking failure, a depression in textile production and mining:

> In the year of our Lord 1315, apart from the other hardships with which England was afflicted, hunger grew in the land .... Meat and eggs began to run out, capons and fowl could hardly be found, animals died of pest, swine could not be fed because of the excessive price of fodder. A quarter of wheat or beans or peas sold for twenty shillings [*In 1313 a quarter of wheat sold for five shillings*], barley for a mark, oats for ten

---

[12] *Considerandum vero est quod cum omnis praedicta adversitas sit per Satan inducta, necesse est confiteri quod Deo permittente Daemones possunt turbationem aeris inducere, ventos concitare, et facere ut ignis de caelo cadat* (Mullady, Brian, tr. Commentary on the Book of Job by Thomas Aquinas, ed. Joseph Kenny. Lander, WY: Aquinas Institute for the Study of Sacred Doctrine, 2016 (opwest.org), p. 25).

shillings. A quarter of salt was commonly sold for thirty-five shillings, which in former times was quite unheard of. The land was so oppressed with want that whe[n] the king came to St. Albans on the feast of St. Lawrence [August 10] it was hardly possible to find bread on sale to supply his immediate household ....[13]

Particularly disastrous was the result for the grain crop of the summer. The cold weather and torrential rains during June, July, and August prevented the growing grains from coming to full maturity and hardening. Thus the autumn seeding of wheat and rye proved a total failure. The spring rains prevented proper sowing of oats, barley, and spelt, and when the time came for these to ripen they fared no better. So great was the rainfall in England during time of harvest that in many places the hay could not be cured. ... Trokelowe relates how thieves who had been imprisoned, but who were neglected and given no food, ferociously attacked new prisoners and devoured them half alive.[14]

Cannabalism outside the walls of prisons, even within families, was also reported: "Four pennies worth of coarse bread was not enough to feed a common man for one day. The usual kinds of meat, suitable for eating, were too scarce; horse meat was precious; plump

---

[13] Tierney, Brian, tr. 'Famine of 1315,' Internet Medieval Sourcebook, January 1996, sourcebooks.fordham.edu; *Anno Domini millesimo trecentesimo quinto-decimo, praeter supradictas angustias, quibus Anglia affligebatur, accrevit fames in terra .... Carnes enim incipiebant deficere, ova et cetera alba evanescere. Capones et aucae inveniri vix poterant; bidentes per morinam deficiebant; porci, prae nimietate caristieae, nutriri nequibant. Quarterium enim frumenti, fabarum, et pisarum, pro viginti solidis vendebatur, braesii pro marca, et avenarum pro decem. Sed quarterium salis pro triginta quinque solidis communiter vendebatur; quod a saeculis praeteritis est penitus inauditum. Unde terra tanta penuria premebatur, quod, cum Rex apud Sanctum Albanum in festo Sancti Laurentii proximo sequente declinaret, vix poterat panis venalis, pro suae specialis familiae sustentatione, inveniri* (Trokelowe, Johannis de. *Chronica et Annales*, ed. H. T. Riley. London: Longmans, Green, Reader, and Dyer, 1866 (lollardsociety.org), p. 92).

[14] Lucas, H. S. 'The Great European Famine of 1315, 1316, and 1317,' *Speculum*, vol. 5, No. 4 (Oct. 1930), pp. 353, 355-356 (jstor.org); *Sed quod horribile est ad futurorum notitiam perducere, incarcerati etiam fures inter eos recenter venientes in momento semivivos devorabant* (Trokelowe, p. 95).

dogs were stolen. And, according to many reports, men and women in many places secretly ate their own children ...."[15]

Shortly thereafter, the Black Death [1347 – 1351][16] spread across Europe from the southeast, eliminating a third of the population in little more than two years. The crisis exposed an alliance of the monarchies with the bourgeoisie in each country. This was felt as a betrayal and a great danger by the nobility and the clergy, while the lowest strata suffered appalling misery.

The old order was crumbling. The Church tried to prop up its regime with an internal crusade that strengthened controls on the simple people. Her natural allies – the nobility – supported an initiative that reinforced its power in the countryside. This chronic civil war does not really upset either kings or the bourgeoisie and will come to fruition over the course of four centuries.

The landscape was certainly full of projective cure-alls. In a confused and passionate climate, the first great campaigns of decontamination will take as *pharmakoi* or sacrificial lambs, the books, before passing on to focus almost monomaniacally upon the witches. Three kinds of the written word are prohibited: a) works on magic; b) classical culture and basically non-distorted Aristotle; c) and religious

---

[15] Tierney, sourcebooks.fordham.edu; *Quatuor autem denariatus de grosso pane non sufficiebant uni simplici homini in die. Carnes quidem communes, et ad vescendum licitae, strictae erant nimis; sed carnes equinae pretiosae eis fuerant, qui canes pingues furabantur; et, ut multi asserebant, tam viri quam mulieres parvulos suos, et etiam alienos, in multis locis furtim comedebant* (Trokelowe, p. 95); the change in weather corresponded to the end of the Medieval Warm Period, perhaps caused by the explosion of Mount Tarawera in New Zealand, and there is speculation that the subsequent cannabalism is the origin of the folktale Hansel and Gretel (Nelson, L. H. 'The Great Famine (13115 – 1317) and the Black Death (1346 – 1351),' vlib.us/medieval/lectures, p. 2/9).

[16] Said to be caused by the bacterium *Yersina pestis*, and to be the cause of "Giovanni Boccacio's The Decameron, a collection of tales written in 1350 and set in a country house where a group of noble young men and women of Florence have fled to escape the plague raging in the city" (Nelson, vlib.us/medieval/lectures, p. 8/9).

literature. Of these three groups the most important is without any doubt the last.

The Muslim struggled against sleep to read the Koran, but for the Christian the problem does not exist. On the contrary, since Christians are not only prohibited from reading heterodox books but their own scriptures as well, when they are not commented upon by some spiritual director. The clergy had come to be so far divorced from their own revealed truth that only by blocking the reading of their own Bible could they safeguard themselves from criticism. As early as 1299, authorities in the south of France prohibited the laity from possessing any of the books of either the Old or the New Testament:

> Canon XIV. We prohibit also that the laity should be permitted to have the books of the old, or the new, testament; unless any one, from motives of devotion, should wish to have the Psalter, or the Breviary for divine offices, or the house of the blessed Virgin; but we most strictly forbid their having any translation of these books.[17]

---

[17] Maitland, S. R., ed., tr. Facts and Doctrines Illustrative of the History, Doctrine, and Rites, of the Ancient Albigenses & Waldenses. London: C. J. G. and F. Rivington, 1832, section 7, Council of Thoulouse. A. D. 1229 (babel.hathitrust.org), p. 194; Can. XIV. "*Prohibemus etiam no libros veteris Testiamenti, aut novi, laici permittantur habere, nisi fortè Psalterium, vel Breviarium pro divinis officiis; aut horas Beatae Marie aliquis ex devotione habere velit: sed ne praemissos libros habeant in vulgari translatos arctissimè inhibemus*" (Cabassutii, Joannis. *Noticia Ecclesiastica Historium, Conciliorum, & Canonum*, editio secunda. Lugduni: Es Officina Amissoniana, joannis posuel, & Claudii Rigaud, 1685 (GB), *Concilium Tolosanum an. 1228*, p. 463); Szasz, Thomas. Ceremonial Chemistry. Garden City, NY: Anchor Press, 1974 (archive.org), pp. 184-185.

Figure 93. Offering to the Devil, frontispiece to the French translation of the Tractatus contra sectam Valdensium, by Jean Tincton. In 1440, the pope exhorted the faithful to attack "those people known as sorcerers or waldensians."

> [Oxford suspended any] one for the future [who should] hold, teach, preach, or defend ... the heresies or errors aforesaid or any of them, even under sophistical cavilling; nor to admit to preach, hear, or harken to John Wycliff, Nicholas Hereford, Philip Rappyngdon, canon regular, or John Aston or Lawrence Bedeman, who are vehemently and notoriously suspect of heresy, or any of them so suspect or defamed, or to favor them publicly or in secret, but rather immediately flee and avoid, as a serpent spitting pestiferous poison; and, moreover, we suspend said suspects from every scholastic act until they have purged their innocence in this matter before us ....[18]

A bit later, William de Berton, chancellor of the university of Oxford, added the "punishment of imprisonment and suspension from every scholastic act, and also under punishment of the greater excommunication" to those preaching heretical opinions either "in the schools or outside in this university."[19] By 1407, however, that which had not been previously approved was prohibited, including "the reading of any theological tract, whether of Wyclyf's authorship or otherwise, already published in his day or since or still to be published, unless it was first approved by the university of Oxford or of Cambridge."[20] In 1428, on orders from Pope Martin V, "44 years after Wyclyf's death, his bones were dug up" and burned.[21]

The translators and editors, guilty not only of consumption but trafficking, will be brought to the bonfire and on occasion punished like regicides, with a show that included various days of torture, followed by dismemberment and the burning of their remains.[22] The ecclesiastic majesty is the only one authorized to read and expound upon the divine word.

---

[18] Dahmus, J. H. The Prosecution of John Wyclyf. New Haven: Yale University Press, 1952, pp. 110-111.

[19] Dahmus, p. 131.

[20] Dahmus, p. 152.

[21] Dahmus, p. 154.

[22] There is, for example, a minutely detailed story of this kind of torture in Foucault (1978, pp. 11-13).

tendi volumus ⁊ mandamus ⁊ ap
pellatione postposita firmiter ob-
seruari.

Liber quartus. De sponsa
libus ⁊ matrimoniis.
Ex concilio triburiensi.

O
E francia quī
dam nobilez
mulierem de
saxonia lēge
saxonum du-
xit in vxorem
verū quia nō
hisdem vtun-
tur legibus saxones ⁊ francigene:

Figure 94. The Decretales of Gregory IX,
the first official and universal code for the church.

B. The Opening of the Internal Crusade

One of the first social decontaminations through the transference of evil to a collective in the Middle Ages has as its object the "people of a fertile region of Oldenburg, called Stedingerland ..."[23] who had recently begun to refuse to pay taxes to the archbishop. In his Papal Rule of 1232, which converts a witchhunt into a crusade, Gregory IX accuses them of "depreciating the sacraments, persecuting the faithful, being in league with the Devil, making waxen images and consulting witches."[24] A second papal bull from this same pontiff describes a sabbat with all the details that are going to be repeated mechanically over the next half millennium. This particular sabbat involved the ingestion of the secretions of certain members of the genus *Bufo* or *Rana* followed by an orgy:

---

[23] *Los naturales de una región fértil de Oldenburgo, llamada Stedingerland, estaban obligados a pagar ciertos diezmos al arzobispo de Brema por una donación que había hecho Enrique IV. En 1197, algunos clérigos que fueron a recaudarlos salieron maltrechos de su empresa. El arzobispo, en consecuencia, excomulgó a los stedinger, declarándolos heréticos. Estos no hicieron caso de la condena y entonces el arzobispo pidió a Roma autorización para levantar una cruzada contra los mismos. Luego parece que hubo un acuerdo provisional. Pero treinta años después del alboroto volvió a estallar un conflicto entre el prelado y sus feligreses rebeldes* (Baroja, Julio Caro. Las brujas y su mundo. Madrid: Alianza Editorial, 1966, p. 104); see also Baroja, 1971, p. 75: "The inhabitants of a fertile region of Oldenburg, called Steingerland, were obliged to pay certain tithes to the archbishop of Brema .... In 1197 some clergyman who were sent to collect the tithes were assaulted. The archbishop, in consequence, excommunicated the inhabitants of Stedingerland, declaring them heretics. ... They paid no attention ... and the archbishop asked the Pope to give permission to raise up a crusade against them. A temporary compromise was reached between the parties. But thirty years after the original revolt trouble broke out again [tr. gwr]."

[24] Baroja, 1971, p. 75; *En la bula acusaba a los stedinger de despreciar los sacramentos, persequir a los religiosos, tener comercio con el demonio, hacer imágenes de cera y consultar a las hechiceras* (Baroja, 1966, p. 104).

When a novice is to be initiated and is brought before the assembly of the wicked for the first time, a sort of frog appears to him; a toad according to some. Some bestow a foul kiss on his hind parts, others on his mouth, sucking the animal's tongue and slaver. Sometimes the toad is of a normal size, but at others it is as large as a goose or a duck. Usually it is the size of an oven's mouth. The novice comes forward and stands before a man of fearful pallor. His eyes are black and his body so thin and emaciated that he seems to have no flesh and be only skin and bone. The novice kisses him and he is as cold as ice. After kissing him every remnant of faith in the Catholic Church that lingers in the novice's heart leaves him.[25]

As it would.[26]

Later appear the bulls of John XXII – especially the *Super illius specula* (1320) – "which seems to mark the beginning of a new era in witchcraft. Many historians have considered the effects of this bull to have been decisive."[27] The bulls of John XXII "condemned magic in all its forms" and "urged the inquisitors to keep a careful watch on

---

[25] Baroja, Julio Caro. The World of the Witches, tr. Nigel Glendinning. London: Phoenix Press, 2001, p. 76; *Huius pestis initia talia perferuntur: nam dum novitius in ea quisquam recipitur et perditorum primitus scholas intrat, apparet ei species quedam rane, quam bufonem consueverunt aliqui nominare. Hanc quidam a posterioribus et quidam in ore damnbiliter osculantes, linguam bestie intra ora sua recipiunt et salivam. Hec apparet interdum indebita quantitate, et quandoque in modum anseris vel anatis, plerumque furni etiam quantitatem assumit. Demum novitio procedenti occurrit miri palloris homo, nigerrimos habens oculos, adeo extenuatus et macer, quod consumptis carnibus sola cutis relicta videtur ossibus superducta; hunc novitius osculatur et sentit frigidum sicut glaciem, et post osculum catholice memoria fidei de ipsius corde totaliter evanescit* (Rodenberg, Carolus, ed. *Epistolae Saeculi XIII E Regestis Pontificum Romanorum*, selected by G. H. Pertz, vol. I. Berlin: Apud Weidmannos, 1883, (*dmgh.de*, *Monumenta Germaniae Historica*), no. 537, "*Vox in Rama*," p. 433).

[26] The Sonoran Desert Toad (*Bufo alvarius*), for example, secretes bufotenin (5-hydroxy-N, N-dimethyltryptamine, similar to 5-MeO-DMT) in the skin on its back and in its venom (erowid.org). Devotees of DMT will not find it surprising that one's faith in any little bit of reality should be questioned during such an excursion. Gregory receives his distorted information secondhand via a priest's confessional from a parishoner who has clearly participated in such a ceremony.

[27] Baroja, 2001, p. 84.

such activities"[28] but with the *Super illius specula* not only is the Inquisition consolidated as an institution but also various professions connected to the discovery and liquidation of persons related to witchcraft. After these proclamations there is a mighty river of analogous precepts flowing directly from Rome[29] that bestow plenary indulgence and economic benefits to those who aid Christianity in its battle with the demons.

The most perfect model of these decrees, "and the one to which both civil and ecclesiastical judges appealed as the supreme authority,"[30] is the *Summis desiderantes affectibus* of Innocence VIII (1484) which accuses the witches of a multitude of crimes:

> [I]t has come to our notice ... that ... a number of persons of both sexes ... have given themselves up to devils in the form of incubi and succubi. By their incantations, spells, crimes and infamous acts they destroy the fruit of the womb in women, in cattle and various other animals; they destroy crops, vines, orchards, meadows and pastures, wheat, corn and other plants and vegetables; they bring pain and affliction, great suffering and appalling disease (both external and internal) upon men, women and beasts, flocks and other animals; they prevent men from engendering and women from conceiving; they render both wives and husbands impotent; they sacrilegiously deny the faith they received in Holy Baptism; and they do not abstain from committing other fearful excesses and foul crimes, endangering their souls, mocking God and causing a serious scandal, at the instigation of the Enemy.[31]

---

[28] Baroja, 1971, p. 84.

[29] "Eugene IV gave orders for such repressive measures in 1437 and 1445, Calixtus II in 1457 and Pius IV in 1459. These were later followed by Alexander VI in 1494, Julius II and Leo X in 1521, Hadrian VI in 1523 and Clement VII in 1524" (Baroja, 2001, p. 94, quoting H. Ch. Lea, A History of the Inquisition of Spain, IV, p. 208).

[30] Baroja, 1971, p. 94; *De todas aquella disposiciones pontificias la que más fama ha tenido, la que se consideró como básica durante mucho tiempo en las actuaciones de jueces, eclesiásticos y civiles, es la bula «Summis desiderantes affectibus» de Inocencio VIII, fechada a 9 de diciembre de 1484 y dirigida a varios prelados alemanes, en cuyas diócesis estaba muy extendido el mal* (Baroja, 1966, p. 127).

[31] Baroja, 2001, p. 94, quoting from the introduction to the *Malleus*; see also Baroja, 1966, pp. 127-128.

Further, the two friars sent to investigate, who would later collaborate in writing the Malleus Maleficarium (1486), were given "plenary powers from Rome."[32]

Before the policy of internal crusade was dreamed up, rural witches in the High Middle Ages were anomolous and infrequent characters. With the transition toward the Lower Middle Ages, the existence of collective pagan rituals, executed with the help of drugs and orgiastic objectives, is newly suspect, as exemplified by the *Canon episcopi* (XI century). Starting with the bulls of Gregory IX, one can observe this not only in the declarations of ecclesiastical and civil magistrates, but also in texts like the *Roman de la Rose* (1277), published some fifty years after the *Canon episcopi*, which assures its readers that "*lamiae* or *mascae* who flew under cover of darkness committing all kinds of atrocities, constituted a third of the female population of France."[33] After the bull of Innocence VIII and the all-encompassing powers conceded to the Inquisitors, the Holy Office of the Inquisition, speaking of Germany, says in 1486 that "there does not exist even the smallest farm where women do not try to play dirty tricks on others, drying up the milk of their cows by means of spells and, frequently, until they cause them to die."[34]

In the sixteenth century, two hundred years after the start of the hunt, the epidemic is declared global and devastates the New World as well as the Old. Denunciations can be made not only freely and in secret but are also obligatory, the punishments are of an

---

[32] Baroja, 1971, p. 95: "At the same time we give instructions in our Apostolic Letters to our beloved brother the Archbishop of Strasburg, for him or others to publish this most solemnly whenever it shall seem necessary to him, or whenever one or both of the Inquisitors shall require it. Nor shall he allow the Inquisitors to be molested in their work;" see also Baroja, 1971, p. 275, n. 46.

[33] Baroja, 1971, p. 90, citing Jean de Meung, *Roman de la Rose*, line 18624; Hansen, *Zauberwahn*, pp. 147-150; Cf. also Jean Français, *L'Eglise et la sorcellerie*, p. 17 (1971, p. 274).

[34] Huxley, 1972, p. 129.

unheard of cruelty, the people had been convinced of the intrinsic abomination of witchcraft and yet the reprobates did not cease to increase in number. To be exact, it is in this century and the following one when the majority of people are burned publicly in Europe, a totality – according to the calculations of C. H. Lea – that will round out at half a million,[35] though later studies reduce this figure to some 60,000 executions and something like double that number of trials (terminating nearly always in the plundering of the possessions of the accused).

The ineffectiveness of the persecution in attacking the problem seems evident and is of great theoretical interest, as it occurs at the same time as its grandiose success, if (thinking like an Inquisitor) we understand by this success the locating and extermination of so many witches, a not depreciable percentage of the European population altogether. But before inquiring about the ultimate causes of the success/failure observed in the crusade, it is important to analyze the nature of the accusations and the relationship they have to the use of drugs.

1. Drugs and Apostasy. Having erased the distinction between necromants, wizards and herbalists from the time of the Salic Law (424), by way of Charlemagne – and perhaps much earlier – not only can one now speak of diabolic plants in generic terms, but also opium in particular as one of them. Other drugs considered diabolic in the tenth century are some solanaceas like the spiny apple (*Datura stromonium* L.) that is condemned as a "satanic philter in the hands of brothel workers, party animals and shameless procurers of skirts."[36] Over the course of time this condemnation is

[35] The work of Lea (1939, three volumes) continues to be considered the most documented global investigation (see also Harris, 1980, p. 181). Nevertheless, it has also been the object of a recent revision, for example, in Levack, 1995.

[36] Brau, 1973, p. 80.

going to be solidified and amplified at the same time, and with the arrival of the Lower Middle Ages the connection between witchcraft in general and ebriety with non-alcoholic drugs becomes overwhelming. However, to present the subject in this fashion would suppose an analytical coldness foreign to the aims of the Holy Office as well as its practical operation. As a consequence, it continued to be not at all clear in the orthodoxy whether there was something effectively supernatural within malevolent herbs – an authentic demon within – or only that they were employed by those admirers of the demons; in effect, in the process of deciding if the satanic power of drugs was real or merely symbolic, the followers of Augustine of Hippo and those of Thomas de Aquinas continued to dispute the issue. But ecclesiastic judges are conscious that certain substances – both simples and compounds – are the most effective elements in the magic arsenal used in witchcraft, and that to condemn their possession disarms in good measure their adversary. This, together with some attempts made to describe the effects of the drugs, is what we will see reiterated from the fourteenth century on.

During the Inquisitional processes of the decade of the 1330s in Carcassone, where for the first time the *sabbat* appears under that name, one can read in the transcript of depositions the following:

> There she found a huge he-goat and after greeting him she submitted to his pleasure. The he-goat in return taught her all kinds of secret spells; he explained poisonous plants to her and she learned from him words for incantations and how to cast spells during the night of the vigil of St. John's day, Christmas Eve, and the first Friday of every month. ... She boiled together in a cauldron, over an accursed fire, poisonous herbs and substances taken from the bodies of animals or humans which she had sacrilegiously and foully taken from the consecrated ground of cemeteries to use for her spells; she frequented the gallows-trees by night stealing shreds of clothing from the hanged, or taking the rope by which they were hanging, or laying hold of their hair, their nails or flesh.[37]

[37] Baroja, 1971, p. 85.

In the same transcript, one can notice that Ms. Anne-Marie Georgel, "having been denounced by respectable persons," at first "denied" the accusations against her and "would not confess" until "forced."[38]

Likewise, Catherine, "the wife of Pierre Delort of Toulouse," declared that she

> has made certain harmful concoctions and potions which cause men and beasts to die. Every Friday night she fell into a strange sleep during which she was carried to the Sabbath. ... There she worshipped the he-goat and served his pleasure and that of all those who were present at that loathsome feast.[39]

Ms. Delort also was "forced to confess by the means we have power to use to make people speak the truth ... although she protested her innocence for a long time and made several false declarations."[40] Both women were described as being "advanced in years."[41]

Deprived of mythical apparel, the women in question copulated or were believed to copulate with a man covered in the skins of animals (or fantasized such under the effects of some kind of drug), who then instructed her in herbs and drugs in the first case or who was already adept in the second. Satisfied with both, they then went on to to exercise their offices until bumping into the Inquisitors. A Spanish law from these times appears to foresee similar apprenticeships when it states laconically: "'a woman who is a witch or a sorceress shall either be burnt or saved by iron.' In this case, the context makes it clear that this was an individual and not a group problem."[42]

In the same period – specifically in 1324, four years after John XXII promulgated the papal bull *Super illius specula* – an Inquisitional

---

[38] Baroja, 1971, p. 85.

[39] Baroja, 1971, p. 86.

[40] Baroja, 1971, p. 86.

[41] Baroja, 1971, p. 84.

[42] Baroja, 2001, p. 82, citing Section 1, Article 35 of the Second Book of the *Fuero de Cuenca*, Rafael Ureña (ed.), Madrid, 1935, p. 329.

prodeeding declares: "On inspecting the attic of the woman a tube of unguent was found, with which she greased a broom handle, upon which she would roam about and gallop over every obstacle wherever and however she wished."[43]

The detail of the broom, reiterated in a thousand other places, also has a pharmacological explanation, and it is one of the nearly invariable details until the seventeenth century. A proceeding from 1470 states: "The vulgar believe, and the witches confess, that on certain days and nights they annoint a broomstick and mount it to go to a special place, or rather they annoint themselves under the arms and other places where hair grows."[44]

The other places where hair grows – on a woman – certainly coincide with those that would be in contact with the broomstick when mounted upon it. The broomstick was used to rub or insert the unguents into zones of which the modesty of the Inquisitor avoids speaking. The probibited areas are those that some unfortunate wretches also called diabolic parts in a confession extracted around 1540:

> [A]nd they confessed – according to that stated in its procedure – that had known many times carnally the devil; and asked in particular if they had known some particular delight in their nether parts they responded constantly no, and that it caused an incomparable coldness to be felt in the diabolic parts, for which also it seemed to them they went back to a humor cold as ice, like hailstones, in the bowels.[45]

A later document describes how an old woman activated her diabolic parts with a powerful ointment:

---

[43] Schultes and Hofmann, 1982, p. 88.

[44] J. Bergamo, in Hansen, 1901, p. 199.

[45] Laguna, in Font Quer, 1982, p. 568.

After stripping and rubbing herself with the oinment, she threw back her head and was asleep in an instant. With the help of the Devil she dreamed of the lustful Venus and other superstitions in a form so realistic that let out a cry and gesticulating with her hands she rolled from the foot (of the bed) where she was found.[46]

A contemporary anthropologist is probably right when he affirms that the famous brooms of the witches were chemically reinforced dildos, which, "without discarding its phallic symbolism, served to apply the atropine extracts to sensitive vaginal membranes."[47] In effect, from the information preserved, it could be said that there were two basic methods in which these drugs were administered: one, collective and rural, which both sexes attended – linked to initiation and seasonal ceremonies and the learning of a religious office – and the other, solitary, within the context of a ritual of a more mastabatory type, dependent upon the market for unguents, probably sold for a good price by urban and rural witches.

That is why, though on the subject of court appearances required for *sabbats*, an Inquisitor explains the connection between apostasy in witchcraft and the consumption of drugs. Any use of a pomade requires justification. In his *Instrucciones a los jueces en materia de brujeria* – written in preparation for his *De la Demonamonie des Sorciers* (1580) – the celebrated civil magistrate Jean Bodin[48] warns:

[46] J. Nider, 1692, in Harner, 1972, pp. 131-132.

[47] Harner, 1972, p. 131.

[48] The "renowned lawyer and political writer" (Baroja, 1971, p. 115) Jean Bodin also wrote on the history of political science, founding the concept of national sovereignty (by way of the old sacred royalty). In the field of demonology, however, "Bodin reached the conclusion that the Devil is one and the same everywhere and that the Sabbath, too, is everywhere identical" (Baroja, 1971, p. 115). He established that the witches are guilty of fifteen crimes, no more and no less: "1. Denial of God. / 2. Cursing God and blaspheming. / 3. Giving honour to the Devil by worshipping him and making sacrifices. / 4. Dedication of children to the Devil. / 5. Murdering children before they have been baptised. / 6. Pledging to Satan children who are yet in the womb. / 7. Spreding propaganda about the cult. / 8. Honouring oaths sworn

Figure 95. Linda maestra, Etching #68, from the series Las caprichos of Goya.

---

in the name of the Devil. / 9. Incest. / 10. Murdering men and little children to make broth. / 11. Disinterring the dead, eating human flesh and drinking blood. / 12. Killing by means of poisons and spells. / 13. Killing cattle. / 14. Causing famine on the land and infertility in the fields. / 15. Having sexual intercourse with the Devil" (Baroja, 1971, pp. 115-116, citing Jean Bodin, *De la Demonomanie des Sorciers* (Paris, 1580), f. 199 v). In the third section of the work, "ways of eliciting statements are enumerated and the penalties corresponding to each crime are listed" (Baroja, 1971, p. 116). "Bodin, as a man of law, never doubted that magic was within the proper scope of the law" (Baroja, 1971, p. 116).

If the subject is found with certain greases, this is an indication for torture, and more if she cannot justify such greases, since it is well known that the witches use such drugs communally in their maleficient ceremonies.[49]

The phenomenon of metamorphosis or transformation is also attributed to the virtue of psychoactive preparations. De Nynauld, author of a treatise entitled *De la lycanthropie, transformation et extase des sorciers* [On lycanthrophy, transformation and the ecstasy of witches], distinguishes three types of unguents: "1) an unguent that makes the witches believe that they are really going to an *aquelarre*, but that acts only upon the imagination; 2) an unguent that permits a true transformation, with the permission of God; 3) an unguent that gives the witches the illusion of an animal transformation."[50] While the vulgar continue to believe in fantastic legends of wolf-men, the Inquisitors now think – with some reason – that the metamorphosis has a pharmacological origin. Even so, in De Nynauld and in almost all the others one can observe this interesting alternation between a secular point of view and superstition, distinguishing between unguents that only modify consciousness and unguents that induce modifications of the external world.

---

49 Brau, 1973, p. 43.

50 *Pour obuier à cecy le Diable caut & rusé, leur a persuadé qu'elles y iroient seulement en esprit; à condition qu'elles s'oignissent d'un onguent composé de son artifice; par la vertu duquel l'ame se separeroir du corps pour quelques heures, & s'en iroient au lieu par luy assigne, le corps demeurant en leurs licts .... Venons maintenant au second onguent, par la vertu duquel le Diable persuade aux Sorcieres apres s'é estre ointes pouvoir en mettant un balay, ou baston entre les jambes chevaucher en l'air, & aller en leur synagogues d'une vistesse incredible en passant par la cheminee. ... Car il faut noter que le Diable peut ce faire, entant que Dieu a liuré des ja telles gens en sens reprouvé, de sorte qu'estans faicts eselaues du Diable .... Reste finalement a parler du troisiesme que le Diable donne aux Sorcieres, leur persuadant qu'apres qu'elles s'en seront oingtes, elles seront vrayement transformees en bestes, & ainsi pourront courir les champs* (Nynauld, I. de. De La Lycanthropie, Transformation, et Extase des Sorciers. Paris: Chez Nicolas Rousset, 1615, archive.org, pp. 27, 28, 36, 38, 48).

It can, then, be affirmed that if there are various recurring indications of witchcraft, such as the possession of certain books, the existence of signs,[51] precedents of kinship or family demons, and other more episodic details, no proof was more solid or continuously accepted than the possession of lotions and potions. The *denomonomania* of the witches defined by Bodin and his colleagues in the civil or ecclesiastic magistracy is in the first instance a *toxicomania* proven or suspected. Justly for this the humanists insist on the thesis that the unguents alone are psychoactive (type one of De Nynauld), because if the voyage was due to the natural effects of natural substances the persecution for apostasy would seem to lack foundation.

But no less inadmissible for orthodoxy was the very idea of the *pharmakon*, an especially secular concept which from the beginning – when the Christian struggle was not only directed against cults based upon entheogens, but also generally against the pagan attitude to certain drugs (euphoria as an end in itself, voluptuousness, euthanasia) – disappeared as if by magic from the world. Although the unguents with supernatural power (type two of De Nynauld) perhaps were not credible to the majority of the Inquisitors, their existence had to be defended at all costs – and it was – for two reasons of the greatest importance: one was to maintain intact the *theological* basis of the crusade, avoiding that it should seem a strategic policy in times of crisis for its authority; the other motive, more profound, is an inextricable relationship between any kind of ecstatic ebriety and Satan, consolidated already in the first centuries, when a mystery religion with Dionysiac elements betrays its original entheogenic promise (to eat and

---

[51] Signs of Satanic affiliation understood practically any non-habitual characteristic, like birthmarks or congenital defects, points insensible to the prick of a needle, even warts in some cases. Lacking other evidence, a woman that had a third nipple was condemned because "a cat or Satanic toad could suck from it and grow fat" (Huxley, 1970, p. 126).

drink the god), transforming itself into a dogmatic ritualism that attempts a hatred of everything physical.

For this reason – thanks in part to its own persecution – the phenomenon of witchcraft represents a vigorous return of the repressed and, to be precise, of a repression with maximal horror and maximal hypocrisy: the cult of the flesh and the earth. In this specific aspect a complex phenomenon like an epidemic of witches is a disorderly clamor and even a delirium, though directed toward the reconciliation of man with the here and now, a proposition that defines the Renaissance as such.

Figure 96. An aquelarre on Mount Brocken, Eastern Germany.

2. Eroticism as Pharmacological Aim. Beginning with the Great Hunt (1330 – 1340), encouraged by the generous papal bulls of John XXII, the preparation of certain ingredients and harmful potions is a fixture in the judicial processes. But it is also a constant that sex appears as well and that female criminals adopt attitudes strangely similar to the Greek and Roman Bacchants. From the start their crime is the sin of lust, apostasy specifically connected to sensuality. One of the earliest mentions of a *sabbat* (in Stedingerland, ca. 1232) describes acts of pagan veneration followed by orgies:

> When this ceremony is over the lights are put out and those present indulge in the most loathsome sensuality, having no regard to sex. If there are more men than women, men satisfy one another's depraved appetites. Women do the same for one another.[52]

It is very much the same sexual accusation made by the consul Postumius in 186 BC, the same wielded by the mythical Pentheus. We ought to distrust any confession extracted by torture, and it is likely that part of the picture we have today was added by the persecutors, besieged by phantasms born of their own sexual repression. But this will not discount the coherence of so much testimony, coming from different places and times, nor the fact that destroying the dikes of Puritanism would have been in the air. The musicians invite to the

---

[52] Baroja, 1971, p. 76, translating a Papal Bull describing a 'Secret Society' formed by the inhabitants of Stedingerland, using a "text given by Soldan, [*Geschichte der Hexenprozesse*], I, pp. 161-3. The relevant section begins on page 159" (Baroja, 1971, p. 272, n. 12); ... *doy aquí una traducción de los pasajes más importantes relativos a la sociedad secreta que los mismos stedinger formaban. «Terminaba semejante ceremonia apagan las luces y se abandonan a la lubricidad más abominable, sin consideración al parentesco. Si hay más hombres que mujeres, los hombres satisfacen entre ellos su depravado apetito. Las mujeres entre sí hacen lo mismo. Verificados estos horrores se encienden de nuevo las candelas y todo el mundo se encuentra en su sitio ...»* (Baroja, 1966, pp. 104-105).

dances those who would celebrate the mysteries of the flesh, not those who damn their lives.

Heartbreaking from the eschatological point of view, the ceremony represents the sacred only in reverse. The "ignoble kiss on the rear"[53] opens the door to a series of excrements that begins with a parody of the mass or the black mass. In the same way that there can only be one Church and one God – comments the judge De Lancre, the most implacable of the civil Inquisitors – there can be only one Satan and one Witchcraft. But the dogmatic assertion is correct in a sense never foreseen by its formulator. Just as monotheisms are always supported by dogmas, the natural religions are always founded in ecstacy; just as ritualism will always demand faith, the mysteries of fertility will always need the trance; just as the cult of pure liturgy will always demand an iron discipline, so the cult of the Earth will always need relaxation and intermixing, the melting of inhibitions; just as the lover of control will ever share formal communions, so the lover of freedom will ever share substantial communions. We can, then, doubt that the *akelarre*, the Walpurgis nights and the Nordic *sabbats* consciously would have imitated the ancient Bacchanals.

But all these ceremonies respond to the same basic human need, whose roots are buried in the origin of the species. This need can be found as much in the sacreligious imitators of the High Church mass as in the astonished judges and mayors organized to strike against their perpetration, because on each side are human beings who dispute the nature of the pure and the impure; for some the impure is the glorification of the flesh, and for others the impure is its mortification. The flesh continues to exist, and one can give it life in periodic ceremonies or continue to try to repress it at every moment.

---

[53] The officer at these events often wore the two-faced mask of Janus, and what was kissed was the back part of the mask. It is possible that the "ignoble kiss" may be a clerical addition.

The caricature of the *sabbat* represents it as an orgiastic rite that includes giant toads, black cats the size of a large dog and the same Satan transfigured, half-man and half-animal.[54] "From the point of view of its composition," comments Julio Caro Baroja, one of the great scholars on this subject, "such a group would seem to recall adepts of a mystery cult more than anything else, and many of these had sprung up in Greece and Rome at one time or another."[55]

The humanist Pedro de Valencia considered this possibility in his first *Discourso*, maintaining the proposition with regards to the meetings at Zugarramurdi that they were

> merely real gatherings of vicious people who 'have invented those meetings and evil mysteries – in which one person, the boldest of them all, pretends to be Satan himself and puts on the horns and other foul and obscene attire which are referred to – because they desire to commit fornication, adultery or sodomy.'[56]

He compares them to "the bacchanals, especially those described by Euripides" and to those "which took place in Rome" in 186 BC.[57] These, he says, were the "'works of man and natural inventions of

---

[54] Baroja, 1971, p. 76 (1966, pp. 104-105); as noted, pharmacologically, one of the discoveries derived from Medieval witchcraft appears to be the powerful psychoactivity of the skin of certain toads, especially the so-called Bufo toad, which contains bufotine or 5-hydroxy – N, N – dimethyltripamine (DMT) as well as 5-methoxy – N, N- dimethyltriptamine, indolic alkaloids of the visionary type.

[55] Baroja, 1971, p. 77; *Desde un punto de vista estructural podría decirse que un grupo constituido de esta suerte, a lo que más se parece es a los asociados a un culto misteriosófico, como aquellos que se multiplicaron en Grecia y Roma a partir de épocas determinadas* (Baroja, 1966, p. 106).

[56] Baroja, 1971, p. 181, citing *Discurso de Pedro de Valencia â cerca [sic] de los quentos de las/ Brujas y cosas tocantes a Magia dirigido al* Illmº. Sr. D. Berdº. de Sandobal y Roxas Cardenal Arcpoº de Toledo Inquisidor/ General de España. Department of Manuscripts, Biblioteca Nacional, Madrid, MSS 9087, f. 262 v.

[57] Baroja, 1971, pp. 181-182, citing the first *Discurso*, ff. 263 v. – 265 r., 266 r. – 267 r., and Livy, XXXIX, 9, 13, 15 and 41.

seducers, consisting of crimes and evil deeds of men and women, without visible magic or supernatural agency being involved.'"[58]

Another possibility that Pedro de Valencia discusses in his first *Discurso* is that

> everything that is said to take place at the meetings – sexual inercourse, banquets, etc. – is only a vision that occurs in dreams brought on by the Devil with oinments, poisons and other substances. ... [P]arts of the visions may simply be due to the natural powers of ointments ....[59]

In his second *Discurso*, he returns to the theory that the orgies are real and are for the purpose of committing "sins of the flesh."[60]

To summarize the common theme to these ceremonies the following description has some value:

> The Devil was found represented in the person of a man who had inherited, or perhaps acquired, the honor of being the incarnation of the god of two faces of the Dianic cult. The devotees render homage to the god kissing his posterior face, with a furry mask, which is worn under the tail of an animal as the rear part of the Devil. There he had a place in the ritual copulation with the god, which for such purposes he was equipped with an artificial phallus. The ceremony was followed by a Romeria with its dances, which was celebrated out-of-doors, under the trees and among sacred rocks. And it ended all together with an orgy of sexual promiscuity that primitively had been, without doubt, an operation of magic oriented to augment the fertility of the animals that assured the subsistence of the hunters and farmers of those times.[61]

In fact, all over Europe today there are still similar Romerias, with idols more or less retouched so as not to offend the ecclesiastic hierarchy.

---

[58] Baroja, 1971, p. 182, citing the first *Discurso*, f. 267 r.

[59] Baroja, 1971, p. 183, citing the first *Discurso*, ff. 270 r. – 274 r.

[60] Baroja, 1971, p. 183, citing the *Segundo discurso de Pedro de Valencia acerca de los brujos y de sus maleficios*," *Revista de Archivos, Bibliiotecas y Museos*. Madrid: Tip. de la Revista de Archivos, Bibliotecas y Museos, 1906, pp. 445-454.

[61] Huxley, 1972, p. 137.

Nevertheless, eroticism and drugs were not limited to collective rural ceremonies. Along with this festive use by campesinos is an urban use amply documented, where the unguents are not applied by an artificial phallus of an official but by broomsticks or simply rubbed upon the prohibited parts. During the Renaissance Bartholomew della Spina (1475? – 1546?) mentions three cases where there is nothing resembling an old rural herbalist, or a master of ceremonies with Druidic overtones, though it does have eroticism supported by drugs:

Don Augustin de Turre, from Bergamo, the most experienced among the physicians of his time, told me that once when he was a student he returned home late at night. And as no one responded nor opened the door, he made a ladder and was able to enter by a window. He went to look for the concierge and found her in her room, fallen upon the ground, as naked as a cadaver and totally unconscious. When the morning arrived and she came in, Don Augustin asked her what happened the night before. She confessed that she had been transported on a voyage .... Also the doctor Petro Cella, before vicar to the Marques de Como, told me a similar thing had happened with his concierge. But also it was told between us that when the Inquisition was operating in the diocese of Como, in the walled city of Lugano, the spouse of a notary of the Inquisition was formally accused of being a witch and practicing witchcraft. Her husband suffered indescribably, though he was considered a saint. Then, by the will of God, he was one day in the pigsty because he could not find her anywhere. There he found her naked in a corner, exhibiting her pudenda, completely unconscious. Unsheathing his daggar, in a sudden wrath, he wished to kill her, but he recovered and put away his daggar in order to see what would be the result of all this. And a little later she came in to see him. When she saw that her husband was threatening to kill her, she prostrated herself before him and promised that she would reveal to him the truth. She confessed then that that night she had gone on a voyage, etc. Hearing these things, the husband departed at that moment and accused her before the Inquisitors, so that she would be brought to the fire.[62]

---

[62] Spinei, F. Bartholomaei. *Quaestio de strigibus, una cum tractatu de praeeminentia Sacrae Theologiae, &quadruplici Apologia de Lamiis contra Ponzinibium* (An Investigation on wittches with a treatise on the Supremacy of Sacred Theology and A Fourfold Defense from Ponzinibio's on Witches). Romae: In Aedibus Populi Romani, 1576, ch. 2, archive.org, pp. 4-5: *Dominus Augusti de Turre, Bergomen sis; medicus suo tempore*

It is clear, then, that not only attending *sabbats* or practicing magic was considered witchcraft. The simple administration of a drug was now punished with the bonfire, some centuries before the Chinese emperors punished the consumption of opium with strangulation. To experience the voyage and to be accused of the apostasy of witchcraft are the same thing for the theological lawyer, at least from the thirteenth century onward, and probably much earlier. In Europe the prohibited is not just limited to opium; it embraces also the solanaceas and, in fact, any diabolical potion; it covers any substance suspected of altering consciousness, which means – given the ecclesiastic ignorance on questions of toxicology – even those only apparently useful for inducing a trip. It seems impossible to conceive of a wider prohibition.

---

celebratissimus, mihi superioribus annis in domo sua Bergomi retulir, quod cum iuuenis Paduae studeret, quadam nocte circa sextam horam domum cum sodalibus suis rediens, & pulsans, com nemo responderet, aut aperirer; tandem per fenestram, scala conscendens, domum intrauit: & ancillam inquirens, reperit iacentem in cubili super terram supinam, nudatam veluti mortuam, & penitus insensibilem, ita ut nulla potuerit arte per ipsum excitari. Facto mane, ab ipso, quae ad sensum redierat, sciscitata, quidnam illa nocte passa fuisset; tandem confessa est se delatam ad cursum. Ex quo manifeste pater, quod no corporaliter, sed in spiritu vel in somnis ita deluduntur, ut putent se longius deferri, quae immobiles domi residet. Huic simile mihi Salutijs retulit superioribus annis D. Petrus Cella, olim vicarius Marchionarus Salutiaru, qui superest adhuc, de quadam sua etiam ancilla similia passa, similiterque ab eo deprehensa deludi. Sed & fama publica apud nostros fertur, quod cum in dicecesi Cumana officium inquisitionis exerceretur a nostris, contigit in castro, quod Luganum appellatur, usorem notarij inquisitionis iudicialiter accusari, quod esset strix, atque malefica. Turgbaatus est autem mirum inmodum vir eius, eo quod sanctam esse putaret. Dispositione aute domini mane dici Veneris sancti, dum usorem uo invenieret, in stabulum porcorum concessit, & ibit nudam verendque praemonstroantem, & penitus insensibilem in quodam angulo reperit limo porcorum respersam. Iam igitur certior ferme factus de eo quod credere no poterat, arrepto gladio subita ira voluit eam occidere. Sed in se rediens, paululum substitit ut videret finem. Et ecce post modicum temporis ad sensus suos illa reversa, uiso marito sibi mortem intentare, coram eo prostrata est: & veniam perens promisit quod omnem ei veritatem panderet, et confessa est, quod iuisset illa nocte ad cursum &c. Maritus aute haec audiens starimqwue recedens, eam apud Inquisitorem accusauit ut ignibus traderetur; in Harner, 1972, p. 133.

Figure 97. The Witches' Kitchen (ca. 1610),
Frans Francken the Younger (1581 – 1642),
Kunsthistorisches Museum, Vienna.

Spina does not indicate how old these unhappy wretches were, though the lack of an express mention of their age suggests that they might have been young or middle aged. A contemporary of Spina was Franz Francken, whose well-known work *The Witches' Kitchen* shows a young nude woman and two others who have stripped her of her clothes in order to rub her with unguents; the ladies are dressed very well and stand out from the old witches in rags who prepare the ointments in another part of the room. The work is a noble precedent with so many contemporary illustrations – not so far away from the original – where young women appear tempted to try the drug.

The lustful effect that these pomades exercise on the feminine sex during this epoch – on ladies no one suspects of witchcraft – was witnessed by the celebrated Andres de Laguna, physician to the pontiff Julius III and Carlos V. While in Metz he "annointed from the foot to the head the wife of the executioner, who, from the jealousy of her husband, had totally lost sleep and ran about almost frenetically."[63] Laguna obtained the ointment from a certain baliff, who in turn had gotten it from a pair of witches condemned some time before, and tells how – after falling into a profound stupor that lasted a day and a half (an evident case of an overdose) – the woman woke up saying:

> Why have you woken me at the worst time, as I was surrounded by all the pleasures and delights of the world? And turning her eyes on her husband (who had just carried out a hanging) she said to him smiling: Tacaño, you should know that I have put upon you the horns, and with a galant younger and better hung than you. And while saying many other strange things, we took our leave and left her to return to her sweet sleep.[64]

Later, Giambattista della Porta will explain the use of unguents because "the women hope to be carried to banquets, concerts, dances and to be accompanied by young men, a thing they desire above everything."[65] The Inquisitor Johannes Nider (1380/85 – 1438), author of a treatise entitled *Fornicarius* [The Ant Colony], insists upon the point of view *ad nauseum* that the unguents are not the cause of apostasy due to their supernatural virtues but only because they induce a lustful ecstacy, a sin even more serious than other magical feats.[66]

---

[63] Laguna, 1555, VI, 75, pp. 421-422.

[64] Laguna, p. 422.

[65] Porta, 1562, II, 27, p. 197.

[66] Bailey, M. D. "Johannes Nider," Iowa State University Digital Repository (2006), p. 827: "[W]omen were more prone to the temptations of the Devil, due mainly to their weaker phyical, metal, and moral nature."

Figure 98. Der Liebeszauber (the Love Charm), ca. 1470, by an unidentified Lower Rhenish master, Museum der bildenden Künste, Leipzig. On the floor are plants related to witchcraft.

C. Lotions and Potions.

Perhaps we shall never know if the recipes employed in the lower Middle Ages and the beginnings of the Modern Age were ever known in antiquity. If we are inclined to think that they came from a pre-Christian epoch, their variety and potency suggest as probable (and not merely hypothetical) the use of non-alcoholic drugs in the mystical Hellenistic rites. Be that as it may, there are a great number of these preparations in circulation from the thirteenth century on, the majority of them made up to be administered cutaneously, and it is reasonable to think that many more were forgotten, when they did not become specifics sold by the herbalists later.

1. Composition. The physician, mathematician, astrologer, philosopher, gambler and author of over 130 books Jerome Cardan (1501 – 1576) examined the recipes of reputed witches for producing dreams or visions, something with which he was well acquainted. As a boy, upon waking or going to sleep, he "commonly saw figures ... and wild shapes that represented nothing he had ever seen before ...."[67] From the age of four to seven, before rising from his bed in the morning, he routinely experienced hallucinatory visual phenomena:

> For I used to vision, as it were, divers images of airy nothingness of body. They seemed to consist of very small rings such as compose vests of chain mail – although up to that time I had not yet seen a linked cuirass. These images arose from the lower right-hand corner of the bed, and moving upward in a semicircle, gently descended on the left and straightway disappeared. They were images of castles, of houses, of animals, of horses with riders, of plants and trees, of musical instruments, and of theaters; there were images of men of divers costumes and varied dress; images of flute-players, even with their pipes as it were, ready to play, but no voice nor sound was heard. Besides these visions, I beheld soldiers, swarming peoples, fields, and shapes like unto bodies which even to this day I recall with aversion. There were groves, forests, and other phantoms .... Even flowers of many a variety, and four-footed creatures, and divers birds appeared in my visions; but in all this exquisitely fashioned pageant there was no color, for the creatures were of air.[68]

---

[67] Morley, Henry. The Life of Girolamo Cardano, of Milan, Physician, vol. I. London: Chapman and Hall, 1854, archive.org, p. 36.

[68] Cardan, Jerome. Book of My Life (De Vita Propria Liber), tr. Jean Stoner. New York: E. P. Dutton & Co., Inc., c. 1930, archive.org, pp. 147-148, ch. 37: "Certain Eccentricities, and Marvels, Among Which, Dreams."

As a man of the budding Renaissance, sometimes called "the first psychologist [and] a scientist of the first order,"[69] he studied various psychotropic plants, even classifying them by the kinds of hallucinations they induced. In Book XVIII of his work, *De Subtilitate* (On Subtlety), he inquires into the composition of the so-called flying ointment and relates it to his own personal experience with unguents:

This is the source of the belief in bogeys, which make people who feed on celery, chestnuts, beans, onions, cabbage, and French beans seem to be conveyed in a dream to various places, and there be influenced in various ways, according to their individual temperament. They are assisted in this by an ointment with which they coat themselves all over. It is thought to consist of the fat of children dug from graves, and juice of celery and aconite, also of cinquefoil and a soft kind of wheat. It is beyond belief what huge things they convince themselves they are seeing: now happy things, theatres, garden plots, fisheries, clothing, finery, dances, handsome youths, and sexual intercourse of the kind they particularly desire, kings too, and magistrates with their escorts, and all the glory and pomp of humankind, and many other distinguished things, such as appear in dreams and in pictures, things larger than those nature has to offer. And instances on a contrary basis: grief, ravens, prisons, solitude, torture. And this is to be expected, although linked to sorcery, for it must be converted to natural causes. I have frequently tried the often-celebrated ointment called 'populeon,' from poplar fronds, on the arteries of my feet and hands; some people even say also on those of the liver and temples, to achieve sleep in most cases, and in the greatest part of these to display cheerful dreams, because the juice of fresh fronds cheers the soul, and exhibits sights imbued with its clarity and colour; there is no colour more cheerful than green.[70]

---

[69] Cardan, Jerome (c. 1930), p. x, introduction.

[70] Forrester, John M., ed. The *De Subtilitate* of Girolamo Cardano. Tempe, AZ: Arizona Center for Medieval and Renaissance Studies, 2013, Book 18, "On Marvels, and the Way to Represent Diverse Things Beyond Belief," pp. 907-908; *Inde ab his natam opinio nem lamiarum, quae apio, castaneis, fabis, cepis, caulibus, phaselisque victitantes, videntur per somnum ferri in diversas regiones, atque ibi diversis modis affici, prout uniuscuiusque fuerit temperies. Iuuantur ergo ad haec unguento, quo se totas perungunt. Constat ut creditur puerorum pinguedine e sepulchris eruta, succisque apij aconitique tum pentaphylli filigineque. Incredibile dictu quanta sibi videre persuadeant: modo laeta, theatra, viridaria, piscationes, vestes,*

At first glance, the recipe requires certain picturesque/frightening ingredients, as if it had been thought up by the simply credulous. Unfortunately, "the unambiguous botanical identification of a plant mentioned in a sixteenth century text is far from being straightforward."[71] For example, the original Latin has *phaselisque victitantes*, or "living beans," usually translated as "French beans," also "kidney beans."[72] But just below in the same seventeenth century dictionary we find *Phaseoles espineux*, or "The common rough Bindweed."[73] Bindweed is an older name for wild morning glory, and morning glory (*Ipomea violacea* L.) seeds contain LSA, a natural analogue

---

ornatus, saltationes, formosos juvenes, concubitusque eius generis quales maximé optant: reges quoque & magistratus cum satellitibus, gloriamque omnem ac pompam humani generis, multaque alia praeclara, velut & in fornijs & picturis quae maiora sunt quàm quae natura praestare possit. Velut & contraria ratione tristia, coruos, carceres, solitudinem, tormenta. Neque id mirum, quanquam veneficū, ad naturales enim causas traduci debet. Quandoquide expertus sim sepevulgatus unguentum quod Populeon à frondibus populi dicit, arterijs pedum acmanuu, quida etiam dicunt iecori, tum temporu, in plerifque; somnu cociliare, arque in horum maxima parte laeta ostendere insomnia, que succus frondiu nouaru populi anima exhilaret, & imagines claritate sua & colore infectas ostendat. Nullus enim color viridi laetior (Hieronymus Cardanus. Hieronymi Cardani Mediolanensis Medici, de subtilitate Libri XXI. Basileae: Cum gratia & privilegio Caefareae maiestatis, Heinrich Petri, 1560, e-rara.ch, Universitäts bibliothek Basil, p. 500); in an early French translation, *apio* in the Latin becomes "the juice of black poppies, called opium" [*du suc de pavot noir, dit opium*] (Le Blanc, Richard, tr. *Les Livres de Hierosme Cardanus, Medecin Milannois, intitulez de la Subtilité, & subtiles inventions, ensemble les causes occultes, & raisons d'icelles*. Rouen: Chez la Vefue du Bosc, dans la Court du Palais, 1642, archive.org, ch. 18, p. 435 verso); in classical mythology the *Lamia* (or bogeys) were women who devoured children.

[71] Piomelli, D. and Antonino Pollio. "*In upupa o strige.* A Study in Renaissance Psychotropic Plant Ointments," *Hist. Phil. Life Sci.*, 16 (1994), p. 257.

[72] Forrester, ed., p. 907; Howell, James. A French and English Dictionary, composed by Mr. Randle Cotgrave. London: Printed for Anthony Dolle, 1673 (archive.org), "Pha – Phy;" see also Fuschs, Leonart. *L'Histoire Des Plantes*. Lyon: Chez Guillaume Rouille, 1558, p. 489: *Les fueilles & fruicts des Phaseoles espineux hont une proprieté & efficace contre les poisons mortifieres si on les boit devant, ou aprés.*

[73] Howell, "Pha – Phy."

of LSD.[74] Celery (*apio*) has been identified as "the poisonous umbelliferous herb, *Conium maculaturm* L. (hemlock)" but also a "wild variety of the widespread *Apium graveolens* L. (*Umbelliferae*). Innocuous at weak doses, the extracts obtained from the seeds or from the leaves of *Apium* may have, at stronger ones, a series of pharmacological actions ranging from mildly psychoactive to drastically emmenagogue."[75] Aconite (*Aconitum napellus* L.) is probably Wolf's Bane, "a deadly poison, known as such by Theophrastus and Pliny, and banned by both Greek and Roman law."[76] Cinquefoil (*Potentilla reptans* L.) was a "favorite of plant folklore ... [to which was] attributed all sort of magical and purificatory powers."[77] *Filigine* is sometimes derived from *fuligo* (soot)[78] but othertimes from *siligo* (a soft kind of wheat),[79] though this is also known as corn smut, related to the fungus ergot (*Ustilago maydis*).[80] As for the engaging/disturbing detail of "fat of children dug from graves," from a

---

[74] Cox, H. R. The Eradication of Bindweed, or Wild Morning-Glory. Washington, D. C.: Government Printing Office, 1909, p. 368; erowid.org.

[75] Piomelli, et al., p. 258.

[76] Piomelli, et al., p. 261.

[77] Piomelli, et al. (1994), p. 262.

[78] Piomelli, et al. (1994), p. 262, 263: "Likewise, the inclusion of soot may be attributed less to a direct pharmacological action of this substance than to its ability to enhance the passage of organic bases (such as the alkaloids contained in *Atropa belladonna* and *Aconitum* sp.) through intact skin and other mucosae. The positive ionic charge present on alkaloids at neutral pH hinders their penetration throguh the hydrophobic layers of the epidermis. However, a weakly alkaline environment is normally sufficient to neutralize this charge, and to allow diffusion of the active principles into the bloodstream. (The same pharmacokinetic principle is exploited by Peruvian coca chewers, who mix in their mouths the cocaine-containing leaves of *Erythroxylon coca* with alkaline cinders.)"

[79] Forrester, ed. (2013), p. 908.

[80] Dossie, Robert. Memoirs of Agriculture and other Oeconomical Arts, vol. 2. London: J. Nourse, 1771, p. 161 (GB).

pharmacological standpoint, it is certain that a lipophylic extract of leaves, roots or berries of *Atropa belladonna* and other allied *Solanaceae* would cause marked effects on the central nervous system, even when administered as a topic ointment .... The active principles variously present in these plants (atropine, hyosciamine and scopolamine, potent receptor antagonists of the neurotransmitter, acetylcholine) are slowly absorbed through the skin, and their penetration may be enhanced by the presence of small abrasions, inflammation or by slight alkalinization of the applied salve.[81]

Cardano is also coy about the unguent he experimented with, made as he says from poplar leaves. But he omits the other ingredients in this common medieval hynotic salve:

An ointment make of poppy, henbane and nightshade (*onguent populeum*). It is composed of the fresh buds of black poplar, one pound, which you leave to macerate for twenty-four hours in fat, ready and molten, three pounds. You keep it till the suitable season, to mix it with fresh, crushed leaves of poppy, deadly nightshade, henbane and garden nightshade, of each four ounces. This ointment has a lovely green color, and the smell of poplar buds.[82]

It was without doubt effective for engendering both sleep and visions, as it contained both opium and the extracts of solanaceas. The sleep-inducing effects of *Papaver somniferum* L. are well known; deadly nightshade is usually identified with *Atropa belladonna* L., of which "[l]arge doses paralyze, small doses stimulate the nervous system."[83] Henbane (*Hyoscyamus niger* L.) contains the "powerfully intoxicating anti-cholergenic" alkaloid hyoscyamine, that can "induce intensely real hallucinations populated with 'numerous fully formed images of autonomous intelligences' not unlike the demons and dancers reported

---

[81] Piomelli, et al. (1994), pp. 259-260.

[82] Piomelli, et. al., p. 251, citing J. B. Kapeler and J. B. Caventou's Manuel des Pharmaciens et des Droguistes. Paris: Brosson et Chaude, 1821, p. 527.

[83] Felter, H. W. and J. U. LLoyd. King's American Dispensary, vol. I. Cincinnati, OH: The Ohio Valley Company, 1906, archive.org, p. 336.

at the witches' feast."[84] Perhaps Cardano is avoiding the censure of the Inquisition by giving only part of the well-known recipe.

Figure 99. Simples used in the elaboration of witches' unguents: henbane, datura, mandrake.

[84] Ostling, "Babyfat and Belladonna," (2016), p. 37, quoting Schultes and Hoffmann.

Figure 100. Belladonna, sapo toad and Amanita muscaria.

A similar flying ointment is given in two recipes by Giovan Battista Della Porta, "the most famous natural magician of the mid-sixteenth-century"[85] in the first edition of his *Magia Naturalis* (1558):

> Although they [the witches] mix in a great deal of superstition, it is apparent nevertheless to the observer that these things can result from a natural force. I shall repeat what I have been told by them. By boiling children's fat in a copper vessel, they get rid of its water, thickening what is left after boiling and remains last. Then they store it, and afterwards boil it again before use: with this they mix celery, aconite, poplar leaves and soot. Or, in alternative: sium, acornus, cinquefoil, the blood of a bat, solanum and oil.[86]

Though the same recipe shows up again in an edition printed at Antwerp (1560), the expanded editions from twenty years later (from which the English translation was taken) no longer contain any references to the flying ointment of the witches.[87]

---

[85] Ostling, Michael. "Babyfat and Belladonna: Witches' Ointment and the Contestation of Reality," *Magic, Ritual, and Witchcraft* (Summer 2016), University of Pennsylvania Press, p. 44.

[86] Piomelli, D. and Antonino Pollio. "*In upupa o strige.* A Study in Renaissance Psychotropic Plant Ointments," *Hist. Phil. Life Sci.*, 16 (1994), p. 253; *Lamiarum unguenta, Quae quanquam ipsae superstitionis plurimum admiscent, naturali tamen vi euenire patet intuenti; quaeque ab eis acceperim, referam. Pueroroum pinguedinem ahaeno vase decoquendo ex aqua capiunt, inspissando quod ex elixatione ultimum, nouissimumque subsidet, inde condunt, continuoque inseruiunt usui: cum hac immiscent eleoselinum, aconitum, frondes populneas, & fuliginem. Vel ALITER sic: Sium, acorum vulgare, pentaphyllon, vespertilionis sanguine, solanum somniferum, & oleum* (Porta, Io. Baptista. *Magiae Naturalis, sive De Miraculis rerum Naturalium*. Neapoli: Apud Matthiam Cancer, 1558, Book II, chapter 26, *Laminarum unguenta*, pp. 101-102, reader.digitale-sammlungen.de; as for the child condensed in a pot, Porta does not appear to believe his old informant at any moment.

[87] See *Magiae Naturalis* (1560), *liber secundus*, p. 85, archive.org; look for it in vain, for example, in Natural Magick by John Baptista Porta, A Neopolitane: in Twenty Books. London: Printed for Thomas Young, and Samuel Speed, 1658, book eight, archive.org, pp. 217 et seq.

This self-censorship, like that of Cardano, was no doubt the result of a "brush with the Holy Office ... [as] popular herbal lore and folk-medicine were becoming a favorite target of the Catholic Church's attempts to eradicate deep-seated pagan practices and to secure a more complete Christianization of the natural world."[88] In 1580, Porta was publicly accused by Jean Bodin in his treatise De la Démonomanie des Sorciers, a charge Porta refutes: "A certain Frenchman in his Book called Daemonomania, Tearms me a Magician, a Conjurer, and thinks this Book of mine, long since Printed, worthy to be burnt, because I have written the Fairies Oyntment, which I set forth onely in detestation of the frauds of Divels and Witches."[89] In the expanded version, Porta confines himself instead to listing the ingredients of the popular medieval soporific sponge:

A Sleeping Apple

For it is made of Opium, Mandrake, juice of Hemlock, the Seeds of Henbane; and adding a little Musk, to gain an easier reception of the Smeller: these being made up into a ball, as big as a mans [sic] hand can hold, and often smelt to, gently close the eyes, and binde them with a deep sleep.[90]

A little later he mentions an ointment composed exclusively of solanaceas (mandrake, stramonium, henbane and belladonna) "[t]o make a man believe he was changed:"[91]

For by drinking a certain Potion, the man would seem somtimes to be changed into a Fish; and flinging out his arms, would swim on the Ground: sometimes he would seem to skip up, and then to to dive down again. Another would believe himself

---

88 Piomelli, D. et al., pp. 254-255.

89 Porta, John Baptista. Natural Magick. London: Young and Speed, 1658, archive.org, preface, p. 3.

90 Porta, Natural Magick, 1658, book eight, chapter one, p. 218.

91 Porta, Natural Magick, 1658, book eight, chapter two, p. 219; M. Harner brings interesting documentation about drugs and metamorphoses, painted in the *Caprichos* of Goya.

turned into a Goole, and would eat Grass, and beat the Ground with his Teeth, like a Goole: now and then sing, and endeavour to clap his Wings. And this he did with the aforementioned Plants: neither did he exclude Henbane from among his ingredients .... I remember when I was a young man, I tried these things on my Chamber-Fellows.[92]

The black cat was out of the bag, however, and Porta's original recipe for the flying ointment was copied by Johan Wier, translated into English by Reginald Scot, repeated by Bacon[93] and shows up dramatized as late as the nineteenth century in the lines written by Thomas Middleton for his witch Hecate:

Hec. There, take this unbaptized brat;
[*Giving the dead body of a child.*]
Boil it well; preserve the fat ...
I thrust in eleselinum lately,
Aconitum, frondes populeas, and soot –
You may see that, he looks so b[l]ack i' th' mouth –
Then sium, acorum vulgare too,
Pentaphyllon, the blood of a flitter-mouse,
Solanum somnificum et oleum.[94]

De Nynauld also lists a number of simples "with which the Devil troubles the senses of his Slaves" including the root of belladonna, the furious mushroom, the blood of the flying mouse, henbane, hoopoe (*Upupa epops*) blood, aconite, opium, poppy, hemlock, poplar leaves and "magical gemstones for summoning the gods below

---

[92] Porta, Natural Magick, book 8, ch. 2, p. 219.

[93] Ostling, p. 45.

[94] Bullen, A. H., ed. The Works of Thomas Middleton, vol. 5. London: John C. Nimmo, 1885, *The Witch*, Act I, Scene II, pp. 366-368.

and the gods above."[95] Another recipe very similar can be found in J. Wier.[96]

The oscillation between pathetic formulas and effective formulas is a constant, making one think of diversionary maneuvers on the part of the witches, and the powers of fantasy grounded in ignorance. Sometimes the recipe partakes of both lines, as when Shakespeare, in Macbeth, fills the cauldron of the witches:

Round about the cauldron go;
In the poisoned entrails throw.
Toad, that under cold stone
Days and nights has thirty-one
Sweltered venom, sleeping got,
Boil thou first i' the charmed pot.
...
Fillet of a fenny snake,
In the cauldron boil and bake;
Eye of newt and toe of frog,
Wool of bat and tongue of dog,
Adder's fork and blindworm's sting,
Lizard's leg and owlet's wing,
For a charm of powerful trouble,
Like a hell-broth boil and bubble.
...
Scale of dragon, tooth of wolf,
Witches' mummy, maw and gulf
Of the ravined salt-sea shark,
Root of hemlock digged i' the dark,

---

[95] Nynauld, I. de (1615), ch. 2, archive.org, pp. 24-25: *[D]esquels le Diable se sert pour troubler les sens de ses Esclaves ... la racine de la belladonna, morelle furieuse, sang de chauve sourris, d'huppe. l'Aconit, la berle, la morelle endormate, l'ache, la suye, le pentaphilon, l'acorum vulgare, le perfil, fueilles du peuplier, l'opium, l'hyoscyame, cygue, les expeces de pavot, l'hyuroye, le Synochytides, qui fait voir les ombres des Enfers, c.d. les mauvais esprits, comme au contraire, l'Anachitides faict apparoir les images des saincts Anges*; Ostling (2016), pp. 66-67.

[96] Wier, 1885, II, 17; Ostling (2016), p. 65.

Liver of blaspheming Jew,
Gall of goat, and slips of yew
Slivered in the moon's eclipse,
Nose of Turk and Tartar's lips,
Finger of birth-strangled babe
Ditch-delivered by a drab,
Make the gruel thick and slab.
Add thereto a tiger's chaudron
For th' ingredience of our cauldron.
Double, double, toil and trouble;
Fire burn, and cauldron bubble.
Cool it with a baboon's blood,
Then the charm is firm and good.
...
Pour in sow's blood, that hath eaten
Her nine farrow; grease that's sweaten
From the murderer's gibbet throw
Into the flame.[97]

The widespread urban recreational use – for the purposes of dreaming and solitary sexual ecstacy – together with the orgiastic cults celebrated in the countryside, without forgetting the strict medical use, also suggests a considerable commerce in potions and lotions, with all the repercussions this entails: a motivation to continue investigating new recipes, phenomena of adulteration and even a market of resale in the hands of the bailiffs and the witch-hunters.

Manifest is a psychopharmacology of disconcerting richness, after a millennium of pious silence. The formulas not only contain opium and all the active solanaceas, but also highly sophisticated drugs like toad skin and flour contaminated with cornezuelo, as well as mushrooms and other fungi. With this variety of ingredients, together with the potency derivable from their diverse combinations, it's clear

[97] Bevington, David, ed. The Complete Works of Shakespeare, updated Fourth Edition. New York: Longman, 1997, pp. 1242-1243.

that a competent European witch had available a wide choice of means to induce all kinds of trips, trances and modifications of the psyche. Did the rural healers and the urban witches have such an arsenal from the beginning of the Middle Ages, which were then simply discovered starting in the thirteenth century? Instead, was it something that arose later, during the transition between the High and Low Middle Ages, out of desperation faced with the model of life propounded by Christian orthodoxy? Could it be that the crusade itself stimulated the disinterment of practices until then relatively inhabitual, conferring upon them the aura of the prohibited and the bait of a market profit? None of these hypotheses really seem to exclude the others.

2. Verification. Just after the beginning of the twentiety century, an expert in occultism prepared a sample of an ointment, following to the letter the instructions of Porta and fell rapidly asleep, dreaming of "flying in spirals, visiting strange places,"[98] though he did not mention any erotic encounters. Both the fabulist C. Castaneda[99] and the writer G. Schenck[100] have related experiments of this same type, with slight or no sexual overtones. However, the most conclusive experiment – for being made in a collective, using a pomade extracted from a recipe book of the fifteenth century and suggested for just such an experiment – was done by a professor at the University of Gottingen in the 1970s. He and other colleagues rubbed themselves on the napes of their necks and in their armpits, falling into a "stupor of twenty-four hours, where they dreamed of audacious flights, frenetic

98 Harner, 1972, p. 139.

99 He tested datural metel or the "herb of the devil" prepared for him by a Yaqui shaman: "I enjoyed a freedom and lightness as I had never known. The marvelous darkness produced in me a feeling ... of yearning" (1968, p. 91).

100 Schenck inhaled the smoke from beleno seeds: "A drunken sensation of flying. The anguished certainty that my end was near, due to a dissolution of my body, was counterposed against an animal jubilation of flight" (Schenck, 1955, p. 48).

dances and other extravagant adventures of a kind connected to medieval orgies."[101]

Though eroticism and phallic symbolism do not appear to have a comparable prominence in more recent experiments as in the medieval ones, it is possible either that modern communicants maintain a certain reserve or simply that there exists today more freedom, conferring less importance to these types of fantasies. Where all coincide – and also coincide with extensive experiments since then – is in the experience of flight and of lightness, witnessed by an infinity of campesinos and traditions, ancient as well as contemporary. They also coincide in that the most active solanaceas produce hallucinations and delirium in the strict sense, in logical accord with the psyches and cultural symbols of each individual.

Rare cases where solanaceas (*Datura stromonium* or *toloache*) continue to be employed in collective ceremonies occur among the Maya of Sinaloa and the Yaqui of Sonora, whose women periodically celebrate rituals close to the maenadic, with unguents that they rub on their breasts and bellies; it seems, the event includes very long sessions of frenetic dancing, followed by a "heavy stupor, interrupted by voluptuous dreams."[102]

It's interesting to take into account that where plants with visionary and plants with hallucinogenic alkaloids are consumed – for example, among the Jibaros of Eastern Ecuador – the shamans consider the second kind too strong, and never use them in ordinary rituals or celebrations; for these only the first kind are used. They only employ daturas among themselves or with their successors, as a kind of ordeal that demonstrates their strength in the face of obstacles that would be excessive for a commoner. In the opinion of M. Harner, from his field work with the Jibaro:

---

101 Krieg, 1966, p. 53

102 Perez de Barradas, 1957, pp. 310-311.

One of the principal characteristics of Medieval and Renaissance witchcraft in Europe helps to distinguish it from common shamanism. It is the fact that the witches cast their spells and actions of mutual aid when they were NOT in a trance, but only as part of a ritual reunion called esbat ... clearly different in name and substance from the sabbat or sabbath, where they would fly and participate in orgiastic encounters with demons. I believe the reason for this distinctive feature of European witchcraft resides in the nature of the drugs they were using. The hallucinogens in the solanaceas are so powerful that it is essentially impossible for the user to sufficiently control his mind and body to accomplish a ritual activity at the same time.[103]

Compared with the wizards and South American shamans, perhaps the European witches suffered a very hard ethnobotanical fate: to celebrate festivals and rites of their incumbency with sharp drugs, highly toxic and hardly useful as vehicles of knowledge, due to the amnesia before and after that they provoked.[104] Nevertheless, the Europeans did have available cannabis and opium, henbane and belladonna, drugs unknown to the American before the Conquest.

Although the European witches seem to have been poor insensate brutes, beset by misery, the solanaceas and persecution, a

---

[103] 1973, p. 46.

[104] According to the historian – and academic – J. Berruezo, "the Basque campesinos learned to obtain lysergic acid, LSD, and this substance was what made them fly" (Y. Osses, ABC, 8/11/1986, p. 42). The data – if the report of his meeting is true – illustrates the degreee of pharmacological ignorance that still characterizes specialists in Medieval history. The diethylamide of lysergic acid (LSD) was discovered in 1939 by Albert Hofmann and it is completely impossible that anyone in the fifteenth century could have known how to produce a semisynthetic substance. If the campesinos and medieval European witches would have had available preparations composed exclusively of visionary alkaloids (like the amide of lysergic acid, present in cornezuelo), they would never have flown, fallen into long stupors, nor demonstrated total amnesia or absolute credulity. Between the Medieval sabbat and the collective ceremonies of ingesting peyote or teonanacatl of many American tribes there is the same distance as between the frensi of voodoo and the experiences described by the pilgrims to Eleusis.

certain craftiness cannot be denied to European witchcraft as an institution. The policy of inventing fantastic ointments, mixing mythology and pharmacology, was combined to perfection with the lack of scientific curiosity of the Inquisitors, leaving them not a few times convinced that the trips were born of the pure bad will of certain people, supported by the providential aid of Satan. This explains why the Inquisition would not decide to directly persecute the cultivation of plants. In the judicial procedure of the witches of Zugarramurdi, for example, they confiscated twenty-two jars and a number of potions, unguents, powders and concoctions. Examining this material by way of an outlandish procedure – giving the substances to the animals that would accept them – the authority in charge resolved to think just what he most desired to think, declaring in the end that

> it was shown by experiments and by the evidence of doctors, as well as by the statements of the witches themselves that the properties of each and every one of them was sheer invention and deceit, and that they had been made by ridiculous methods and with absurd ingredients.[105]

Perhaps the witches had time to hide the true pharmacological vehicles and it is even possible that the people of the town were victims of a substitution. But there is not any doubt that in this era there existed hundreds of psychoactive preparations, and that trials with animals (even checking to see they received an adequate dose) hardly have value for judging the effect of certain psychoactive substances on the human nervous system. On the other hand, certain customs – like the one in Central Europe permitting the witches to drink a brew of the seeds of henbane before being burned to a

---

[105] Baroja, 1971, pp. 185-186, citing Alonzo de Salazar y Frías, *Relación y epílogo de lo que a resultado de la visita q hizo el sancto offiº. en las montañas del Reyº de Navarra y otras partes con el hedito de gracia concedido de los que ouiesen yncurrido en la secta de Brujos conforme A las relaciones y papeles que de todo ello se an Remitido al Consejo*, f. 129 r.

cinder[106] - indicates that the authorities knew something about these potions.

Between the risory and the bitter is written one final fact. The alkaloids of the psychoactive solanaceas are not today considered stupefacients. The offical pharmacopeias include them as useful drugs, non-addictive, with a high but manageable[107] toxicity; in fact, they were singularly appreciated as so-called truth drugs used in interrogations. As for the plants themselves, the most hallucinogenic solanaceas are not even considered psychotropic substances. A whole host of factors that govern something in principle as feasible as determining the objective effects of a given drug are highlighted given that from 1330 to 1700 the extracts of these plants represented for the authorities the incarnation of Satan, generated a considerable number of users, created in the majority of people a blind faith in the supernatural powers of lotions and potions made from them, and of course, led to the torture and burning at the stake of uncountable human beings.

The picture of clergy, notaries of the Inquisition, witchhunters, maidservants, young ladies of good families and old go-betweens using drugs that called for the outfit of Eve and the conduct of Venus, which transported them to icy orgies by means of broomsticks or phallic horns annointed with green greases, is a landscape somewhere between the horrible and the comic, apt for psychoanalytical disquisitions on the pathology of repression. As Huizinga said, summing up the end of the Middle Ages: "An enormous insincerity rules over everything."[108]

From another perspective, this evidence is also admitted by the bishop Ciruelo: "The devil many times comes into the monasteries of friars and nuns to the beds where they sleep, and makes some of them

---

106 Font Quer, 1982, p. 576.

107 On the medicinal use of scoplamine and hyoscamine (atropine), see Goodman and Gilman, 1970, v. II, ch. 1 and 2.

108 1962, p. 111.

touch themselves dishonestly, and others in many ways will not let them sleep calmly."[109]

D. Practice and Aspiration of Medicine

One could say, then, that all the non-alcoholic drugs were prohibited for recreational or religious uses, but that this distinction had nothing to do with their chemistry. An important part of their perversity is derived from the pomade, and the rest from the user. It was perfectly possible to end up being burned alive for the possession of a pomade for dislocations or aching joints, so long as the person was suspicious for some other indication, or simply because they had enemies. Of course, any list of unguents and potions in the house of an ecclesiastic, a magistrate or a noble was understood to be justified. What Bodin and De Lancre call a drug, connected inevitably to an essencially Satanic content, is not a physically defined body, but something half way between the guilty aspiration of a person (lust, libations to demons) and objective features of impiety in physical nature. If the Vedic tradition saw many of the non-alcoholic psychoactive drugs as drops of ambrosia fallen from the sky for the solace of humanity, Christianity sees a kind of exact opposite, implicitly understanding that the non-alcoholic drugs are drops of bitter bile oozing up from hell for the perdition of mankind.

Thus the war on the greases, on the harmful ingredients, on the ointments, on diabolic plants, on malevolent herbs, and on witches' brews never blossoms into notions of toxicology. The Inquistitors saw as equal the expert on drugs and the poisoner, though they knew that the work of the witches would never have continued to exist if they had only employed preparations to kill. But – and this is outstanding, because it will last in one way or another down to our days – their preparations did not need to harm the body, nor create a victim in

[109] Ciruelo, 1538 (1977), p. 56.

Figure 101. Illustration from the medieval codex Tacuinium Sanitatus in Medicina. An herbolist offers a remedy.

empiric terms. The victim is the soul. Whether one prepares any of these ingredients or administers them, she incurs chiefly a thought crime, in the offense of risking the spiritual by closer contact with the same abomination, which remains as silent and dark as the mouth of hell.

However, by the fact of its being a crime of risk or danger – a challenge to the divine majesty and not an aggression toward a person – the same plants, the same potions and the same ointments could be represented also as perfectly innocuous things, healthy and even necessary. This explains why from the eleventh century so many of the solanaceas as with opium and cannabis will be employed by respectable physicians and herbalists for various ailments. It is dangerous, but already from the end of the first crusade to the Holy Land the Arab pharmacopeia is considered a very valuable aid. Sometime later the reception of the GrecoRoman legacy will tilt the balance toward attitudes of tolerance, so long as the patients and therapists are always above any suspicion.

In the twelfth century the so-called *Antidotarium Nicolai* recommended the use of the soporific sponge as an anaesthetic. The rebirth in Western medicine, that is prepared in the Universities of Montpellier, Bologna, Padua and Paris, begins in the so-called School of Salerno, which proposed from the beginning – with all due discretion – the use of opium. Miguel Escoto, one of the representatives of Salerno, was who first dared to publish the recipe for the *spongia* – equal parts opium, beleno and mandragora ground and macerated in water – said: "When you wish to saw or cut on a man soak a rag in this and apply it to the nose for some time."[110]

Toward the end of the fourteenth century the medicinal use of opium is widely enough defused and produces a series of interesting notices. In 1391 Amadeo VII of Saboya dies, due perhaps to an overdose of the substance, a thing which leads to the execution of the

[110] Crombie, 1974, v. I, p. 205.

surgeon. The following year the lead physician of the monarch, A. Guainerio, launches a diatribe against his Piamontane colleagure in the treatise *De fluxibus*, accusing them of using enemas and suppositories of opium in doses capable of killing. Guainerio does not attack the substance itself, but the unconscious or incompetent use of it. But the theological/moral criterion quickly shows up, presented by the physician G. A. della Croce, who measures by the same yardstick all analgesics and discards chemical euphoria: "Only when the pain is insupportable and many things have been tried to no avail can narcotics be used, those which cause stupid dreams or quit them totally."[111]

Pain can only be mitigated and then only in exceptional cases. Its annulment excites guilty passions, what della Croce calls euphemistically stupid dreams. A little later Porta will be processed for encouraging the use of opium in surgery and speaking too much of drugs. Yet its use as an analgesic continues to spread, beginning to be sold in triacas in the drugstores and – as a stroke of grace – the republics of Genoa and Venice decide to commercialize the product on a great scale, importing it again from Alexandria, in the same way as did the Roman Empire. From this moment one could say that the irresistible ascension of opium to therapeutic panacea in the West begins. But it will still have to win some battles. The first and most serious is the frightening insecurity that accompanies the use of psychoactive drugs and even the non-psychoactive. Any person without a high social position can be processed, tortured if they refuse to confess, and of course, be burned alive for suspicions so much more indefensible when they are not founded upon toxicological concepts. A similar situation inconvenienced greatly the physicians and herbalists, and they will become a force for the separation of pharmacology and magic. The path is to develop untouchable therapeutic professions, not of the people but only of the universities,

---

[111] Leonicio, 1971, p. 110.

that can carry forward its responsibilities without threats from the dominant spiritual power. This ideal only begins to be fulfilled starting in the sixteenth century, thanks to Paracelsus and his disciples, who confer social validity on the narcotics as a thing of scientific nature, inaugurating a step toward chemotherapy such as it is. The irony is that Paracelsus was the greatest wizard of his day, a magician par excelence.

But not only the Hippocratics used and would use in the future drugs of great activity. Various types of curanderos will manage to subsist adopting edifying clothing and achieving sometimes a status superior to all the galenics. Within this category entered, for example, the faithhealers,[112] who have a recognized specialty in Spain from a rule promulgated by the Catholic Kings in 1477. Said text puts on the same level physicians, surgeon-barbers and herbalists, stipulating that they should be – as they themselves are – examined by a panel of doctors. The faithhealers like the midwives, druggists and spicers manage themselves so well that a half century later in 1523, their prestige exempts them from going through these proofs of sufficiency, as stated a pragmatica of Juana la Loca and her son Carlos.[113] Hippocratic medicine inclined toward respect for the *physis* only when it did not stop them earning some severe critics and a strict vigilence.

Besides the clergy there were, then, good witches who through prayers and drugs were considered effectively capable of healing others. However, what was considered a dignified profession at one moment and place could appear in another, with omnipresent arbitarity, as a sign of Satanic compromise. Though Carlos I exempted

---

112 In the *Tesoro de la lengua castellana* S. Covarrubias defines the profession in the following manner: "To pray is a certain way of curing by prayers, sometimes alone and other times applying with them some remedies .... Sometimes it means to split ones head open, because it is necessary to ... some bandage on the head, blessing it first and making with it certain crosses over the bloody or wounded part. They are called prayers because traditionally they use verses from Salterio."

113 Perez de Barradas, 1957, p. 9.

them from examination, the first bishop of Granada, fray Hernando de Talavera, called them infamous sinners, and the archbishop of Toledo decreed that no person shall heal with holy prayers, on pain of great excommunication. The unfortunate Franciso de Aguirre, one of the first governors of Chile, was accused by the Inquisition of curing the toothache with certain words, for example, while the priest Pedro Simon – an historian of the Indies and his contemporary – defended the grace of health as something incontrovertibly demonstrated by the faithhealers and approved in the first Epistle of Paul to the Corinthians.[114]

It is important to mention these two types of therapies, because in the course of time – when the liberal revolutions suspend the obligatory ecclesiastical tutelage – a great war between the Hippocratics and the other therapeutic schools will ensue, centered specifically on resolving whether or not the former should enjoy a monopoly on the elaboration and dispensing of drugs capable of altering the soul.

E. The Aguardientes and Alcohol

The alquimists never discovered the philosopher's stone, but they did perfect the alcohols. The simple still was known in the Mediterranean area from the GrecoRoman era, well-understood in Alexandria, probably by way of India and China. It was an instrument that functioned at relatively low temperatures and was used to distill substances like mercury, arsenic, sulfur and turpentine. The Arabs perfected the technique introducing a gallery of various alembiques, producing thus on a small scale substances like the essence of roses or naphtha.

However, to distill more efficiently and on a larger scale the spirit of wine or alcohol required a method of refrigeration that neither the Egyptians nor the Arabs knew. This method – the serpentine coil

114 Simon, 1892, 6a. Not., XII.

that passed through a cold medium – was the contribution of Medieval Europe, and revealed something unsuspected until then: "On mixing pure and very strong wine with three parts salt, and heating it in vessels appropriate to the task, one obtains an inflammable water that burns without consuming the material [in which it is soaked]."[115] These are the terms of the oldest known European exposition of the process, which appears in the *Mappae Claviculae*, a technical treatise from the twelfth century. As is known, the art of distilling alcohol is based upon the different boiling points of alcohol (78.5 degrees C) and water (100 degrees C). One hundred years later the Italians prepare through simple distillation the *agua vitae* (with 60 percent alcohol), and by even further distillation (to 96 percent alcohol) the *agua ardens* for industrial and chemical ends.

The Mallorquin R. Llull (1232 – 1315) introduced rectification using limestone and beginning in the fourteenth century the aguardientes like the alcohols are markets of noteworthy importance. Alcohol is used as a dissolvant in the preparation of perfumes and the manufacture of drugs; later it was used also as an anaesthetic. In the middle of the sixteenth century ether was discovered, using alcohol and sulfuric acid.

The success of the aguardientes can only be compared to the velocity and spread of tobacco. Being four or five times more active than wine – in exchange for elevating in the same proportion its toxicity – the new drinks offered the user an economy of time and quantity, a more rapid and more prolonged drunk with less liquid and more varied aromas. Already in the sixteenth century they arrived in China, where they provoked a spectacular rise in venereal disease in the court and outside of it, which suggested the imposition of severe restrictions on their sale.[116]

---

115 Crombie, 1974, v. I, pp. 126-127.

116 Huard and Wong, 1972, v. I, p. 183.

Figure 102. Illustration from Teniers' El Alquimista.

In Europe the distillers formed a union in the fifteenth century, before that of the physicians, and they have not ceased to prosper to this very day. However, with what happened in America, Africa and China it is appropriate to deduce that easy availability in the West never ceased to cause a commotion. An ambitious European endeavor which attempted to confront the flood of dipsomaniacs created by distilled beverages was a society promoting temperance, presided over by, among others, the principal German electors, the landgrave of Hesse and the bishops of Wurzburg, Strasbourg, Spire and Regensburg, noted more for its good intentions than any serious practical measures.[117] Some religious orders, like the Cartujans and the Benedictines, began very early to manufacture liquors that achieved great popular acceptance and continue to do so.

In general terms, the Middle Ages and the Renaissance are epochs where the consumption of alcoholic drinks achieved Bacchic levels. In the monasteries they composed songs of Dionysian style like the *Catulli Carmina* or the *Carmina Burana*, within an almost religious exaltation toward wine that writers like Boccaccio or Rabelais frequently describe. In fact, the antipuritan impulse that one observes in the lustful/sorcery use of drugs has its orthodox correspondence in festivals where they drank tumultuously, to the sound of licentious songs, as now one celebrates *Corpus Christi* or the Passion week. In the middle of the fourteenth century the official acts of the Council of Strasbourg show that there were distributed every year some 1200 liters of Alsatian wine among those who passed the night of San Adolfo in the cathedral, "lighting candles and praying."[118] However,

---

[117] Lewin, 1964, p. 191: "In 1524, the Electors of Treves and the Palatinate, the five Counts Palatine of the Rhine, the margrave Casimir of Brandenburg, the landgrave of Hesse, the bishops of Würzburg, Strasbourg, Speyer, Regensburg, etc., founded a temperance society which not only bound them to proselytize. They also pledged themselves instantly to dismiss functionaries in their service who drank, and to note the cause of the dismissal on their certificates."

[118] Huizinga, 1962, p. 226.

expensive wine and liquors were not affordable for the common person, except during festivities, their principal consumers being the clerical estate, the nobility and the bourgeoisie. In the home of the artesan, the serf and the campesino perhaps the head of the family might drank these at meals, and rarely outside of them. Yet there was no lack of legal norms of great severity[119] – superior in rigor to those of ancient Islam – to repress alcoholic excesses in public.[120]

It is difficult to decide what would have been the opinion of the GrecoRoman world to abundant quantities of a flammable *aguae*. Its inconveniences were already evident in wine when consumed in an immoderate manner, and it is doubtful that the ability to drink it in a more concentrated form would have changed the opinion of Euripides, Philon or Plutarch on the Dionysian nectar. Pliny passes by the subject blithely:

> In the second degree of excellencie, are ranged the wines of the Falerne territorie, and principally that which came from the vineyards of Faustian .... And to say a truth, this Faustian wine is inferiour to none in reputation: so piercing and quicke it is, that it will burne of a light flame, a propertie that you shall not see in any other wine.[121]

---

[119] Lewin, 1964, pp. 191-192: "In France, in the reign of François I, an edict of the year 1536 stipulated that anyone who appeared in public in a state of intoxication should on the first occasion be imprisoned on bread and water, on the second chastised with birch and whip, and on the third publicly flogged. Should further relapses occur the delinquent was to have an ear cut off and suffer banishment. Exemption from punishment for infringement of the laws during the state of inebriety was quite out of the question."

[120] None of which seemed to work: "All these numerous and infinitely varied measures taken in recent centuries against alcoholism, like the modern forms of prohibition, have hardly ever achieved any appreciable result, for the reasons already stated" (Lewin, 1964, p. 192).

[121] Holland, Philemon, tr. The Historie of the World, commonly called the Naturall Historie of C. Plinius Secundus. London: Printed for Adam Islip, 1601, pp. 403-428, book IV, the Booke of the Historie of Nature, penelope.uchicago.edu.

The others would have thought perhaps the same that they opined about the cordial or the betraying vine, that is, that in individual nature is found continence or excess, and that the *pharmakon* is only the gift of these contrary elements. The medieval European temporal and spiritual authority thought the same.

In his *Essays* (1533 – 1592)[122] makes some commentaries on the loss of control when drinking beyond measure, considering drunkenness

[122] "He is the first essayist, a skeptic, and acute student of himself and of man, a champion of a man-based morality, a vivid and charming stylist, and many other things besides. ... Self-sufficient though he was, he had an imperious need to communicate. The Essays are his means of communication ..." (Frame, "Introduction," 1957, p. v). "I think the great pleasure we take in Montaigne's Essays comes from the great pleasure he took in writing them, a pleasure we feel, so to speak, in every sentence" (Andre Gide, "Introduction," in Ives, 1946, pp. xxix, 1). "Montaigne's closest bond, his friendship with Etienne de La Boétie ... lasted four or five years before his friend died and made his later life seem hollow. He devoted himself to his friend's memory, never quite replaced him, never ceased to mourn him. La Boétie satisfied his deepest need, for complete communication. The lack of this later was one of Montaigne's reasons for writing the Essays" (Frame, Donald M. Montaigne A Biography. New York: Harcourt, Brace & World, Inc., 1965, p. 63). "[As with drinking, his] attachment to moderation in all things fails him when it comes to La Boétie, and so does his love of independence. He writes, 'Our souls mingle and blend with each other so completely that they efface the seam that joined them, and cannot find it again.' ... As he wrote in a marginal addition: 'If you press me to tell why I loved him, I feel that this cannot be expressed, except by answering: Because it was he, because it was I'" (Bakewell, Sarah. How to Live – or – A Life of Montaigne in One Question and Twenty Attempts at an Answer. New York: Other Press, 2010, pp. 93-94). "When he started his book [the Essays] he had lost a dear friend ... to whom he had been able to express, as he never could to any one person again, his every thought, view, and feeling. ... [T]he reader takes the place of the dead friend" (Frame, 1957, p. v). "This is an honest book, reader" (Montaigne, "To the Reader," in Ives, 1946, p. 1).

> a gross and brutish vice. ... [Yet, my] taste and constitution are more inimical to this vice than my reason. For, quite aside from the fact that I easily submit my beliefs to the authority of ancient opinions, I find it a loose and stupid vice, but less malicious and harmful than the others, which almost all clash more directly with society in general. And if we cannot give ourselves pleasure without its costing us something, as they maintain, I find that this vice costs our conscience less than the others. Moreover, it is not hard to prepare for and find: a consideration not to be despised.[123]

Drunkenness represents neither a sickness nor an epidemic nor a crime, but only a vice,[124] a lack of virtue which ends by man losing the "knowledge and control of himself."[125] Carried to its extreme, it is a pleasure that engenders its opposite, in the long run causing pain. But with a mix of disappointment and ridicule he declares himself a partisan of drinking deep, looking for the enthusiastic delirium of the Greek, in order to truly relax the soul:

> It is certain that antiquity did not strongly decry this vice. Indeed, the writings of several philosophers speak of it very mildly, and even among the Stoics there are some who recommend that we allow ourselves sometimes to drink our fill, and get drunk in order to relax the soul: "In this contest like others, so they say, / The great Socrates bore the prize away." -- Maximianus.[126]

In his old age, he was no supporter of drinking moderately:

---

[123] Frame, Donald M., tr. The Complete Works of Montaigne. Stanford, CA: Stanford University Press, 1957, pp. 245, 247, Book II, Essay II, "Of Drunkenness."

[124] "The other vices modify the understanding; this one overturns it and dulls the bodily senses" (Ives, George B., tr. The Essays of Michel de Montaigne, vol. I. New York: The Heritage Press, 1946, p. 450, book II, ch. 2, "Of Drunkenness").

[125] "The worst condition of man is when he loses knowledge and control of himself" (Frame, 1957, p. 245).

[126] Frame, 1957, p. 246.

> [T]o drink French style, at two meals and moderately, for fear of your health, is to restrain the god's favor too much. You need more time and persistence. The ancients spent whole nights at this exercise, and often added the days. And so we should make our daily drinking habits more expansive and vigorous. ... The pleasure we want to reckon on for the course of our life should occupy more space in it. Like shop apprentices and workmen, we should refuse no chance to drink, and have this desire always in our head. ... The discomforts of old age, which need some support and refreshment, might reasonably make me wish to be a better drinker; for drinking is almost the last pleasure that the years steal from us.[127]

In the end he mentions the euthanasia by wine of Stilpo and Arcesilaus as a resolve of wise men: "They say that the philosopher Stilpo, weighed down with old age, deliberately hastened his end by drinking undiluted wine. The same cause, but not by his own design, also stifled the worn-out vital forces of the philosopher Arcesilaus."[128]

Certainly, the French seem to have followed his advice. But what shines through in Montaigne is an irrestible return to the criteria of the pagans. Alcohol is that compromise between a gift of God and a stupid vice, between the loss of sense and the relaxation of the soul, betwen the ruin of one's health and the ultimate pleasure. Finally, with drunkenness, man is only once more before a challenge to his virtue: he is at once both an actor and the author of his own fate.

---

[127] Frame, 1957, pp. 247-248.

[128] Frame, 1957, p. 249.

Figure 103. Antique alembiques.

Bibliography for Volume Two, Part One

Adams, Hannah. A View of Religion in Two Parts, 3rd ed. Boston, MA: Manning & Loring, 1801.

Adlington, W., tr. Apuleius: The Golden Ass. London: W. Heinemann, 1924.

Allbutt, T. Clifford. Greek Medicine in Rome. New York: Benjamin Blom, Inc., 1970.

Al-Nowaihi, Magda M. The Poetry of Ibn Khafaja: A Literary Analysis. Leiden: E. J. Brill, 1993.

Alpago, Andrea. *Avicennae Liber canonis de medicinis cordialibus et cantica*. Venice: Apud Juntas, 1555.

____________, ed. *Tractatus de Theriaca*, in *Averrois Cordubensis Colliget, Libri VII*, tr. Armegando Blasio. Venice: Apud Juntas, 1552.

Anawati, Georges C. "*Le Traite D'Averroes sur la Theriaque et ses Antecedents Grecs et Arabes*," *Quaderni Di Studi Arabi*, 5/6, 1987.

Aquinas, Thomas. The "Summa Theologica" of St. Thomas Aquinas, literally translated by The Dominican Fathers. London: Burns Oates & Washbourne, Ltd., 1922.

Arendeen, J. P. "Encratites," The Catholic Encyclopedia, vol. V, "Diocese – Fathers," Herbermann et al, eds. New York: Robert Appleton Company, 1909.

Arendonk, C. van. "Kahwa," in The Encyclopaedia of Islam, ed. E. van Donzel, et al, vol. IV, Iran-Kha. Leiden: E. J. Brill, 1978.

Arnot, Robert, ed. The Sufistic Quatrains of Omar Khayyam. New York: M. Walter Dunne, 1903.

Aurelius, Marcus Lucius. The Meditations, Book I, tr. George Lang. //classics.mit.edu.

Bacqué-Grammont, Jean-Louis, "*Autour des premières mentions du café dans les sources ottomanes*," in *Le commerce du café avant l'ère des plantations coloniales*, ed. Michel Tuchscherer. Cairo: Institut Français d'archéologie orientale, 2001.

Baigrúe, Brian S., ed. The Renaissance and the Scientific Revolution: Biographic Portraits, vol. I. New York: Charles Scribner's Sons, 2001.

Bailey, M. D. "Johannes Nider," Iowa State University Digital Repository (2006).

Bakewell, Sarah. How to Live – or – A Life of Montaigne in One Question and Twenty Attempts at an Answer. New York: Other Press, 2010.

Baluzius, Stephanus. *Capitularia Regum Francorum*, vol. I. Paris: Ex Typis Francisci-Augustine QUILLAU, Typographi Serenissimi Principis CONTII, via vulgo dicta, du Fouarre, 1780.

Baroja, Julio Caro. The World of the Witches, tr. O. N. V. Glendinning. Chicago, IL: University of Chicago Press, 1964.

_______________ *Las brujas y su mundo*. Madrid: Alianza Editorial, 1966.

_______________ The World of the Witches, tr. O. N. V. Glendinning. Chicago, IL: University of Chicago Press, 1971.

Basore, John W., tr. Seneca Moral Essays, vol. II. Cambridge, MA: Harvard University Press, 1965 (Loeb).

Beeton, Samuel Orchard. Beeton's Science, Art and Literature, vol. II. London: Ward, Lock & Tyler, 1870.

Bell, Gertrude L. Poems from the Divan of Hafiz. London: William Heineman, 1897.

Bernard, L. and T. B. Hodges, eds. Readings in European History. New York: The MacMillan Company, 1958.

Bernhard, J. *Le Thériaque: Étude historique et pharmacologique*. Paris: *J.-B. Baillière et Fils*, 1893.

Bevington, David, ed. *The Complete Works of Shakespeare*, updated Fourth Edition. New York: Longman, 1997.

Bingham, R., ed. *The Antiquities of the Christian Church*, Book XVI, in *The Works of the Rev. Joseph Bingham*, vol. VI. Oxford: At the University Press, 1855.

Birnbaum, E. "Vice Triumphant," *The Durham University Journal*, December 1956, New Series, Vol. XVIII, No. 1 (Vol. XLIX, No. 1), p. 22, n. 7.

Blackwell, R. J. "Democritus," *New Catholic Encyclopedia*, vol. IV, Com to Dys. New York: McGraw-Hill, 1967.

Boretius, Alfredus, ed. *Capitularia Regum Francorum*, vol. I, in *Monumenta Germaniae Historica*, ed. Societas Aperiendis Fontibus, Legum Sectio II. Hannover: Bibliopolii Hahniani, 1883.

Bostock, J. and H. T. Riley, trs. *The Natural History of Pliny*, vol. V. London: Henry G. Bohn, 1856.

Bourke, Vernon J., tr. *Saint Augustine Confessions*, in *The Fathers of the Church*, vol. 21. New York: Fathers of the Church, Inc., 1953.

Bronfenbrenner, Martha Ornstein. *The Rôle of Scientific Societies in the Seventeenth Century*. Chicago, IL: University of Chicago Press, 1975.

Bryce, Archibald Hamilton and Hugh Campbell. *The Seven Books of Arnobius Adversus Gentes*. Edinburgh: T. and T. Clark, 1871.

Buli, Jean Marc, tr. "Of Imperial Lands and Imperial Courts," *Readings in European History*, vol. I, ed. James H. Robinson. Boston, MA: Ginn & Co., 1904.

Bullen, A. H., ed. *The Works of Thomas Middleton*, vol. 5. London: John C. Nimmo, 1885.

Burkhardt, J. *The Civilization of the Renaissance in Italy*, Middlemore, S. G. C., tr. London: S. Somenschien, 1904.

Burton, Joan B. *Theocritus's Urban Mimes: Mobility, Gender, and Patronage*. Berkeley, CA: University of California Press, 1995.

Burton, Richard F. The Book of the Thousand Nights and a Night, vol. I. Teheran Edition, Number 738: Printed by the Burton Club for Private Subscribers Only, 1885.

Butler, H. E., tr. The Apology and Florida of Apuleius of Madaura. Oxford: At the Clarendon Press, 1909.

Butterworth, G. W. Clement of Alexandria. London: William Heinemann, 1919.

Cabassutii, Joannis. *Noticia Ecclesiastica Historium, Conciliorum, & Canonum*, editio secunda. Lugduni: Es Officina Amissoniana, joannis posuel, & Claudii Rigaud, 1685.

Candolle, Alphonse de. Origin of Cultivated Plants. New York: D. Appleton and Company, 1885.

Candolle, A. P. de. *Flore Française, ou Descriptions succinctes de toutes les plantes qui croissent naturellement en France, tome cinquième, ou sixième volume.* Paris: Chez Desray, 1815.

Cardan, Jerome. Book of My Life (De Vita Propria Liber), tr. Jean Stoner. New York: E. P. Dutton & Co., Inc., c. 1930.

Carneau, Etienne, Francois le Comte, trs. *Troisiesme Partie des Fameux Voyages de Pietro della Valle*, Letter 12 from Persia. Paris: Chez Gervais Clouzier, 1653.

Carpenter, W. S. and P. T. Stafford, eds. Readings in Early Legal Institutions. New York: F. S. Crofts & Co., 1932, p. 79, taken from W. A. Hunter. Roman Law. London: William Maxwell & Son, 1885.

Cartledge, Paul. Democritus. New York: Routledge, 1999.

Causape, Maria del Carmen Frances. "*Dioscoride, Andrés Laguna et la Pharmacie*," *Revue d'histoire de la pharmacie*, vol. 79, Issue 291 (1991).

Cave, Roy C. and H. H. Coulson. A Source Book for Medieval Economic History. NY: Biblio and Tannen, 1965.

Chapman, John. "Monophysites and Monophysitism," The Catholic Encyclopedia, vol. 10, "Mass to Newman," Charles G. Herbermann, et al., eds. New York: Robert Appleton Company, 1911.

Chelebi, Kātib. The Balance of Truth, tr. G. L. Lewis. London: George Allen and Unwin, Ltd., 1957.

Chen, Li-wei, "The Mountain without the Old Man: Xishiji on Ismailies," in the *Proceedings of the 2nd International Ismaili Studies Conference "Mapping a Pluralist Space in Ismaili Studies,"* held March 9-10, 2017, at Carleton University, Ottawa, Canada, edited by Karim H. Karim.

Ciruelo, Pedro. *Reprobacion de las Supersticiones y Hechizerias*. Medina del Campo, España: Casa de Guillermo de millis, 1551.

Clough, A. H., ed., rev. Plutarch's Lives, vol. 2. London: J. M. Dent & Sons, Ltd., 1910.

Conybeare, F. C., tr. Philostratus: The Life of Apollonius of Tyana, vol. I, book 2. London: William Heinemann, 1912.

Corcoran, Thomas H., tr. *Naturales Quaestiones*, vol. II, in Seneca in Ten Volumes, vol. X. Cambridge, MA: Harvard University Press, 1972 (Loeb).

Covel, Dr. John. "Extracts from the Diaries of Dr. John Covel (1670 – 1679)," in Early Voyages and Travels in the Levant, ed. J. Theodore Bent. NY: Burt Franklin, ____.

Cox, H. R. The Eradication of Bindweed, or Wild Morning-Glory. Washington, D. C.: Government Printing Office, 1909.

Cunningham, J. G., tr. Letters of St. Augustine. New York: The Christian Literature Company, 1892.

Dahmus, J. H. The Prosecution of John Wyclyf. New Haven: Yale University Press, 1952.

De Sacy, Silvestre. *Chrestomathie Arabe*, vol. I. Paris: A L'Imprimerie Royale, 1826.

_______________, tr. *Relation de L'Égypte, par Abd-Allatif, Médecin Arabe de Bagdad*. Paris: De L'Imprimerie Impériale, 1810.

Devins, J. B. An Observer in the Phillipines. Boston: American Tract Society, 1905.

Dods, Marcus, tr. Basic Writings of Saint Augustine, vol. II, ed. Whitney J. Oates. New York: Random House, 1948.

Dossie, Robert. Memoirs of Agriculture and other Oeconomical Arts, vol. 2. London: J. Nourse, 1771.

Downey, Glanville. A History of Antioch in Syria. Princeton, NJ: Princeton University Press, 1961.

Drabkin, I. E., tr. Caelius Aurelianus: On Acute Diseases and On Chronic Diseases. Chicago, IL: University of Chicago Press, 1950.

Duff, J. D., tr. Lucan The Civil War (Pharsalia). London: W. Heinemann Ltd., 1969.

Dunlop, John Colin. History of Roman Literature from Its Earliest Period to the Augustan Age, vol. I. London: Longman, Hurst, Rees, Orme, Brown, and Green, 1823.

Du Pin, Lewis Ellies. A New Ecclesiastical History, vol. X. London: Abel Sibal & Timothy Child, 1698.

Edwards, Edward. "Libraries," Encyclopedia Britannica, vol. XIII, 8th ed. Edinburgh: Adam and Charles Black, 1857.

_______________ Memoirs of Libraries, vol. I. London: Trubner & Company, 1859.

Efendi, Evliya. Narrative of Travels in Europe, Asia and Africa in the Seventeenth Century by Evliya Efendi, tr. The Ritter Joseph von Hammer. London: Oriental Translation Fund of Great Britain and Ireland, 1834.

Eliade, M. *Le chamanisme et les tecniques archaiques de l'extase*. Paris: Payot, 1968.

The Encyclopaedia Britannica, vol. XV. Chicago: R. S. Peale & Co., 1890.

Fairclough, H. Rushton, tr. Virgil, vol. I, rev. ed. Cambridge, MA: Harvard University Press, 1974.

Fakhry, Majid. Averroes (Ibn Rushd): His Life, Works and Influence. Oxford: Oneworld Publications Ltd., 2001.

Farmilo, C. G. "Detection of Morphine in Papaver setigerum DC," *UNODC Bulletin on Narcotics*, 1953, Issue 1 – 004.

FEDĀ'Ī, Encyclopaedia Iranica, iranicaonline.org.

Felter, H. W. and J. U. LLoyd. King's American Dispensary, vol. I. Cincinnati, OH: The Ohio Valley Company, 1906.

Fierz, Marcus. Girolamo Cardano (1501 – 1576), tr. Helga Niman. Boston: Birkhäuser, 1983.

Finkel, Caroline. Osman's Dream: The History of the Ottoman Empire. New York: Basic Books, 2005.

Fitzgerald, Edward, tr. Rubáiyát of Omar Khayyám / Six Plays of Calderon. London: J. M. Dent & Son Ltd., 1948.

Fitzmaurice-Kelly, James. "Introduction," Celestina or the Tragicke-Comedy of Calisto and Melibea Englished from the Spanish of Fernando de Rojas by James Mabbe, 1681. London: David Nutt, 1894.

Forrester, John M., ed. The *De Subtilitate* of Girolamo Cardano. Tempe, AZ: Arizona Center for Medieval and Renaissance Studies, 2013.

Frame, Donald M. Montaigne A Biography. New York: Harcourt, Brace & World, Inc., 1965.

_______________, tr. The Complete Works of Montaigne. Stanford, CA: Stanford University Press, 1957.

Fuschs, Leonart. *L'Histoire Des Plantes*. Lyon: Chez Guillaume Rouille, 1558.

Galland, Antoine. *De l'origine et du progres du cafe*. Caen: Chez Jean Cavelier, 1699.

Gayangos, Don Pascual de, ed. *Biblioteca de Autores Espanoles*. Madrid: M. Rivadeneyra, 1860.

Gibbon, Edward. History of the Decline and Fall of the Roman Empire, vol. III. New York: Modern Library, 1932.

Gilman, Stephen. The Spain of Fernando de Rojas. Princeton, NJ: Princeton University Press, 1972.

Gómez de Ortega, Casimiro. *Continuacion de la Flora Española, ó Historia de las plantas de España, que escribia Don Joseph Quer*. Vol VI. Madrid: D. Joachîn Ibarra, 1784.

Gow, A. S. F., tr. The Greek Bucolic Poets. Cambridge: At the University Press, 1953.

Graves, Robert. "The Universal Paradise," Difficult Questions Easy Answers. New York: Doubleday & Company, Inc., 1973.

____________ and Omar Ali-Shah, trs. The Original Rubaiyyat of Omar Khayaam. Garden City, NY: Doubleday & Company, Inc., 1968.

Greenhill, W. A., tr. A Treatise on the Small-Pox and Measles by Abú Becr Mohammed ibn Zacaríyá ar-Rází. London: Printed for the Sydenham Society, 1848.

Gregory, John. The NeoPlatonists: A Reader. London: Routledge, 1999.

Guizot, F. The History of Civilization: the Book of Judges, vol. II, tr. William Hazlitt. New York: D. Appleton & Company, 1864.

Gurdon, Edmond. 'Denys the Carthusian,' The Catholic Encyclopedia, vol. 4, ed. C. G. Herbermann. New York: Robert Appleton Company, 1908.

Haenel, Gustavus. *Pauli Sententiarum*, in *Lex Roman Visigothorum*. Leipsig: *Sumptibus et typis* B. G. Teubner, 1849.

Haight, Gordon S., ed. The Rubaiyat of Omar Khayyam, rendered into English quatrains by Edward FitzGerald, the five authorized versions. New York: Walter J. Black, 1942.

Halperin, David M. Before Pastoral: Theocritus and the Ancient Tradition of Bucolic Poetry. New Haven, CN: Yale University Press, 1983.

Hammer, J. J. *Histoire de L'empire Ottoman, depuis son origine jusqu'a nos jours*, tr. J.-J. Hellert, vol. 9. Paris: Bellizard, Barthès, Dufour et Lowell, 1837.

Harrison, Stephen et al., trs. Apuleius Rhetorical Works. Oxford: Oxford University Press, 2001.

Hasan, Ahmad, tr. *Sunan Abu Dawud*, eleventh edition, vol. III (chapters 1338 – 1890). New Delhi: Kitab Bhavan, 2012.

Hattox, Ralph S. Coffee and Coffeehouses: The Origins of a Social Beverage in the Medieval Near East. Seattle, WA: University of Washington Press, 1985.

Healy, Patrick J. "Tatian," The Catholic Encyclopedia, vol. 14, "Simony – Tournély," eds. Herbermann, et al. New York: Robert Appleton Company, 1912.

Henderson, Ernest F., ed. Select Historical Documents of the Middle Ages. London: G. Bell and Sons, Ltd., 1912.

Heron-Allen, Edward. "An Analysis of Edward FitzGerald's Translation of the Quatrains of Omar Khayyam," in Arnot, 1903.

Heschel, A. Maimonides: A Biography, tr. J. Neugroschel. NY: Farrar, Strauss, Giroux, 1982.

Heseltine, Michael, tr. Petronius, rev. E. H. Warmington. Cambridge, MA: Harvard University Press, 1969 (Loeb).

Hieronymus Cardanus. *Hieronymi Cardani Mediolanensis Medici, de subtilitate Libri XXI*. Basileae: Cum gratia & privilegio Caefareae maiestatis, Heinrich Petri, 1560.

Hoffmann, R. Joseph, tr. "Introduction," Celsus On the True Doctrine A Discourse Against the Christians. Oxford: Oxford University Press, 1987.

__________________ Julian's Against the Galileans. New York: Prometheus Books, 2004.

Holland, Philemon, tr. The Historie of the World, commonly called the Naturall Historie of C. Plinius Secundus. London: Printed for Adam Islip, 1601.

Howell, James. A French and English Dictionary, composed by Mr. Randle Cotgrave. London: Printed for Anthony Dolle, 1673.

Humphries, Rolfe, tr. Ovid Metamorphoses. Bloomington, IN: Indiana University Press, 1967.

Huizinga, Johan. *El otoño de la Edad Media*, fourth edition, tr. José Gaos. Madrid: Alianza Editorial S. A., 1982.

Hunter, W. A. Roman Law. London: William Maxwell & Son, 1885.

Ibn-Sina, Hakim. *Al-Qānūn Fi'l-Tibb*, Book II (*Materia Medica*), supervising translator Hakeem Abdul Hameed. New Delhi: Department of Islamic Studies, *Jamia Hamdard* (Hamdard University), 1998.

Ives, George B., tr. The Essays of Michel de Montaigne, vol. I. New York: The Heritage Press, 1946.

Jacob, H. E. Coffee: The Epic of a Commodity, tr. Eden and Cedar Paul. Short Hills, NJ: Burford Books, 1998.

James, Montague Rhodes, tr. The Apocryphal New Testament. Oxford: At the Clarendon Press, 1955.

Jayyusi, Salma Khadra. "Nature Poetry in Al-Andalus and the Rise of Ibn Khafaja" in The Legacy of Muslim Spain, S. K. Jayyusi, ed. Leiden: E. J. Brill, 1992.

Jones, W. H. S., tr. Pliny Natural History, vol. VII. Cambridge, MA: Harvard University Press, 1966 (Loeb).

Joseph, Isya. "Bar Hebraeus and the Alexandrine Library," *The American Journal of Semitic Languages and Literatures*, vol. XXVII, October 1910-July 1911. Chicago, IL: University of Chicago Press, 1911.

Kahl, Oliver. The Dispensatory of Ibn at-Tilmīd. Leiden: Brill, 2007.

Kahn, Charles H. The Art and Thought of Heraclitus. Cambridge, UK: Cambridge University Press, 1979.

Khiari, Farid. *Licite, illicite? Qui dit le droit en islam?* Aix-en-Provence, FR: Edisud, 2005.

Kluger, Rivkah Schärf. Satan in the Old Testament, tr. Hildegard Nagel, Studies in Jungian Thought, ed. James Hillman. Evanston, IL: Northwestern University Press, 1967.

Knatchbull, Wyndam, tr. Kalila and Dimna, or The Fables of Bidpai. London: Longman, Hurst, Rees, Orme, and Brown, 1819.

Knysh, A. D., tr. Al-Qushayri's Epistle on Sufism. Reading, UK: Garnet Publishing Ltd., 2007.

Kopf, L. tr. The English Translation of the History of Physicians by Ibn Abi Usaybi'ah. Bethesda, MD: National Library of Medicine, MS C 294, 1971.

Kurtz, Paul. "Intellectual Freedom, Rationality and Enlightenment: The Contribution of Averroës," in Averroës and the Enlightenment, eds. M. Wahba, M. Abousenna. Amherst, NY: Prometheus Books, 1996.

Laguna, Andres Fernandez de, tr. *Pedacio Dioscorides Anazarbeo, Acerca de la Materia Medicinal, y de los Venenos Mortiferos*. Antwerp, NL: Casa de Juan Latio, 1555.

Lane-Poole, Stanley. Saladin and the fall of the Kingdom of Jerusalem, ch. X, Truces and Treaties (1176 – 1181). NY: G. D. Putnam's Sons, 1906.

L'arroque, M. The History of the Eucharist, tr. Jos. Walker. London: George Downes, 1684.

Le Blanc, Richard, tr. *Les Livres de Hierosme Cardanus, Medecin Milannois, intitulez de la Subtilité, & subtiles inventions, ensemble les causes occultes, & raisons d'icelles*. Rouen: Chez la Vefue du Bosc, dans la Court du Palais, 1642.

Leclerc, L. *Traité des Simples par Ibn El-Beïthâr*, vol. 1, in *Notices et Extraits des Manuscrits de la Bibliothèque Nationale, tome vingt-troisième. Paris: Imprimerie Nationale*, 1877.

Lee, Alex, tr. Aul. Cor. Celsus on Medicine. London: E. Cox, 1831.

Lenorment, Francois. "The Eleusinian Mysteries," part IV, *Contemporary Review*, vol. 38, July – Dec 1880.

Leonicio, U. *El vuelo mágico*. Barcelona: Plaza, 1971.

Lewin, Louis. Phantastica Narcotic and Stimulating Drugs, tr. P. H. A. Wirth. New York: E. P. Dutton & Co., Inc., 1964.

__________ Phantastica Narcotic and Stimulating Drugs. London: Routledge & Kegan Paul, 1964 (1931).

Lewis, Bernard. The Arabs in History. Oxford: Oxford University Press, 2002.

__________ "Maimonides, Lionheart, and Saladin," *Eretz-Israel: Archeological, Historical and Geographical Studies* (1964).

Lucas, H. S. 'The Great European Famine of 1315, 1316, and 1317,' *Speculum*, vol. 5, No. 4 (Oct. 1930).

Luibheid, Colm and Paul Rorem, trs. Pseudo-Dionysius The Complete Works. New York: Paulist Press, 1987, The Ecclesiastical Hierarchy.

Magny, Ariane. "Poetry in Fragments: Jerome, Harnack, and the Problem of Reconstruction," *Journal of Early Christian Studies*, 18. 4 (Winter 2010).

Maitland, S. R., ed., tr. Facts and Doctrines Illustrative of the History, Doctrine, and Rites, of the Ancient Albigenses & Waldenses. London: C. J. G. and F. Rivington, 1832.

Mansi, Johannes Dominicus. *Sacrorum Conciliorum Nova et Amplissima Collectivo*, vol. VIII. Florentiae: Expensis Antonii Zatta Veneti, 1762.

Margoliouth, D.S. The Hibbert Lectures (Second Series), The Early Development of Mohammedanism, Lecture V. London: Williams and Norgate, 1914.

______________ Mohammedism. London: Williams and Norgate, 1920.

Maviglia, A. "*Une lettre de Valerius Cordus sur les trochisques de vipère et sur quelques simples*," *Revue d'histoire de la pharmacie*, 58e *année*, no. 205, 1970.

Migne, J.-P., ed. *Burchardi Womaciensis Ecclesiae Episcopi, Decretorum Liber Decimus, De Incantatoribus et Auguribus, in Patrologiae Cursus Completus*, vol. 140. Paris: Apud Garnier Fratres, 1880.

Morley, Henry. Jerome Cardano: The Life of Girolamo Cardano, Physician, vol. II. London: Chapman and Hall, 1854.

Montesquieu, Charles de Secondat. The Persian Letters, tr. C. J. Betts. London: Athenaeum Publishing Company, 1897.

____________________________ *Lettres Persanes*, ed. Robert Loyalty Cru. New York: Oxford University Press, 1914.

Mooney, James. "Sahagún, Bernadino de," The Catholic Encyclopedia, vol. 13, "Revelation – Simon Stock," Herbermann, C. G., ed. et al. New York: Robert Appleton Company, 1912.

Moule, A. C. & Paul Pelliot, trs. Marco Polo: The Description of the World, vol. I. London: George Routledge & Sons Ltd., 1938.

Mullady, Brian, tr. Commentary on the Book of Job by Thomas Aquinas, ed. Joseph Kenny. Lander, WY: Aquinas Institute for the Study of Sacred Doctrine, 2016.

Munk, Salomon, tr. *Mélanges de Philosophie Juive et Arabe*. Paris: Chez A. Franck, 1857.

Murphy, F. X. "Monophysitism," New Catholic Encyclopedia, vol. IX, "Ma to Mor." New York: McGraw-Hill, 1967.

Murray, Margaret Alice. The Witch-Cult in Western Europe. Oxford: At the Clarendon Press, 1921.

Mustafa, Yassar. "Avicenna the Anaesthetist," aagbi.org.

Musto, D. F. "The History of Legislative Control over Opium, Cocaine, and their Derivatives," druglibrary.org.

Mylonas, G. E. Eleusis and the Eleusinian Mysteries. Princeton, NJ: Princeton University Press, 1961.

Nelson, L. H. 'The Great Famine (13115 – 1317) and the Black Death (1346 – 1351),' vlib.us/medieval/lectures.

Newman, John Henry Cardinal. An Essay on the Development of Christian Doctrine, 16th ed. New York: Longman, Greene & Company, 1920.

Nynauld, I. de. *De La Lycanthropie, Transformation, et Extase des Sorciers*. Paris: Chez Nicolas Rousset, 1615.

Osbaldeston, T. A. and R.P.A. Wood, trs. *Dioscorides: De Materia Medica.* Johannesburg, SA: Ibidis Press, 2000.

Ostling, Michael. "Babyfat and Belladonna: Witches' Ointment and the Contestation of Reality," *Magic, Ritual, and Witchcraft* (Summer 2016), University of Pennsylvania Press.

Paño, María Victoria Escribano. "Heretical Texts and *Maleficium* in the *Codex Theodosianus* (*CTH.* 16.5.34)," Magical Practice in the Latin West, eds. R. L. Gordon and F. M. Simón. Leiden: Brill, 2010.

Parsons, Sister Wilfrid, tr. Saint Augustine Letters, vol. II (83-130), in The Fathers of the Church, vol. 18, ed. Roy Joseph Deferrari. New York: Fathers of the Church, Inc., 1953.

Pascual, Jean-Paul. "*Café et Cafés à Damas: Contribution à la Chronologie de Leur Diffusion au XVIème Siècle*," *Berytus Archaeological Studies*, vol. XLII (1995-1996).

'Patarenes,' The Encyclopaedia Britannica, 11th edition, vol. xx. Cambridge, UK: At the University Press, 1911.

Patrick, D. and F. H. Groome, eds. Chamber's Biographical Dictionary: The Great of All Times and Nations. Philadephia, PA: J. B. Lippincott Company, 1898.

Pharr, Clyde, tr. The Theodosian Code and Novels and the Sirmondian Constitutions. New York: Greenwood Press, 1952.

Pilkington, J. G., tr. Confessions of St. Augustin, in A Select Library of Nicene and Post-Nicene Fathers of the Christian Church, vol. I, ed. Philip Schaff et al. New York: Christian Literature Company, 1892.

Piomelli, D. and Antonino Pollio. "*In upupa o strige.* A Study in Renaissance Psychotropic Plant Ointments," *Hist. Phil. Life Sci.*, 16 (1994).

Porta, Io. Baptista. *Magiae Naturalis, sive De Miraculis rerum Naturalium*. Neapoli: Apud Matthiam Cancer, 1558.

________________ Natural Magick by John Baptista Porta, A Neopolitane: in Twenty Books. London: Printed for Thomas Young, and Samuel Speed, 1658.

Powell, Owen, tr. On the properties of Foodstuffs (*De alimentorum facultatibus*). Cambridge, MA: Cambridge University Press, 2003.

Price, Derek J., ed. Natural Magick: John Baptista Porta. New York: Basic Books, Inc., 1957.

Prioreschi, Plinio. A History of Medicine, vol. II, 2nd ed. Omaha, NE: Horatius Press, 1996.

Rabbinowicz, I.-M., tr. *Traité des Poisons de Maimonide*. Paris: Adrien Delahaye, 1865.

Rafeq, Abdul-Karim. "The Socioeconomic and Political Implications of the Introduction of Coffee into Syria (16th-18th centuries)," *Le Commerce du Café*, ed. Michael Tuchscherer. Cairo: Institut Français d'Archéologie Orientale, 2001.

Rätsch, Christian. The Encyclopedia of Psychoactive Plants, tr. J. R. Baker, et al. Rochester, VT: Park Street Press, 2005.

Ray, John, ed. A Collection of Curious Travels and Voyages in Two Tomes: The First Containing Dr. Leonhart Rauwolff's Itinerary into the Eastern Countries ...., tr. Nicholas Staphorst, 2nd ed., vol. II. London: Printed for J. Wathoe, et al., 1738.

Real Academia Española. *Fuero Juzgo, en latín y castellano, cotejado con los más antiguos y preciosos códices*. Madrid: Ibarra, 1815.

Regino, Abbot. "A Warning to Bishops," *Libri duo de synodalibus*, //bibleapologetics.wordpress.com.

Ribera, J., tr. *Historia de los Jueces de Córdoba por Aljoxaní*. Madrid: Imprenta Iberica, 1914.

Ricordel, Joëlle. "*Le traité sur la thériaque d'Ibn Rushd (Averroes)*," *Revue d'histoire de la pharmacie*, 88e année, no. 325, 2000.

Rist, Anna. The Poems of Theocritus. Chapel Hill, NC: University of North Carolina Press, 1978.

Rittenhouse, Jessie B., ed. The Rubaiyat of Omar Khayyam, comprising the metrical translations by Edward Fitzgerald & E. H. Whinfield and the prose version of Justin Huntly McCarthy. Boston: Little Brown, and Company, 1900.

Robinson, T. M. Heraclitus Fragments. Toronto, CA: University of Toronto Press, 1987.

Rodenberg, Carolus, ed. *Epistolae Saeculi XIII E Regestis Pontificum Romanorum*, selected by G. H. Pertz, vol. I. Berlin: Apud Weidmannos, 1883.

Rojas, Fernando de. *La Celestina*. ----------: Archer M. Huntington, 1909.

_______________ *La Celestina*, first edition. Buenos Aires, AR: Editorial Sopena, 1941.

Rolfe, John C., tr. Ammianus Marcellinus, vol. I. Cambridge, MA: Harvard University Press, 1963 (Loeb).

Rosenthal, Franz. The Herb: Hashish versus Medieval Muslim Society. Leiden, NL: E. J. Brill, 1971.

Rudd, Niall, tr., ed. Horace Odes and Epodes. Cambridge, MA: Harvard University Press, 2004 (Loeb).

Ruden, Sarah. Petronius Satyricon. Indianapolis, IN: Hackett Publishing Co., Inc., 2000.

Safra, Jacob E, chmn. The New Encyclopedia Britannica, vol. 9, 15th ed. Chicago, IL: Encyclopedia Britannica, 2005, "Porta, Giambattista della."

Sahagún, Bernadino de. *Historia general de las cosas de Nueva España*, vol. I, Carlos Maria de Bustamente, ed. Mexico: Alejandro Valdés, 1829.

Sale, George, tr. The Koran, commonly called the Alcoran of Mohammed. London: C. Ackers, 1734.

Sanchez-Albornez, Claudio. *España: Un Enigma Histórico*, tomo I. Barcelona: Edhasa, 1973.

____________________ *La España Musulmana según los autores islamitas y cristianos medievales*, third edition, vol. I. Madrid: Espasa-Calpe, 1973.

____________________ Spain: A Historical Enigma, vol. I, trs. C. J. Dees, D. S. Rehen. Madrid: Fundacion universitaria española, 1975.

____________________ "*El vino y los borrachos en la España mora hace mil años*," in *Ensayos Sobre Historia de España*, first edition. Madrid: Siglo XXI de España Editores, 1973.

Schaefer, Charles G. H. "Coffee Unobserved: Consumption and Commoditization of Coffee in Ethiopia before the 18th century," in *Le commerce du cafe*, p. 24, quoting L. Bartels. Myths and Rites of the Western Oromo of Ethiopia: An Attempt to Understand. Berlin: Dietrich Reimer Verlag, 1983.

Schaff, Philip, ed., et al. Nicene and Post-Nicene Fathers, vol. I, Edinburgh: T&T Clark, 1886.

Schipano, Mario, ed. *Viaggi di Pietro della Valle, Il Pellegrino, Descritti da lui medesimo in Letterre familiari*, *La Persia, parte seconda.* Venice: Presso Paolo Baglioni, 1667.

Scott, S. P., tr. The Civil Law, vol. XVII. Cincinnati, OH: The Central Trust Company, 1932.

Shahnavaz, S. "AFYŪN," Encyclopaedia Iranica, I/6, iranicaonline. org.

Share, Michael, tr. Philoponus Against Proclus's "On the Eternity of the World 1 – 5." Ithaca, NY: Cornell University Press, 2005.

Shehan, T. J. "Council of Agde," The Catholic Encyclopedia, vol. I, Aachen – Assize, ed. Herbermann, C. G. New York: Robert Appleton, 1907.

Showerman, Grant, tr. Ovid in Six Volumes, vol. I.: Heroides and Amores. Cambridge, MA: Harvard University Press, 1971.

Shuckburgh, Evelyn S., tr. The Histories of Polybius, vol. II. London: Macmillan and Co., 1889.

Sigerist, Henry E. The Great Doctors. Garden City, NY: Doubleday & Co., 1958.

Singleton, M. H., tr. Celestina: A Play in twenty-one acts attributed to Fernando de Rojas. Madison, WI: University of Wisconsin Press, 1958.

Siorvanes, Lucas. Proclus Neo-Platonic Philosophy and Science. New Haven, CT: Yale University Press, 1996.

Slane, Baron Mac Guckin De, tr. Ibn Khallikan's Biographical Dictionary, vol. III. Paris: Oriental Translation Fund of Great Britain and Ireland, 1868.

Smith, G. R. and M. A. S. Abdel Haleem, trs. The Book of the Superiority of Dogs over many of Those who wear Clothes by Ibn al-Marzubān. Warminster, UK: Aris & Philips, Ltd., 1978.

Smith, William, ed. A Dictionary of Greek and Roman Biography and Mythology, vol. II. Boston, MA: Little, Brown and Company, 1867.

________________ A Dictionary of Greek and Roman Biography and Mythology, vol. III. London: John Murray, 1876.

________________ and S. Cheetham, eds. A Dictionary of Christian Antiquities, vol. II. London: John Murray, 1880.

Spencer, W. G., tr. Celsus: De Medicina, vol. I. Cambridge, MA: Harvard University Press, 1971 (Loeb).

Spinei, F. Bartholomaei. *Quaestio de strigibus, una cum tractatu de praeeminentia Sacrae Theologiae, & quadruplici Apologia de Lamiis contra Ponzinibium* (An Investigation on wittches with a treatise on the Supremacy of Sacred Theology and A Fourfold Defense from Ponzinibio's on Witches). Romae: In Aedibus Populi Romani, 1576.

Standage, Tom. *A* History *of the* World *in* 6 Glasses. New York: Walker and Company, 2005.

Steel, Carlos. "Proclus," The Cambridge History of Philosophy in Late Antiquity, vol. II, ed. Lloyd P. Gerson. Cambridge, UK: Cambridge University Press, 2010.

Summers, Montague, tr. The Malleus Maleficarum of Heinrich Kramer and James Sprenger. London: John Rodker, 1928.

Szasz, Thomas. Ceremonial Chemistry. Garden City, NY: Anchor Press, 1974.

Tarrant, Harold, tr. Proclus' Commentary on Plato's Timaeus, vol. I. Cambridge, UK: Cambridge University Press, 2007.

Taylor, Thomas, tr. The Arguments of the Emperor Julian Against the Christians. Chicago, IL: Ares Publishing Inc., 1930.

Thatcher, Oliver J., ed. The Library of Original Sources. Milwaukee, WI: University Research Extension Company, 1901.

Thompson, Eben Francis, tr. The Quatrains of Omar Khayyam of Nishapur. London: Privately Printed, 1906.

Tibi, Selma. "Al-Razi and Islamic medicine in the 9th century," *Journal of the Royal Society of Medicine (JRSM)*, 2006 Apr; 99(4).

Tierney, Brian, tr. 'Famine of 1315,' Internet Medieval Sourcebook, January 1996, sourcebooks.fordham.edu.

Trokelowe, Johannis de. *Chronica et Annales*, ed. H. T. Riley. London: Longmans, Green, Reader, and Dyer, 1866.

Ukers, William H. All About Coffee, second edition. New York: The Tea and Coffee Trade Journal Company, 1935.

Urban, Sylvanus. "Curiousities of the Old Church Canons No. 11," *The Gentlemen's Magazine*, vol. XXXVI, New Series, July – Dec. London: John Bouvyer Nichols and Son, 1851.

Valencia, Pedro de. "*Segundo discurso de Pedro de Valencia acerca de los brujos y de sus maleficios*," *Revista de Archivos, Bibliiotecas y Museos*. Madrid: Tip. de la Revista de Archivos, Bibliotecas y Museos, 1906.

Veith, I. "Galen," New Catholic Encyclopedia, vol. VI, Fra to Hir. New York: McGraw-Hill, 1967.

Wacks, D. A. "The cultural context of the translation of Calila E Dimna," Framing Iberia. Leiden: Brill, 2007.

Walker, Stephen F. Theocritus. Boston, MA: Twayne Publishers, 1980.

Wallis, R. E., tr. "On the Jewish Meats," Anti-Nicene Fathers: the writings of the Fathers down to A. D. 325, vol. 5, Alexander Roberts and James Donaldson, eds. Peabody, MA: Hendrickson Publishers, 1995 (1886).

Walsh, Joseph A. Coffee: its History, Classification and Description. Philadephia, PA: Henry T. Coates and Co., 1894.

Warren, Edward W., tr. Porphyry the Phoenician. Toronto, CA: Pontifical Institute of Medieval Studies, 1975.

Weyer, P. H. "Novatian and Novatianism," New Catholic Encyclopedia, vol. X, Mas to Pat. New York: McGraw-Hill, 1967.

Wheelwright, Philip. Heraclitus. New York: Atheneum, 1964.

Whinfield, E. H., tr. "The Quatrains of Omar Khayyam," in Arnot, Robert, ed. The Sufistic Quatrains of Omar Khayyam. New York: M. Walter Dunne, 1903.

Williams, C. Dickerman. "Introduction," in Pharr, Clyde, tr. The Theodosian Code and Novels and the Sirmondian Constitutions. New York: Greenwood Press, 1952.

Wilson, George, tr. The City of God, vol. II, in The Works of Aurelius Augustine, vol. II, Dods, Marcus, ed., tr. Edinburgh: T & T Clark, 1871.

Wilson, W., tr. The Writings of Clement of Alexandria. Edinburgh: T & T Clark, 1867.

__________ Clement of Alexandria, in The Ante-Nicene Fathers, vol. II, eds. A. Roberts and J. Donaldson. Grand Rapids, MI: William B. Eerdmans Publishing Co., 1956.

Withington, E. T. Medical History. London: The Scientific Press, 1894.

Yellin, D. and I. Abrahams. Maimonides. Philadephia, PA: The Jewish Publication Society of America, 1903.

Yonge, C. D., tr. The Roman History of Ammianus Marcellinus. London: George Bell & Sons, 1894 (Bohn).

Zenos, A. C., tr. The Ecclesiastical History of Socrates, surnamed Scholasticus. London: George Bell and Sons, 1874.

__________ Socrates, Sozomen: Church Histories. New York: The Christian Literature Company, 1890.

__________ The Ecclesiastical History of Socrates Scholasticus, in A Select Library of Nicene and Post-Nicene Fathers, vol. II, second series, Socrates, Sozomenus: Church Histories, eds. Philip Schaff, Henry Wace. Grand Rapids, MI: William B. Eerdmans Publishing Co., 1952.

Ziyadah, Ma'am. "Ibn Bajja's Book Tadbir al-Mutawahhid: An Edition, Translation and Commentary." Institute of Islamic Studies, MA Thesis, McGill University, 1968.

Index
for Volume Two, Part One

www.ingramcontent.com/pod-product-compliance
Lightning Source LLC
Chambersburg PA
CBHW030415100426
42812CB00028B/2968/J

* 9 7 8 0 9 8 2 0 7 8 7 7 8 *